A326 Empire: 1492–1975

The Open University

Block 5
Why do empires end?

Block 6
Conclusions and legacies

This publication forms part of the Open University course A326 *Empire: 1492–1975*. Details of this and other Open University courses can be obtained from the Student Registration and Enquiry Service, The Open University, PO Box 197, Milton Keynes MK7 6BJ, United Kingdom: tel. +44 (0)845 300 60 90, email general-enquiries@open.ac.uk

Alternatively, you may visit the Open University website at http://www.open.ac.uk where you can learn more about the wide range of courses and packs offered at all levels by The Open University.

To purchase a selection of Open University course materials visit http://www.ouw.co.uk, or contact Open University Worldwide, Walton Hall, Milton Keynes MK7 6AA, United Kingdom for a brochure. tel. +44 (0)1908 858793; fax +44 (0)1908 858787; email ouw-customer-services@open.ac.uk

The Open University
Walton Hall, Milton Keynes
MK7 6AA

First published 2009

Edited and designed by The Open University.

Typeset in India by Alden Prepress Services, Chennai.

Printed in UK by Bell & Ltd., Glasgow

ISBN 978 0 7492 1712 9

1.1

CONTENTS

BLOCK 5
WHY DO EMPIRES END?

INTRODUCTION TO BLOCK 5

Paul Lawrence

Learning outcomes

When you have completed your study of this block, you should:

- be aware of the diverse ways in which imperial systems are undermined and dismantled
- be able to identify and discuss the metropolitan, peripheral and international factors (both long and short term) driving processes of decolonisation
- be able to engage with some of the historiographical debates that have surrounded these issues.

The mid twentieth century is the period most commonly associated with the 'end of empire'. During the relatively brief period between the end of the Second World War and 1975 (when Angola, previously Portuguese, secured independence) the European maritime empires were dismantled with startling rapidity. By the end of the century, only minor outposts remained. Though even then, as the Falklands or Malvinas War of 1982 demonstrated, the vestiges of empire still had the power to shape foreign affairs dramatically. That said, the mid twentieth century was not the only time when colonies were lost or empires ended. The British empire, for example, was never a static political entity, and had periodically expanded and contracted well before the twentieth century. The loss of the American colonies following the War of Independence (1775–83) marked the end of the 'first' British empire. It started the so-called 'switch to the east', and was followed in the early nineteenth century by the collapse of the French, Spanish and eventually Portuguese empires in the Americas. Equally, the period 1918–25 saw the demise of the Austro-Hungarian, Ottoman and Russian land empires in eastern Europe and the Near East.

However, what exactly do we mean by the 'end of empire'? It is, as John Darwin notes, a 'deceptively enigmatic phrase' (Darwin, 1991, p. 3). Rather than 'end of empire', a term many scholars use is 'decolonisation' – implying that to understand the ending of imperial systems we need to look first at the differing circumstances by which individual colonies are lost. Although coined in academic circles in 1932, the term 'decolonisation' did not pass into general use until the 1960s – a delay perhaps indicative of the way in which the 'end of empire' really only has coherence in retrospect. As Raymond Betts notes, while it was happening, decolonisation was 'not a process but a clutch of fitful activities and events, played out in conference rooms, acted out in protests mounted in city streets, fought over in jungles and mountains' (Betts, 1998, p. 1). While it is, of course, possible to point to specific moments when power was

Decolonisation

transferred, our analyses of imperial endings will not be focused solely on these. After all, the British empire effectively ended long before Chris Patten formally handed Hong Kong back to the Chinese at midnight on 30 June 1997. Decolonisation, the 'end of empire', was always a messy business – a mix of long- and short-term factors, a product of declining influence and interest on the part of the metropole, growing assertiveness on the part of indigenous populations and of the dictates of changing international contexts.

In attempting to explain the complex historical factors – both long and short term – that led to the ends of empires, historians have tended to focus on three main types of explanatory variable. The first type of variable is *metrocentric* – that is to say, focused on the mother country and on decision making and opinion there. For example, early accounts of the end of the British empire often focused on the liberalism of British officials and the 'far-sighted' intentions of British politicians to transform the colonies into 'dominions'. These arguments, advanced by some of the participants themselves, are now rather outdated (Macmillan, 1972). It is certainly possible to point to the reorientation of Britain politically, economically and strategically towards Europe in the period following the Second World War, and to highlight a growing unease with the concept of imperial rule among the British population. That said, it seems that British governments still expected to have their imperial cake and eat it – to shed the burdens of empire by granting self-government in varying degrees, but also to retain its imperial perks in terms of international status and preferential markets. Moreover, arguments that trace the end of empire to metropolitan indifference are virtually impossible to sustain in relation to France and Portugal (as discussed in Unit 20), both of which were prepared to fight hard to keep their territories in Algeria and Angola. Mark Mazower has suggested that the almost universal experience of defeat and eclipse in 1940s Europe made the imperial powers more willing to fight to hang on to their empires: the nearest thing to a victor, Britain, was first to let its go (Mazower, 1998, p. 213).

The second type of variable that is often advanced to explain the end of empires can therefore be described as *pericentric* – that is to say, focused on the periphery and the actions and desires of colonial elites and indigenous populations. In the crudest version of this type of explanation, empires are fatally disrupted by the growing nationalism of indigenous populations who assert their right to independent rule. Clearly, decolonisation in Algeria and Angola came at the end of prolonged and bloody conflict, which could not have been sustained without the willingness of activist groups among the indigenous populations to fight. However, this perspective again cannot provide a complete answer to the question of why empires end. Even in the cases of Algeria and Angola, the French and Portuguese were able effectively to contain the separatist forces. Yet, they still eventually opted for a political resolution, clearly indicating a certain degree of volition on the part of the metropole. Moreover, it is a mistake to view the conflicts that led to the end of imperial relationships as simply metropole versus colony. Circumstances were often much more complex.

Who were the Americans.

Colonial "nationalism"

emerging nation

Indeed, one aspect of decolonisation was the struggle between forces in the colony to define local identity and power structures. At the outbreak of the American War of Independence, for example, it is debateable to what extent the separatists really saw themselves as American, rather than English or British. Even as the war progressed, the British side benefited from significant support from some loyalist colonists. Equally, in India in the twentieth century, the move to independence was strongly shaped by divisions within India as to what the new state should be, especially in terms of the claims of Muslim and Hindu politicians. These divisions were dramatically acted out in the partition of India and Pakistan, which left hundreds of thousands dead in 1947, and the further splintering off of Bangladesh in 1971. Thus, while possibly a precondition for decolonisation, the often contested nature of the development of nationalism within the colonies warns us against any kind of simplistic metropole versus colony dichotomy. The units on America (Unit 17), Austria-Hungary (Unit 18) and India (Unit 19) all show that decolonisation was also characterised by conflict between multiple locally based groups.

These local conflicts can help to explain events in individual colonies. But, beyond that, how do we explain waves of decolonisation, when many territories move towards independence? This is where the third and final variable comes in handy. This is *international forces*, such as international politics and economic changes. Some historians have argued that geo-politics is a major explanatory factor when considering the end of empire (in both specific and general terms). In the aftermath of the Second World War, the new superpowers of America and the Soviet Union were certainly hostile to old-style imperialism and, as Betts notes, 'in the mid-twentieth-century world so re-proportioned by war, gunboat diplomacy, an old colonial tactic, seemed almost quaint in the face of the atomic bomb, a product lethally distributed from the air' (Betts, 1998, p. 19). Perhaps, then, the wider geo-political context, rather than anything intrinsic to empires themselves, sometimes holds the key. It is true that after the Second World War American leaders had a strong dislike for colonial empires, which they saw as inefficient, anti-democratic zones of economic exclusion. This certainly encouraged local resistance, and increased the costs of empire, though it usually still left metropolitan powers the choice of whether or not they were willing to bear those increased costs.

anti-imperialism

Thus, no simple or single type of variable can account for the loss of a particular colony, less still the break up of imperial systems. It seems likely that, as Darwin has suggested, the most convincing way of explaining the dissolution of an imperial system or the 'end of empire' of an individual colony 'is likely to be found by tracing the ways in which events at each level ricocheted off each other' (Darwin, 1991, p. 7).

To help you consider the varying ways in which imperial systems can unravel, this block presents four case studies that highlight diverse imperial endings. Unit 17 considers the move to independence by the American colonies during the period between 1763, when the Treaty of Paris marked a great acquisition of territory for the British, and 1783, when the thirteen British colonies on the eastern seaboard of America were recognised as the independent United States of America. Unit 18 considers the dissolution of the Austro-Hungarian empire – a huge dynastic land empire that encompassed vast swathes of Europe until its eventual dissolution following the First World War. Unit 19 considers India's move to independence – in many ways the precursor to the wider break up of the British empire. Unit 20 compares the decolonisation of French Algeria and Portuguese Angola – in both instances the outcome of hard-fought armed conflicts.

As you work through each unit, you will be encouraged to weigh up the different explanatory variables as outlined above – decisions taken in the metropole or political heartland, the wider context shaping what decisions could actually be taken, and the role of indigenous movements for national independence. Each author stresses different points but, as you read the units and consider the specifics of each case, it will be useful to bear in mind three analytical questions, which I will discuss in the following three sections:

- What was the nature of the relationship between metropole and colony?
- Was the 'end of empire' determined primarily by long- or short-term factors?
- How did events and actions in the colony, the metropole and the wider world interact with each other?

WHAT WAS THE NATURE OF THE RELATIONSHIP BETWEEN METROPOLE AND COLONY?

All empires are complex systems. Thus, when thinking about decolonisation, an important variable to consider is the nature of the relationship between the metropole and the colony. Think back to Fieldhouse's typology of colonies that you encountered in Unit 2. Do you think there is likely to be a difference between (for example) settler and occupation colonies when it comes to the end of empire? Clearly, the inhabitants of settler colonies such as those in America initially thought of themselves as English (or British). By contrast, in India there was only ever a very thin stratum of Europeans. Hence, arguably, while a nascent American identity had begun to develop by the late eighteenth century, it was primarily a series of grievances over economic and political decisions taken in England that 'pushed' the colonists away from the empire. In India, because of the very nature of the imperial relationship, the role of indigenous identity and its search for political expression were likely to be more significant.

Equally, at the macro level, it is also important to consider the nature of the imperial system that was dissolving. Were maritime empires inherently more susceptible to secession nationalisms because the imperial power base was further from the areas ruled? The example of Austria-Hungary would seem to indicate that this was not the case. However, were contiguous land empires like Austria-Hungary perhaps more likely to end 'all in one go', at least in comparison with the more gradual disintegration of maritime empires like the British?

Different types of imperial rule may also have been significant. The British had always tended towards the pragmatic devolution of at least some power, and hence were amenable to the granting of various forms of self-government. The French empire was rather more bound up with the notion of assimilation. Algeria was part of *La France d'outre mer* (France overseas) rather than simply a colonial possession. Did this difference help to account for France's greater tenacity in maintaining its colonial territory? Then again, Algeria was unique within the French empire in having attracted a significant degree of settlement, so was it this that made ultimate decolonisation there so problematic for the French? Asking questions about the nature of the colony–metropole relationship, and about the way in which an empire was governed, are useful precursors to understanding decolonisation.

WAS THE 'END OF EMPIRE' DETERMINED PRIMARILY BY LONG- OR SHORT-TERM FACTORS?

All the instances of decolonisation covered in this block identify certain trigger events that perhaps dealt the fatal blow to imperial rule. In the case of Austria-Hungary, for example, being on the losing side in the First World War was arguably the decisive factor. Certainly, the empire was still functioning beforehand, but was carved up by the victorious allies in 1918. In the case of India, the exigencies of the Second World War were probably instrumental in persuading Britain to promise independence. But to what extent are these trigger events merely the end point of long decolonisation processes? In Unit 18, for example, you will learn that some historians have argued that Austria-Hungary was on the verge of internal collapse *prior* to the decision for war. Equally, in the case of India, Charles Trevelyan noted in 1838 that 'the existing connection between two such distant countries as England and India cannot, in the nature of things, be permanent: no effort of policy can prevent the natives from ultimately regaining their independence' (cited in Stokes, 1959, p. 46).

While the formation of organised political resistance was perhaps a relatively new phenomenon, to what extent was it related to earlier British decisions to introduce western education to India, and to allow Indians into the Indian Civil Service? After all, Trevelyan's brother-in-law Macaulay had recognised this very possibility in 1833, telling the House of Commons that:

> it may be that the public mind of India may expand under our system till it has outgrown that system [...] that, having become instructed in European knowledge, they may, in some future age, demand European institutions [...] Whenever it comes, it will be the proudest day in English history [...] The sceptre may pass away from us.
>
> (cited in Chamberlain, 1999, p. 72)

Clearly, as you will see throughout the block, some long-term and some short-term factors are applicable to all imperial dissolutions. The tricky part is deciding which are particularly significant and which merely incidental.

HOW DID EVENTS AND ACTIONS IN THE COLONY, THE METROPOLE AND THE WIDER WORLD INTERACT WITH EACH OTHER?

In all cases of decolonisation you will read about actions of the imperial power and activities of those pushing for independence in the periphery. While, as already mentioned, a simplistic colony versus metropole distinction is to be avoided, the actions of those in the metropole and those in the colonies do need to be considered in relation to each other, in order to assess which were the more significant. As noted, the French were able successfully to contain the Algerian insurgency in military terms. Why then did a political devolution of power eventually take place? Is it possible to evaluate the comparative significance of metropolitan French public opinion and the political intransigency of the European colonists established there (the *pieds noirs*)?

Just as important as linking events in the colony and the metropole, however, is to remember that decolonisation struggles never took place in a vacuum. There are two ways in which a consideration of the wider geo-political context is important. In first place, of course, international pressure and opinion could influence the course of events, sometimes decisively. In the case of Algeria, for example, the FLN (National Liberation Front) found wealthy patrons in Tunisia and Egypt. Equally, the Soviet Union and communist China were valuable sources of money, arms and training in revolutionary warfare in Angola. The struggle for decolonisation was rarely just waged between colony and metropole – there were often other interested parties.

On another level, international context is significant because individual decolonisations often had a cumulative or knock-on impact. The proclamation of the principle of national self-determination in Europe in 1918, upon which premise the break up of Austria-Hungary was predicated, did not go unnoticed in colonies elsewhere. There have equally been debates as to the extent to which Africa was simply 'following in the footsteps of Asia in her liberation struggles'. As Chief Awolowo of Nigeria wrote in 1945, 'India is the hero of the subject countries. Her struggles for self-government are keenly and sympathetically watched by colonial peoples' (cited in Chamberlain, 1999, p. 11). Looking further back in time, it is possible to argue that educated Indians were aware of the American embargo of British goods that preceded the American War of Independence, and that they created their own version of it in the *swadeshi* movement of the early twentieth century, when Indians were encouraged to boycott European goods in favour of Indian.

With these questions in mind, it is time for you now to move on to consider the case studies in detail. While explanations of decolonisation require detailed analysis of the kind discussed above, the various ends of empire discussed in the units are also snapshots of dramatic, significant, world-shaping events.

REFERENCES

Betts, R. (1998) *Decolonization*, London, Routledge.

Chamberlain, M. (1999) *Decolonization*, 2nd edn, Oxford, Blackwell.

Darwin, J. (1991) *The End of the British Empire: The Historical Debate*, Oxford, Blackwell.

Macmillan, H. (1972) *Pointing the Way, 1959–1961*, New York, Harper and Row.

Mazower, M. (1998) *Dark Continent: Europe's Twentieth Century*, London, Penguin.

Stokes, E. (1959) *English Utilitarians and India*, Oxford, Oxford University Press.

UNIT 17
AMERICAN INDEPENDENCE

W. A. Speck

AIMS

- To consider American independence as a case study in 'settler decolonisation'.
- To enable you to assess the long- and short-term causes of American independence.
- To introduce you to some of the differing explanations of the move to independence advanced by historians.

INTRODUCTION

At the Treaty of Paris, which ended the Seven Years War in 1763, Britain acquired Senegal in Africa, the islands of Dominica, Grenada, St Vincent and Tobago in the Caribbean, and all the territories held by France east of the Mississippi in North America, along with Florida from Spain. With the recognition of its dominion over Bengal in India in 1765, the first British empire reached its zenith.

In the treaties ending the American War of Independence in 1783, Britain lost many of these acquisitions. Senegal and Tobago reverted to France. Florida once again became Spanish. Above all, thirteen colonies on the eastern seaboard of the North American continent were recognised as the independent United States of America. This recognition by Britain is usually taken to mark the end of the first British empire.

How had this great reversal of imperial fortunes come about in only twenty years? It was scarcely conceivable in 1763 when most American colonists shared in the jubilation that greeted the defeat of France on three continents. Although there were some who warned that the expulsion of the French from North America would make the colonies less dependent on British protection, and more inclined to break free of the empire, they were very few in number. And yet their prophecies appear to have been vindicated by the American War of Independence, which led to a humiliation so profound for Britain that its king, George III, seriously contemplated abdication.

Many then came to share the view that the separation of the American colonies from the 'mother country' had been inevitable. The very term 'mother country' implied a parent–child relationship between the two. It indicated that the colonists were not **aborigines** like the subject peoples of the second British empire in Africa and India. The Native Americans did not rise up to throw off the yoke of the British. On the contrary, so many took the side of the British government against the colonists that one clause in the Declaration of Independence (which you can view, if you wish, as Primary Source 17.1 – you will be asked to read it for an exercise later in the unit) was to accuse George III of endeavouring 'to bring on the inhabitants of our frontiers the merciless Indian Savages, whose known rule of warfare is an undistinguished destruction of all ages, sexes and conditions' (p. 3). Rather, the colonists were Creoles, that is, descendants of those who had migrated there from Europe, principally from the British Isles, to form settler societies across the Atlantic.

The mother–child simile also suggested that the children would eventually grow up and thereby become independent. With the benefit of hindsight, it is possible to discern growing maturity on the part of the colonies, and that they were beginning to chafe at their subordination to Britain even before the quarrel between them began in earnest. One measure of growth was the increasing population of the colonies. In 1750, the colonists numbered about a million; by 1770, this had doubled to two million. The population roughly doubled every twenty years, which meant that when Britain recognised the United States they had at least three million inhabitants. At that rate they would not take long to catch up with the British population, which took a century to nearly double its population, increasing from about 5,000,000 in 1700 to just under 10,000,000 in 1800. Given this, you might be tempted to infer that this demographic explosion shattered the stability of the colonies, contributing to their independence from Britain. Yet it seems that this was not the case. Those colonies that received the most migrants were not at the forefront of the movement for independence. As one historian has recently put it 'the challenge to the empire was at first to come not from an ungovernable people but from the disaffection of the elites' (Marshall, 2005, p. 49). Benjamin Franklin, one of the signers of the Declaration of Independence, predicted in 1751 that 'the greatest number of Englishmen will be on this side of the water'. However, he did not anticipate that this expansion of population in the colonies would pose an imperial problem. On the contrary, he concluded that it would be 'an accession of power to the British empire' (Franklin, 1751). It is, however, significant that Franklin thought of the colonists as English rather than American. For though by the middle of the eighteenth century many regarded themselves as Americans, not only geographically but also culturally distinct from Europeans, they still considered themselves to be English (or British) legally and politically. It took the constitutional and political separation from the mother country to transform them from British men and women into Americans. Although some contemporaries predicted that the separation of the two was inevitable, they generally put it forward into a remote future. The actual timing of the event was blamed, at the time and by many historians subsequently, on inept policies by British ministers in Whitehall, who were accused of bringing on 'a crisis twenty or possibly fifty years sooner than was necessary' (Thomas, 1987, p. 99).

The first section of this unit will consider the view that the separation of the thirteen American colonies from Britain was an inevitable outcome from their original settlement. It will assess the case for American exceptionalism – that is, the argument that the colonies differed in fundamental ways from Britain

[handwritten margin note: What did they want. independence from. Parliament? then monarchy as well!]

from the outset. This section will also investigate how far the colonies in fact replicated conditions in England. Subsequent sections will address the thesis that the American colonies could have been contained within the first British empire, but for the actions of politicians on both sides of the Atlantic in the years immediately prior to the Declaration of Independence. The imperial crisis of the years 1763–76 will be examined in detail to determine why the fiscal and other demands of the British government provoked a reaction that resulted in independence.

LONG-TERM CAUSES

The notion that separation was inevitable, and could be predicted long before it came about, has been taken back to the very origins of American colonisation in the seventeenth century. Thus it has been asserted that the people who went across the Atlantic to establish colonies differed in several significant respects from those they left behind in England. The decision to sail 3000 miles away to a wilderness over the ocean, in sailing ships that could take three months to get there, took a degree of determination and even courage, allegedly lacking among those who remained in England. Most early settlers, it was claimed, were middle class, farmers and craftsmen, who did not share the aristocratic values of the ruling class, or the subservience of the labouring poor below them, but were independently minded men and women. They were said to have established middle-class societies in America that differed markedly from the hierarchical social structure of England. Some, especially those who went to New England, or to Pennsylvania and Maryland, were religious refugees, fleeing persecution at home. New England became a haven for Puritans and Pennsylvania for Quakers, both groups of Protestants who could not conform to the established Church of England, while the early settlers of Maryland were mainly Catholics.

Therefore, the type of people who became settlers, it was claimed by historians such as Daniel Boorstin (1988 [1958]), were fiercely independent, rejecting the mother country in the very act of emigration. Even the title of Boorstin's book, *The Americans: The Colonial Experience,* encapsulates the exceptionalist case. The descendants of the first settlers were alleged to have retained their ancestors' psychological, social and religious attributes, and reacted predictably when Britain began to make unprecedented demands on them. Boorstin's book was first published fifty years ago, and though it has never been out of print it has not gone unchallenged. On the contrary there has been a reaction to the concept of American exceptionalism in favour of the notion that early America in many ways replicated English society. We might therefore ask ourselves here how different were the colonies from England?

One of the most striking differences between the mother country and the American colonies was the presence in the latter of large ethnic minorities. The Native Americans, who had inhabited the continent for centuries before the arrival of Europeans, contributed a cultural dimension to colonial history totally absent from the mother country. Although Africans were by no means unknown in England, they were few in number compared with those in America who had been taken there as slaves. The existence of chattel slavery in all the colonies, but especially in the south, was a major difference between them and Britain on the eve of the American Revolution. Dr Samuel Johnson was to drive home the distinction when he posed the question 'how is it that we hear the loudest yelps for liberty among the drivers of negroes?' (Johnson, 1775). By the middle of the eighteenth century, blacks comprised roughly 5 per cent of the population in New England, 10–15 per cent in the middle colonies, 40 per cent in the Chesapeake Bay colonies, and a majority, 60 per cent, in South Carolina. Fears of a slave revolt were a constant fact of life for southern planters. When Lord Dunmore, the last royal governor of Virginia, issued a proclamation offering to emancipate any slave who enlisted in the forces loyal to Britain, he ensured that the slave owners in the colony would take the anti-British side.

Against this view of American exceptionalism, **Atlantic historians** such as David Hackett Fischer (1991) have demonstrated that, in many respects, the conditions of the mother country were replicated in the colonies. Again, the title of Fischer's book, *Albion's Seed*, summarises the thesis that migration to the colonies was marked more by continuity than by change. People in early modern England did not inhabit a geographically static society but were highly mobile, so that the decision to sail to America was not the traumatic one it might appear to have been. There they did not create the world anew but recreated the societies they had left behind. Although the upper ranks of English society did not go to the colonies, labourers certainly did, so colonial society was not just middle class from the outset. Moreover, as time went by, social distinctions became increasingly marked in the colonies, and on the eve of American independence colonial society had become remarkably similar to that of the mother country. For instance, a planter aristocracy had emerged in Virginia and South Carolina who cultivated the lifestyles of their counterparts in England. Thus they built country houses for themselves similar to those of the English gentry. In Virginia, George Washington's Mount Vernon – named after a British admiral – and James Madison's Montpelier were comparable to such Yorkshire mansions as Beningborough and Newby Hall, and were filled with books, furnishings, pictures and other British luxuries. Many sent their male children to be educated in England. The way of life of the business and professional classes in the major towns, Boston, New York, Philadelphia and Charles Town, were even more comparable to those of Bristol, Liverpool and even London. For where the country houses of even the largest landowners in the colonies could not compete with the palaces of the richest aristocrats in Britain, the town houses of the prosperous middle classes resembled those of the same status in the mother country. For instance, the Brice and Paca houses in Annapolis in Maryland are comparable to the Maister and Wilberforce houses in Hull (see Figures 17.1 and 17.2).

Figure 17.1   The Paca House (William Paca House), Annapolis, Maryland, 2008. Photographed by W.A. Speck. Photo: ©
W.A. Speck. The house was built between 1763 and 1765.

Politically and constitutionally, too, most colonies became microcosms of
the mother country. They had a governor, a council and an assembly,
reflecting the British institutions of king, lords and commons. While the
political history of each colony was different, a pattern has been discerned
in many of them whereby the lower houses of assembly sought to gain
power at the expense of the governor and council. In this they consciously
emulated the struggle of the House of Commons against the Stuart kings in
the seventeenth century. The members of the lower houses thus saw
themselves as upholding the rights of Englishmen, which they claimed they
had retained from their ancestors who had crossed the Atlantic. During the
decades before the accession of George III, the rise of the lower houses
went on largely unchecked by the British government. Consequently, as we
shall see, when it set out to reverse the process, it was too late. The
colonists were able to use the representative institutions that had developed
to maturity in previous reigns to resist and ultimately to reject king, lords
and commons combined.

movement to
resist based on confidence
borne out by using

Figure 17.2 The Maister House, Kingston-upon-Hull, East Yorkshire. National Monuments Record, BB66/02783. Photo: © Crown Copyright/NMR. The house was built between 1743 and 1744.

Religious differences between Britain and the colonies, on the other hand, survived. By 1776, most subjects of the crown in England (though not in Scotland) were **Anglicans**, while less than ten per cent were **Protestant dissenters**, which included the denominations of Baptists, Congregationalists, Presbyterians and Quakers. By contrast, over three-quarters of the white settlers in North America were members of these non-Anglican sects. In the dispute between Britain and the colonies, the great majority of Anglicans on both sides of the Atlantic supported the mother country, while the nonconformists in Britain sympathised with their brethren in America. The significance of these religious distinctions in the conflict has provoked controversy among historians. Traditionally, the struggle for independence was seen in a predominantly secular light, as a constitutional and political dispute. Recently it has been asserted that these causes were subsumed in a basically religious discourse.

We shall now consider this issue in more detail. The traditional historiography is ably summarised by Isaac Kramnick in 'The ideological background' (Secondary Source 17.1). Kramnick does not ignore religion, for there is a section on 'Protestantism'. It is mainly confined, however, to the Puritan work ethic and how this was employed to provide a moral justification for the American stance against Britain. J. C. D. Clark takes the role of religion much further in 'The structure of Anglo-American political discourse' (Secondary Source 17.2), making it central to the conflict.

Read these two extracts, then jot down short paragraph answers to the following questions.

1   What role does Kramnick allot to John Locke?
2   What was 'civic humanism'?
3   What role does Clark allot to religion?

[handwritten margin note: movement to resist based on absorbing intellectual / ideological ideas]

1   Kramnick rightly gives Locke pride of place in his account of the ideological background. Locke's *Second Treatise of Government* argued that government was entered into by individuals to protect their life, liberty and property, and when it no longer protected but on the contrary jeopardised them, individuals could legitimately oppose it. This theoretical scenario seemed to fit the circumstances of 1763–76.

2   'Civic humanism' is the term used by some historians of political thought to describe a republican tradition going back through Machiavelli to ancient Greece and Rome, which, they claim, had more influence on the American Revolution than had Locke. Since governments tended to become corrupt, and thereby to lack civic virtue, it was the duty of the virtuous citizen to be constantly vigilant to oppose corruption. In this view the American Revolution was 'a republican commitment to the renovation of virtue'.

3   Clark accepts that the concerns of the 'civic humanists' (such as their fear that liberty was threatened by corruption) informed the colonial critique of the British government. He attributes it, however, not to the republican tradition so much as to 'the folk memories of Protestant denominations'. They saw in independence an opportunity to achieve the ideals of their forefathers who had fled Britain looking for the promised land. In his view 'the translation of this millenarian vision into worldly terms entailed not secularisation but a holy war'.

A RELIGIOUS WAR?

During the course of the eighteenth century, the Anglican Church came to be perceived as a threat to the Protestant sects in the colonies. It was firmly established in the south from Maryland to Georgia. Even the southern colonies witnessed friction between the gentry and the Anglican clergy. Further north, however, the church's apparent moves to become an establishment were viewed with suspicion. The colonies above Maryland were still strongholds of **Calvinism**, as the 'Great Awakening' (see box) of the second quarter of the eighteenth century demonstrated. Presbyterians in the middle colonies and

Congregationalists in New England experienced a revival of Calvinist zeal which increased their suspicions of Anglicanism. These were aggravated by the foundation in 1754 of King's College, which after the American Revolution became Columbia University, in New York City. Like the College of William and Mary established in Virginia in 1693, the main function of King's College was to educate clergymen. For their graduates to be ordained as Anglican priests, however, they required the laying on of hands of a bishop of the Church of England. Since there was no bishop resident in America they had to visit the mother country for this purpose.

Calvinism and the Great Awakening

Calvinism is based on doctrines associated with John Calvin, the sixteenth-century Protestant reformer. He preached that man after the fall of Adam was beyond redemption by his own efforts. Good works could not effect his salvation. This could only be obtained by the unmerited gift of God's grace. Those who received grace became the elect who would enjoy eternal bliss after death. Those who were not recipients of grace would suffer eternal torments. This bleak doctrine of predestination was adopted by Protestant sects such as the Baptists, Congregationalists and Presbyterians. Even the 39 Articles of the Church of England can be construed as Calvinist. Many Anglicans, however, became more inclined to Arminianism, which preached that Christ died for all men and not just for the elect. The corollary of this was that men could reject grace, whereas to a strict Calvinist it was irresistible. The Calvinist revival of the mid eighteenth century known as the Great Awakening was a reaction to Arminianism, which was alleged to have become widespread in the colonies.

Following the accession of George III in 1760, the archbishop of Canterbury assured the president of King's College that he would do his best to create a bishopric in the colonies. You might be wondering at this point why this was so controversial in the colonies. Previously the colonial churches had been largely free from any interference by the mother country. Now the Anglican Church threatened them with intervention from Britain. An investigation of the consequences of this policy concluded that 'it was primarily the constitutional–political implications of Anglican episcopacy that caused the issue of a colonial episcopate to become intertwined with the mounting tensions between Whitehall and the colonies between 1763 and 1776' (Greene and Pole, 1991, pp. 178–9).

To dub the American War of Independence a 'war of religion', however, can be misleading. It identifies it with other religious wars, such as those in France in the late sixteenth century, the Thirty Years War of 1618–48 in Europe, and even the civil wars in the British Isles in the mid-seventeenth century, which are now widely accepted as being in the same category as the French and European struggles. Though there were many motives on both sides in the English Civil War, when push came to shove it was religion that led men to fight. Again, many causes led to the conflict between the colonists and the

British government, including religion. However, when fighting broke out, the cause that rapidly assumed priority among the colonists was not religion but independence. The Protestant sects in North America objected to Anglicanism not because they wished to destroy it, but because it represented the established church in England. Their objections were not theological so much as constitutional. The British referred to their constitution in church and state. This was not a mere form of words, for the established church was inextricably united with the government. Bishops were not just representatives of that church, they were also agents of the government. That the Americans who opposed that government also distrusted Anglicans because of that link became clear after the Revolution. The religious element involved in the hostilities was finally resolved with the first amendment to the Constitution of the United States. This reads 'Congress shall make no law respecting an establishment of religion, or prohibiting the free exercise thereof'. There was to be no established church in the new republic. But there was to be no religious discrimination either. Even Anglicans benefited from this provision, launching the Episcopal Church in 1789.

Long-term developments leading to independence were seen by some contemporaries, as well as by later historians, as being 'things in the womb of time' (Bumstead, 1974). The striking metaphor implies that cultural, economic and social developments in the colonies would inevitably lead to the birth of a nation. Certainly the factors discussed above created necessary, though not sufficient, conditions for independence. As the eighteenth-century progressed, one can detect the colonists becoming more and more aware of themselves as Americans. Politically, however, they continued to regard themselves as English, and this perception actually intensified along with the dispute with Britain. That the long pregnancy ended, not in a miscarriage, but in a healthy offspring, was due to the actions of politicians on both sides of the Atlantic.

SHORT-TERM CAUSES

That the dispute between the American colonies and Britain was primarily constitutional and political is indicated by the Declaration of Independence in 1776. This did not even allude to the religious controversy. Instead it drew attention to an alleged 'long train of abuses and usurpations, pursuing invariably the same Object ... to reduce them under absolute Despotism' (Primary Source 17.1, p. 1). Although no date is given for the beginning of the 'long train', since all the allegations are levelled against George III and his ministers, it apparently went back to the opening years of his reign. Before that, presumably, the framers of the declaration could detect no plans on the part of the British government for asserting more control over the colonies. Modern historians, however, have attributed many of the measures introduced to that end after George's accession to the earl of Halifax, president of the Board of Trade from 1748 to 1761. Thus Halifax advocated making judges, governors and other officials in the colonies independent of the colonial assemblies for their salaries by raising parliamentary revenues in America for that purpose.

The Board of Trade's plans had to be shelved until the end of the war with France that broke out in Europe in 1756. In North America it began in April 1754, when the French seized a British fort near the site of modern Pittsburgh. An expeditionary force consisting of the Virginia militia under the command of George Washington was sent to the trouble spot. After initial successes it was defeated and Washington had to surrender to the French. The British government concluded that colonial forces were unreliable and sent a regular army from Britain to take on the French. It was intercepted by French and Indian forces in western Pennsylvania who routed the army and killed its commander, General Braddock. These opening moves in what became the Seven Years War thus proved to be disastrous for both colonial and British troops.

They also generated friction between the colonists and the army sent to defend them. The regular soldiers treated the colonial militias with contempt, and commandeered supplies, such as much-needed horses and wagons, from the local farmers and traders. The arrogance of the British, coupled with their abject defeat, disillusioned many in the colonies who had been conditioned to perceive the mother country as a benevolent and invincible power. This bred bad feelings on both sides, which has been seen as intensifying a growing conviction among the colonists that they were no longer British but Americans. However, such sentiments dissolved with the shared glory of the closing phases of the war, which culminated in the capture of Canada. On the other hand, the view held by many in Britain that they had borne the brunt of the fiscal burden of the war, while the colonists had not pulled their weight, persisted even after hostilities were concluded in 1763 at the Peace of Paris.

In the peace treaty the British acquired vast new territories in North America. This in itself was a major change in the nature of the first British empire. Previously, despite the settlements along the eastern seaboard (see Figure 17.3), imperial policy across the Atlantic was more commercial than territorial. Indeed, the jewel in the imperial crown was not the mainland colonies but the Caribbean islands, especially Barbados and Jamaica. Their production of sugar was much more lucrative to the West Indian planters, and to the crown, than were even the **cash crop** producing colonies of Maryland, Virginia, South Carolina and Georgia, let alone the more northern settlements. At the end of the Seven Years War there were some advisors of George III who urged him to retain Caribbean sugar islands taken from the French, and Cuba from the Spanish, rather than their possessions on the continent. Instead, these acquisitions were exchanged for Canada and Florida. This gave British ministers another new imperial problem in the form of subjects who were French or Spanish and Roman Catholic, unlike the white colonists on the North American mainland who were British and Protestant. Together with the acquisition of subjects on the Indian subcontinent, who were neither British nor even Christian, this represented a change in the British empire so great that it has recently been described as marking a transition from an 'old' to a 'new' empire (Marshall, 2005, chs 5 and 6).

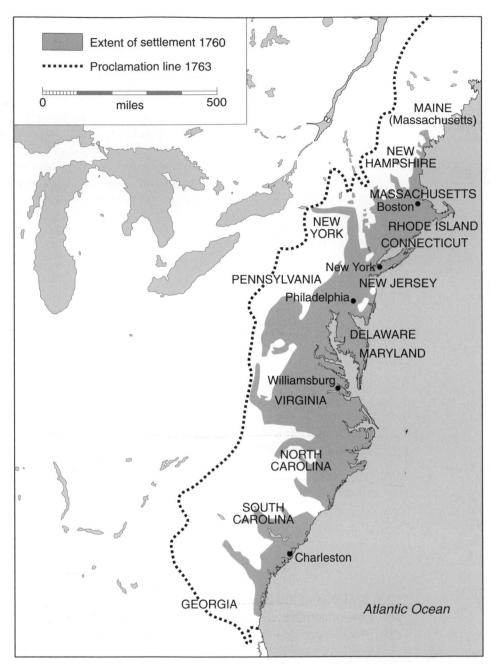

Figure 17.3   British America in 1760, adapted from Wood, G.S. (2002) *The American Revolution: A History*, New York, Modern Library Chronicles, p. xix.

For the American colonists the territorial expansion of the empire also changed their view of the world. Previously they had been largely hemmed in, by the French or the Spanish, to a coastal fringe of settlements. Now they were free to move into the interior, no longer threatened by Europeans, though their encroachments were bound to be challenged by Native Americans. The British government was alarmed by the prospect of warfare between them, and with just cause in the light of the conflict with the Indians in the Great Lakes area from 1763 to 1765 known as Pontiac's uprising. The king took steps to prevent further violent confrontations by issuing the royal proclamation of October 1763 prohibiting settlement west of the Appalachians (see Figure 17.3).

EXERCISE

Read the proclamation (Primary Source 17.2) then answer the following question: What were its objectives?

SPECIMEN ANSWER

The proclamation is often cited merely for its fixing of the western boundary of the colonies on the crest of the Appalachian mountains. Although the proclamation was meant to avoid alienating Indians whose habitations were being encroached upon, its main aim was to provide for the government of the territories in North America gained from France and Spain by carving out three new colonies: Quebec, and East and West Florida.

THE 'NEW' EMPIRE

The royal proclamation was one of the first attempts by the British government to come to terms with the new opportunities, and problems, presented by its acquisition of a territorial empire in North America. It was intended to be a stop-gap measure to restrict the westward expansion of the seaboard colonies. British motives for this were mixed. They were anxious not to alienate the Indians in the new frontier by allowing unfettered migration into the region. They also wished to contain colonists near the Atlantic within the imperial commercial system. Their restriction of colonial expansion westward contributed to the friction between the colonies and Britain. Many colonists who had already made their way over the mountains resented this restriction. In practice, not much could be done to prevent settlers moving westward. However, the proclamation did adversely affect speculators who had invested heavily in western lands, and now found their investments worthless. Many of the Virginian gentry who were to lead the resistance to the British in the American Revolution had been involved in such speculation.

The expansion of the British empire in North America did not merely pose problems of administering the new territories. It also had "financial implications" that were to become a major cause of friction between the colonial elites and the British government.

The decision to station 7500 regular troops in Canada and along the Ohio valley was a more immediate cause of controversy. The cost of maintaining them was estimated at £350,000 a year. The British government baulked at the prospect of laying this burden entirely on taxpayers in Great Britain, especially since the Seven Years War had been extremely expensive, increasing the national debt from nearly £75 million in 1756 to about £148 million in 1763. It seemed reasonable to get the colonists to share at least some of the burden of defending them. This led to the passing of the Sugar Act by the British Parliament in 1764, the avowed aim of which was to raise a revenue in the *taxes –*

revenue

raising.

colonies 'for defraying the expenses of defending, protecting and securing the same' (Greene, 1975, p. 19). This was a new departure in colonial legislation. Although many statutes had been passed regulating commerce between the colonies and Britain, none had previously declared an intention to raise revenue. Now sugar imported into the American colonies from non-British sources was to pay a tax of one pound seven shillings a hundredweight, while molasses were charged at three pence a gallon. There had been previous duties levied on these commodities – sixpence a gallon in the case of molasses – but these had been to protect producers in the British sugar islands rather than to raise revenue. Where these had been widely evaded, the new duties were to be strictly enforced. Those charged with evasion of them were to be tried by a vice-admiralty court set up in Halifax, Nova Scotia. There were some objections raised, principally from those northern colonies where molasses was distilled into rum, though only the Assembly of New York formally complained.

Another measure introduced in 1764 that caused friction was the Currency Act, which regulated the issue of paper money in the colonies, banning new issues. Paper currency issued by some colonies, particularly Virginia, had rapidly depreciated in value. This benefited debtors at the expense of creditors. Since the latter included many British merchants who were paid in depreciated currency by the colonists, they welcomed the Act. Their American customers, on the other hand, felt themselves to be hard hit by it.

Economic DECISIONS + (consequences)

In March 1765, the Stamp Act was put on the statute book. It laid a duty on such legal documents as conveyances, contracts and wills as well as newspapers and pamphlets, thereby taxing lawyers and journalists who swelled the chorus of complaint in the colonies. Even the lower orders felt aggrieved by the duty on items such as marriage licences, playing cards and wills. Many of those affected by the Stamp Act formed themselves into bodies known as the Sons of Liberty. These were behind some of the more violent demonstrations against the Act. In August 1765, the house of Thomas Hutchinson, the lieutenant governor of Massachusetts, was burnt to the ground. The elite sought to harness the grievances of those below them for their own quarrel with Britain.

reaction to the taxes.

Many colonists objected that the stamp duty was unconstitutional since it was a tax levied by a parliament in which they were not and, by the nature of things, could not be represented. The cry went up 'no taxation without representation'. Nine colonies sent delegates to a congress held in New York City in October 1765. The Stamp Act Congress, as it was called, passed a number of resolutions. One maintained 'that it is inseparably essential to the freedom of a people, and the undoubted rights of Englishmen, that no taxes should be imposed on them, but with their own consent, given personally, or by their representatives'. Another asserted 'that no taxes ever have been, or can be constitutionally imposed on them, but by their respective legislatures' (cited in Greene, 1975, p. 64).

During the debates on the Stamp Act in the House of Commons, the prime minister, George Grenville, had asserted that, though the colonies were not actually represented in the Commons, they were represented *virtually*. You might think that this notion of virtual representation is absurd. Certainly it appears so now, when the principle of one adult one vote is the basis of our democracy. Before the establishment of democracy, however, ideas of representation were not based on individual voters. Fewer than a quarter of adult males had the right to vote in England at the time. Rather more enjoyed it in the colonies, where between half and three-quarters of white adult males were enfranchised. Nevertheless, they were entitled to vote by virtue of property ownership even in America. In England, interests rather than individuals were represented in parliament. The social composition of the House of Commons was made up of members who represented, for instance, the landed interest and the monied interest. These were held to be representatives of others involved in the same interests. Thus MPs who were returned from ports such as Bristol, Hull and Southampton virtually represented those from other ports, such as Whitby, which did not return members to parliament. By extension, therefore, in Grenville's view ports involved in the colonial trade, like Liverpool and London, represented colonial merchants. The concept was flawed, however, not because it was undemocratic, but because ports in the mother country competed with rather than complemented such colonial commercial centres as Boston, New York, Philadelphia and Charles Town. The Stamp Act Congress responded to Grenville's claim with yet another resolution stating 'that the people of these colonies are not, and from their local circumstances, cannot be represented in the House of Commons of Great Britain' (cited in Greene, 1975, p. 64).

FRIENDS OF AMERICA?

By the time the Stamp Act Congress met, Grenville had been replaced as prime minister by the marquis of Rockingham. He had to deal with a deteriorating situation in the colonies where distributors of stamps were intimidated from doing their jobs, some by violence. Merchants in Boston, New York and Philadelphia had also begun to boycott British goods. This embargo had a severe effect on exports from Britain to America, leading Rockingham to repeal the Stamp Act early in 1766. To sweeten the pill, since the very members who had passed the Act were now being asked to repeal it, he simultaneously got parliament to pass the Declaratory Act, which declared that it had the right to legislate for the colonies 'in all cases whatsoever' (cited in Greene, 1975, p. 85). Nevertheless, the fact that the Rockinghamites, the most eminent of whom, Edmund Burke, was the marquis's private secretary, had backed down when threatened by the colonists was to lead them to be denigrated as 'friends of America'.

How far colonial complaints were echoed in Britain is hard to gauge. Advocates of repressive measures against the colonies continued to allege that they were succoured by sympathisers in parliament. 'In favour of this exemption of the Americans from the authority of their lawful sovereign' thundered Dr Johnson in *Taxation no Tyranny* (1775) 'very loud clamours have been raised ... These unpatriotic prejudices are the abortions of Folly impregnated by Faction'. (This pamphlet is available for you to download and read from Eighteenth Century Collections Online, accessible through the course website.) By 'faction', Johnson alluded to the Rockinghamites and other 'friends of America' such as Isaac Barré, John Wilkes and William Pitt the elder. Barré, an army officer who had served in North America, warned the House of Commons in February 1765 that the Stamp Act would alienate the Americans, whom he described famously as 'Sons of Liberty'. Some colonists responded by adopting that name. Wilkes, a radical politician, expressed sympathy for Americans who resisted attempts by the British government to tax them. The popularity of the two politicians in America led in 1769 to the naming of a new town in Pennsylvania Wilkes-Barre. Pitt had been prime minister at the height of the Seven Years War when Britain had won its greatest victories over France. He resigned in 1761 in protest at the reluctance of the new ministers appointed by George III, especially the king's favourite the earl of Bute, to continue the war vigorously. Pitt supported the repeal of the Stamp Act, upholding the colonists' insistence on no taxation without representation, agreeing that, since they were not represented in the House of Commons, it had no right to lay an internal tax upon them. He also took exception to the Declaratory Act, and tried unsuccessfully to remove the clause maintaining that parliament had the right to legislate for the colonies 'in all cases whatsoever'. At the end of the day, however, most so-called 'friends of America' accepted that the colonies were subject to Acts of Parliament. The Rockinghamites ruefully acknowledged the rightful jurisdiction of parliament in America even with regard to raising revenues, though they expressed the wish that, while it was valid in theory, in practise it should rarely if ever be exercised. They took some of the sting out of the Sugar Act by reducing still further the duty on molasses to 1d a gallon. But at the same time they imposed it on molasses from British as well as foreign producers, thus emphasising that the policy was based not on commercial but purely on fiscal considerations.

In July 1766, Pitt succeeded Rockingham as prime minister. He was also promoted to the peerage as earl of Chatham and took his seat in the House of Lords. By now his manic depression, or bipolar disorder, incapacitated him so frequently that decisions taken in his name were in fact made by other ministers. Thus the chancellor of the exchequer, Charles Townshend, assumed responsibility for dealing with issues concerning the American colonies.

The first of these was the response made by New York's assembly to a measure of the Grenville administration. This was the Quartering Act of 1765, which made provision for the accommodation of soldiers who could not be accommodated in barracks. Billeting was to be provided in licensed premises and uninhabited buildings – not private houses as some colonists claimed, or feared. They were to be supplied with food, drink, lighting and bedding at the public expense – i.e. the assemblies and not the army were to reimburse the suppliers. This particularly affected New York, where most of the soldiers were stationed. The assembly there refused to supply them as the Act required. The commander-in-chief, General Thomas Gage, informed the British ministers of this defiance, who instructed him to insist that the assembly obeyed the law. When the members refused Townshend undertook to bring in legislation suspending the assembly, unless and until it voted money for the supply of the army in accordance with the Quartering Act. Faced with this threat the assembly reluctantly complied, and the proposed legislation was dropped.

THE TOWNSHEND DUTIES ✈

Townshend also initiated an Act in 1767 for the introduction of duties on a range of commodities imported into the colonies, including glass, paper and tea. The revenue raised by them was intended to pay the salaries of governors and other officials in the colonies. Townshend had first encountered the policy of making officials financially independent of the assemblies when a commissioner of the Board of Trade under Lord Halifax. He now had the opportunity to implement it. In doing so he was mindful of a distinction between external and internal taxes on the colonies that had informed the debates on the Stamp Act in Britain. It had been upheld by Benjamin Franklin when he was questioned in the Commons about them in February 1766. Franklin argued that the colonies had always submitted to external taxes, and objected only to internal taxes, because the former were indirect and could be avoided while the latter were unavoidable. Pitt too shared this view. Townshend's duties were intended to go along with it by placing external taxes on the colonies. By this time, however, colonists denied that the British parliament had any right to impose taxes on them, direct or indirect.

Handwritten margin note: (revenue raised by taxation intended to pay for the colonial officials)

EXERCISE

Objections to British measures were taken up by John Dickinson, a Philadelphia lawyer who also owned land in Delaware, in a series of *Letters from a Farmer in Pennsylvania* (1767–68). I'd like you now to read Primary Source 17.3 – two of Dickinson's letters. As you read, consider the following question: How far did Dickinson deny the doctrine of parliamentary sovereignty?

SPECIMEN ANSWER

The first letter drew attention to the Quartering Act, which Dickinson thought was just as pernicious as the Stamp Act. He insisted that 'the people of New York cannot be legally taxed but by their own representatives'. The second letter took the Townshend duties into consideration. While Dickinson accepted that parliament could pass laws to regulate colonial trade, he insisted that it could not raise a revenue in the colonies and made no distinction between external and internal taxes.

THE ROLE OF THE CROWN

In his third letter, Dickinson expressed the wish that his fellow 'countrymen' would pursue 'the constitutional modes of obtaining relief'. He therefore advocated petitioning the king for redress. 'We have an excellent Prince' he

assured them 'in whose good dispositions towards us we may confide'
(Dickinson, 1774, p. 33). At this stage the colonists looked to the crown to
protect them from parliament. They did so in reaction to the view expressed by
members of both Lords and Commons that parliament had the right to legislate
for them 'in all cases whatsoever'. This notion, which even the so-called
'friends of America' accepted, was based on the concept that sovereignty
throughout the British empire lay with the king in parliament. Dickinson
reflected the views of others opposed to parliamentary taxation that the
colonies were subject to the crown but not to parliament. The charters, by
which they exercised their right to have assemblies that could pass laws and
raise revenues, had been granted by the crown and not by parliament. This
claim implied that there were two constitutions within the king's dominions.
One related to his kingdom of Great Britain, in which sovereignty did indeed
lay with the crown in parliament. But the other applied to the empire, in which
it resided in the crown alone. This appeal to what has been described as 'the
imperial constitution' has received some support from modern historians. It has
even been claimed recently by Brendan McConville that the colonists were
more ardent in their loyalty to the Hanoverian monarchs than were their British
subjects. Clearly this raises problems for the view that the colonists came to
desire independence from Britain simply because they opposed the claim of
the British parliament to tax them. It is possible that they were happy at this
stage to remain subjects of the British king.

EXERCISE

We will now consider this point in a little more detail. Read the extract from
Brendan McConville's *The King's Three Faces* supplied as Secondary Source 17.3.
When you have read this, answer the following question: How far were the colonists
loyal to George III before 1776?

SPECIMEN ANSWER

Obviously Dickinson was not alone in describing George III as 'an excellent Prince'.
As McConville points out, the colonists were devoted to the monarchy. There was
very little overt republicanism in the colonies before 1776. It was not until it
dawned on them that the king was inextricably attached to the doctrine of
parliamentary sovereignty that they were to become disillusioned. Then they were
to react bitterly against him.

THE REPEAL OF THE TOWNSHEND DUTIES

An attempt to repeat the boycott of British goods, which had been so
successful against the Stamp Act, received little support except in New York. It
was lifted by most colonies when news that the Townshend duties had been
repealed, with the exception of that on tea, reached America in the spring
of 1770.

The success of the embargo on British goods as a reprisal against the Stamp
Act, and the relative ineffectiveness of the attempt to impose another against
the Townshend duties, have been given an economic explanation. The earlier
prohibition took place against a backdrop of a postwar recession in the

colonies, which reduced the demand for imports, so that a ban on them made sense economically as well as politically. But by the time the Townshend duties were levied the recession was over and demand for imports was strong, making non-importation an unprofitable option. The resort to such sanctions raises the question of how far economic as well as ideological motives were involved in colonial resistance to British rule. Certainly many Americans were indebted to British creditors, including a significant number of the Virginian gentry. Their indebtedness has been seen as providing part of the motivation that led the upper classes of Virginia to rebel against British rule. It was not that they were crudely using the political crisis to repudiate their debts. They blamed the British government for their plight by restricting their trade in ways that reduced the profitability of their tobacco. As you may recall from Unit 5, a series of Navigation Acts passed by parliament in the seventeenth century obliged the Virginia planters to export their tobacco directly to England, even though the bulk of it was destined for other European markets. They claimed that this monopolistic stranglehold on their cash crop drove down its price. The Navigation Acts thus placed a financial burden on them which meant that they contributed at least their fair share to the British economy. Economic historians disagree about whether or not the Acts in reality had a beneficial or an adverse effect on colonial commerce. While most accept that, on the whole, their impact was positive, this was not how they were perceived by most colonists. As they saw it, the Acts had a negative impact on the colonial economy, so that the unprecedented demand for extra contributions in the form of parliamentary taxation was unfair. By adding to the burden of debt they were already carrying, it was the straw that broke the camel's back. The repeal of the Townshend duties therefore came as a welcome relief.

Navigation Acts

Starting with an ordinance passed by the so-called Rump Parliament in 1651 during the Interregnum, a series of Acts was put on the statute book in England to regulate colonial commerce. The aim was to ensure that trade with the colonies benefited the mother country. The Act passed in 1651 required all colonial produce to be exported to England in English or colonial ships. Goods conveyed to the colonies from Europe had to be carried in ships belonging either to their country of origin or to English owners. After the restoration of Charles II in 1660 it was re-enacted, with a new proviso that certain enumerated products, which included tobacco, could only be exported to England, paying a duty in an English port. European goods destined for the colonies had to go there by way of England according to the Staple Act of 1663. An Act of 1696 introduced vice-admiralty courts into the colonies where those who defied the Navigation Acts could be tried without juries.

The repeal had been decided in December 1769. It was one of the last decisions made by the ministry headed by the duke of Grafton, who had replaced Chatham (Pitt the elder) as prime minister the year before. Grafton urged the cabinet to repeal all the Townshend duties, but by a vote of five to four, in which the prime minister was in the minority, it insisted on retaining duty on tea as a symbol of parliamentary sovereignty over the colonies. It is interesting to speculate as to whether the American War of Independence might have been averted if one of the majority had voted the other way! On such small hinges can empires turn. In January 1770, Grafton resigned, recommending the chancellor of the exchequer, Lord North, as his successor. Lord North's administration was to last until 1782, producing ministerial stability after a decade that had seen six prime ministers. In April 1770, North implemented the decision to repeal the Townshend duties.

THE BOSTON MASSACRE

The years of open confrontation, which began with the colonial response to the Stamp Act, culminated in 1770 with the so-called Boston Massacre. The troops sent to the town by General Gage became targets for hostile demonstrations, the first occurring on 2 March. On 5 March the violence escalated when a crowd of between thirty and sixty townsmen harangued a sentry guarding the custom house in King Street. A party of eight soldiers was sent to rescue the sentry. Faced with a larger body of hostile Bostonians defying them to fire, they retaliated by firing into the crowd, killing three people immediately and wounding eight, two of whom later died. Fearing an escalation of the violence, the governor of Massachusetts, Thomas Hutchinson, acted to defuse the situation. Soldiers were ordered to withdraw into the barracks in Castle William in Boston harbour away from the streets of the town. Captain Preston, who had been in charge of the men ordered to the customs house, was detained on a charge of manslaughter.

Preston was eventually brought to trial in September along with the men he had commanded. John Adams, a lawyer prominent among the critics of British policy in Massachusetts, nevertheless undertook to defend them. Adams was able to persuade the jury that Preston had not ordered them to fire and he was acquitted. Two men who had fired into the crowd were found guilty of manslaughter, but instead of being executed were branded on the thumb. Preston's acquittal by a Boston jury indicates that passions had subsided by the time the trials were held.

EXERCISE

Study Paul Revere's print of the Boston Massacre, which appears as Plate 3.2 in the Visual Sources Book. How does this depiction of the event differ from the account given above?

SPECIMEN ANSWER

The depiction of the British soldiers lined up and obeying their commander's order to fire into an unarmed crowd was a blatant exercise in anti-British propaganda. As we have seen, Preston had not given any such order. The situation was far more confused than the orderly lining up of the troops against the crowd depicted in the print.

1770 - 1774

THE 'PERIOD OF QUIET'

The repeal of the Townshend duties heralded a hiatus in the dispute between
the colonies and the mother country. For nearly four years there was what has
come to be known as a 'period of quiet'. There were, to be sure, quarrels
between governors and assemblies in several colonies, particularly in
Maryland, North and South Carolina, and Georgia. But such disputes were part
and parcel of colonial political history. Without the benefit of hindsight that the
revival of the imperial crisis at the end of 1773 bestows, they would not have
been given any more weight than being signs that politics had returned to
normal. But for the decision by the British government to retain the
Townshend duty on tea, the final confrontation with the colonies might have
been deferred indefinitely. For little was heard of colonial complaints against
Britain between 1770 and 1773 outside New England. There the *Gaspee*
incident in Rhode Island, and the dispute between Governor Thomas
Hutchinson and the Massachusetts House of Representatives, kept the
controversy with the mother country alive.

In Rhode Island, a customs schooner called the *Gaspee* ran aground in June
1772. It had been employed in investigating breaches of the Navigation Acts
(see box), and its crew had earned notoriety by seizing vessels allegedly
infringing them. Given the opportunity provided by its being grounded, men
who felt aggrieved by its overzealous use boarded it, forced the captain and
crew to go ashore, and then set it on fire until it was completely gutted.
The British government responded by offering a reward of £500 for
information leading to the arrest of the perpetrators and by launching a royal
commission in 1773 to investigate the incident, but nobody was ever charged
with the crime.

In the summer of 1772, Thomas Hutchinson announced that he would in future
receive his salary as governor of Massachusetts from the crown and not from
the colony. This led to a Boston town meeting on 20 November, which
criticised this arrangement as yet another infringement of their rights. The
meeting also set up a committee of correspondence on the suggestion of Sam
Adams, who was commissioned by it to write a pamphlet on *The State of the
Rights of the Colonists*, in which he asserted that the British parliament could
not tax them. Governor Hutchinson addressed the House of Representatives on
6 January 1773 to denounce the pamphlet. He declared that he knew 'no line
that can be drawn between the supreme authority of parliament and the total
independence of the colonies' (cited in Greene, 1975, p. 185). His frankness
caused consternation, even in England. The earl of Dartmouth, who had
replaced Hillsborough as secretary of state for the colonies, admitted to
Benjamin Franklin that he and his ministerial colleagues wished Hutchinson
had not put it quite so starkly. The Massachusetts assemblymen, led by Sam
Adams and John Hancock, argued that the colonies were 'by their charters
made distinct states from the mother country' (Greene, 1975, p. 187). They
were dependent on the crown alone, being in the same position with regard to

England as Scotland had been under the Stuarts before the Union of 1707. They had the same king but different legislatures.

THE EMPIRE STRIKES BACK

The decisive shift in the attitude of the colonists to the British government came about in reaction to its policy not towards America but towards India. Thus the very success of the first British empire in encompassing the globe was to contribute to its downfall in America. Before the Seven Years War of 1756 to 1763, British interests in the Indian subcontinent had been largely confined to trading posts of the East India Company (EIC) in Bombay, Calcutta and Madras. During the war, there had been significant territorial expansion from Madras and above all from Calcutta, where the British acquired Bengal. Yet the EIC was still charged with the responsibility for administration and justice in British India. This proved to be financially onerous, and by 1772 the EIC was virtually bankrupt.

To rescue it from its difficulties, North passed a Regulating Act in 1773, which transferred some of the administrative burden from the EIC to a governor-general for all British possessions in India. North also undertook to improve the company's finances by passing a Tea Act. Previously the EIC had had to ship tea directly to Britain even if its ultimate destination was overseas. When the tea entered a British port it was liable to a duty, though three-fifths of this was paid back to the exporter on its being re-exported. Now the whole duty was to be reimbursed. Also, the EIC was to be allowed to ship tea directly to the American colonies rather than through Britain.

The opportunity to drop the Townshend duty on its importation into the colonies was declined, guaranteeing resistance to the importation of tea into America by the EIC. Nevertheless, exempted from all other British duties, the tea sold at very low prices in America. The EIC was permitted to designate merchants who could import its tea into the ports of Boston, New York, Philadelphia and Charles Town. These were at a distinct advantage over other traders, and even over smugglers who had previously handled the bulk of all cargoes of tea arriving in the colonies. British interference in colonial commercial activity provoked intense resentment from all Americans trading in tea, legitimately or otherwise. The result was to renew the outcry against the tea duty as being taxation without representation. All four designated ports organised protests against the measure. That in Boston became the most notorious (see Figure 17.4).

Parliament interfering

On 16 December 1773, a party of colonists disguised as Native Americans boarded an EIC ship and threw 342 chests of tea, valued at £9000, into the harbour. 'The Boston Tea Party', as it became known, created consternation when news of it reached England. Lord North moved quickly to punish the perpetrators. They were to be apprehended and put on trial. Thomas Hutchinson was replaced as governor of Massachusetts by General Gage. An Administration of Justice Act was passed which allowed the new governor

A New Method of MACARONY MAKING, as practised
217   at BOSTON in NORTH AMERICA.
Printed for Carington Bowles, Nº 69 in St Pauls Church Yard. London. Published 12 Octr 1774.

Figure 17.4 'A New Method of Macarony Making, as practised at Boston in North America', 12 October 1774, mezzotint on paper, 15.2 × 11.3 cm, printed for Carington Bowles, London. British Museum, London, Prints & Drawings, J,5.67. Photo: © The Trustees of the British Museum. This mezzotint attacked the 'patriots' who tarred and feathered John Malcolm, a customs commissioner, and forced him to drink tea. A 'macarony' was a contemporary term for a fashionable dandy. Number 45 associates the patriots with the English radical John Wilkes, whose symbol it became after his prosecution for seditious libel for publishing *The North Briton* number 45 in 1763. Stripping a victim naked and pouring hot tar over his body, then sticking feathers to it, was a violent act which could prove fatal. The print was accompanied with a verse:

For the custom house officer's landing the tea
They tarred him and feathered him just as you see.
And they drenched him so well both behind and before,
That he begged for God's sake they would drench him no more.

to have capital crimes tried in a colony other than Massachusetts or even in Britain. Other 'Coercive Acts' were passed in retaliation for the Tea Party. The Boston Port Act closed down Boston harbour until the EIC had been compensated for the destruction of its property. The Quartering Act provided for uninhabited buildings to be appropriated for barracks. The Massachusetts Government Act was perhaps the most contentious, for where the others could be explained as retribution for the Tea Party, this went much further. (See Figure 17.5.)

Figure 17.5   'The able Doctor, or America Swallowing the Bitter Draught', 1 May 1774, etching on paper, 10.3 × 16.8 cm, from the *London Magazine*, vol. 43, p. 184. British Museum, London, Prints & Drawings, 1855,0609.1926. Photo: © The Trustees of the British Museum. Lord North, the prime minister, with the Boston Port Bill – one of the Coercive Acts – protruding from his pocket, forces tea into the mouth of America, represented as a Native North American women (a conventional mode of representing the colonies). Lord Mansfield, lord chief justice of the court of King's Bench, holds her arms, while the earl of Sandwich, 1st Lord of the Admiralty, holds an ankle in one hand while lifting her skirt to peer up her legs with the other. Sandwich, nicknamed 'Jenny Twitcher' from the character in John Gay's *Beggar's Opera*, had a reputation for lechery. Britannia averts her gaze while a Scot holding a sword labelled 'Military Law' encourages the ministers. France and Spain look on. In the background Boston is 'cannonaded' while in the foreground a petition from the town lies on the ground, torn up.

The Act amended the royal charter granted to the colony in 1691. Although the latter stipulated that the governor should be appointed by the crown where previously he had been elected, the council was still chosen by the lower house of assembly. This anomaly had been criticised as being largely responsible for the intransigence of the Bay colony long before the Boston Tea Party. Now the council too was to be chosen by the king. North over-reacted by punishing all colonists throughout Massachusetts for the actions of a handful of them in Boston. His notion of confining the controversy to one colony was also a serious error of judgement. 'If the Boston Port Bill and the other proceedings against that province have been founded on a supposition that the other colonies would leave them to struggle along' a correspondent in Philadelphia warned him 'I do assure you there never was a greater mistake' (cited in Geiter and Speck, 2002, p. 199). (See Figure 17.6.)

Another measure, not meant to be in retaliation for the Tea Party, also ensured that Lord North's American legislation would rouse the ire of all the colonists and not just those in New England. This was the Quebec Act, which only by coincidence was passed in the same session as the others. The stop-gap measures taken for the government of the Canadian province in the proclamation of 1763 had proved abortive. An assembly had not been set up because not enough Protestants had migrated to it to ensure a non-Catholic, non-French majority of assemblymen. The inhabitants of Quebec were still overwhelmingly Roman Catholics. They could no longer be left in a legal limbo and so the Act established the Catholic Church and recognised French civil law. The recognition of 'popery' and a legal system that did not allow for trial by jury caused a paranoid reaction from the colonists, coming as it did simultaneously with the Coercive Acts to which the Quebec Act was added by the Americans. 'Popery and arbitrary power' had been a potent slogan to Protestant Englishmen at the time of the Glorious Revolution in 1688. While anti-Catholicism was no longer as potent a force among the British governing classes, as the passage of the Quebec Act demonstrated, it was still pervasive throughout all ranks of society in the colonies, as the reaction to the Act showed. A more material reason for objecting to the Quebec Act was that it extended the province's border to the Ohio river. This dealt a greater blow to the hopes, and pockets, of land speculators in that vast region than the proclamation of 1763; some of these speculators had even obtained the consent of the crown in 1772 to settle a new colony to be called Vandalia. The Act also meant that the settlers who had moved there found themselves no longer subject to English common law but to French civil law. The empire was generally perceived as being British, Protestant and free. Now it included subjects who were not British, not Protestants and, in the eyes of the American colonists, not free. Hence the hysteria that the Quebec Act gave rise to in the colonies.

economic consequences.

The Coercive Acts polarised the issues between the colonists and the crown. They seemed to prove Thomas Hutchinson's view that there was no compromise between parliamentary sovereignty and the independence of the colonies. When they heard of the passing of the 'Intolerable Acts', as the so-called 'Coercive Acts' also became known to the Americans, the Committee of Correspondence in Boston sent a circular letter to its counterparts in other colonies calling for a boycott of British commerce.

Figure 17.6 'America in Flames', 1 January 1775, woodcut on paper, 14.6 × 9.2 cm, from *Town and Country Magazine*, vol. 6, p. 659. British Museum, London, Prints & Drawings, 1868,0808.10067. Photo: © The Trustees of the British Museum. This woodcut sympathises with the colonists' plight. A Scot (possibly the earl of Bute, though if so it shows him influencing events long after he fell from favour at court), Lord Mansfield (another Scot) and the Devil fan the flames. Scottish influence in the counsels of George III was often depicted in prints as urging coercive measures such as the Quebec Act and the Massachusetts Bay Act here represented as bellows. Figures representing radicals – one of them John Wilkes – attempt to extinguish the fire. Lord North, holding the Boston Port Bill, looks on.

This had become the almost knee-jerk reaction to measures taken by the imperial government regarded as hostile to colonial interests. On this occasion, however, the response was not to impose a trade embargo but to convene a general congress to meet in Philadelphia in September 1774. Thus a series of legislative initiatives on the part of the British parliament tapped into pre-existing anxieties about sovereignty, taxation and religion.

[handwritten top] 'COLONIAL' Nationalism not as important a factor as in India, in shaping decolonisation. The leftes took advantage of mistakes made by / to call for a country free of interference & restrictions.

THE DIE IS CAST

By the time the Philadelphia congress met, the British government too had decided that the time had come to make a stand. 'The die is now cast' George III wrote to Lord North on 11 September 1774, 'the colonies must either submit or triumph' (cited in Black, 2006, p. 215). The fond hope that the crown would act as an impartial broker between the colonies and parliament proved to be no more than that. In reality, the king had never accepted the distinction between the sovereignty of parliament in Great Britain and that of the crown in the empire. Throughout the imperial controversy he had always upheld the view that parliament was the sovereign power. His support for parliamentary sovereignty over the colonies was made crystal clear when he gave his assent to the Massachusetts Government Act. No previous statute had altered a colonial charter. Charters had always been issued, recalled and amended by the crown. It was largely on this basis that colonists argued that there was an imperial constitution in which the king and not parliament was sovereign. Such a distinction was clearly not shared by George III himself.

[handwritten margin] Colonists thought 'empire' was dependent upon the monarch for their legitimacy

It took a while for the realisation that the king was not a friend of America to change into a conviction that he was its foe. Before that, Americans fell back on the constitutional convention that the king could do no wrong, only his ministers could. In September 1774, the First Continental Congress petitioned George III, avowing their loyalty and declaring 'that the present unhappy situation of our affairs, is occasioned by a ruinous system of colony administration adopted by the British Ministry'. They also appealed to the British people, hoping:

[handwritten margin] Who were the Americans?

> that the magnanimity and justice of the British Nation will furnish a Parliament of such wisdom, independence and public spirit, as may save the violated rights of the whole empire from the devices of wicked Ministers and evil Counsellors whether in or out of office, and thereby restore that harmony, friendship and fraternal affection between all the Inhabitants of his Majesty's kingdoms and territories, so ardently wished for by every true and honest American.

> (*Journals of the Continental Congress*, 1774)

They thus put their hopes in the British general election which took place that September. 'The people of England will soon have an opportunity of declaring their sentiments concerning our cause' they observed. 'In their piety, generosity, and good sense, we repose high confidence' (*Journals of the Continental Congress*, 1774).

The results of the British general election, which was held while the congress was in session, must have been a disappointment for most Americans. Whereas their own electorates did provide a reasonable indication of public opinion, the electoral system in Britain ensured that the outcome in most constituencies, which were small and had restricted franchises, was no gauge of it. In these, the American crisis played little or no part in the result. There were some large constituencies in which issues could affect a contest; in many of these there was indeed some appeal to the views of the electors on the government's policy towards the colonies. Pamphlets, such as Joseph Priestley's *Address to Protestant Dissenters*, which sympathised with the colonists, and Dr Johnson's *Taxation no Tyranny*, which supported the government, were aimed at these voters. (These pamphlets are available for you to download and read from Eighteenth Century Collections Online, accessible through the course website.) The results suggest that, where it had a choice, the electorate was more inclined to Johnson's view. Indeed Lord North had got the king to dissolve parliament in June, six months before a dissolution was strictly necessary, in order to capitalise on the perceived popularity of the Coercive Acts. The outcome of the election justified his decision, as his main opponents, the Rockinghamites, lost ground while he increased his majority. Disappointment at the result was to be reflected in the reference in the Declaration of Independence to 'our British Brethren'. 'We have appealed to their native Justice and Magnanimity' it declared. 'They too have been deaf to the Voice of Justice and of Consanguinity' (see Primary Source 17.1). This was a harsh verdict on the many friends of America up and down the country who had petitioned the crown for the conciliation rather than the coercion of the colonies. Like the colonists, they too had been disappointed, for their pleas had fallen on deaf ears.

The Continental Congress not only petitioned the king and addressed the people of England. It also passed a series of resolutions denying the sovereignty of parliament and announcing measures to put pressure on that body to relinquish claims to it. These included a ban on British imports effective from 1 December 1774 and on exports to Britain after 10 September 1775 if their demands had not been met by that date. It then adjourned its session until the following May.

By the time congress met again, the situation had deteriorated into open hostilities. On 19 April 1775, the first shots were exchanged between colonial and regular troops at Lexington and Concord. The regulars retreated to Boston, which was besieged by their opponents. When the delegates to the Second Continental Congress met in Philadelphia on 10 May, they had to deal with the problem posed by the siege. They did so by putting the colonies on a defensive footing and despatching George Washington to Boston as commander-in-chief of 'the American continental army.' On his arrival in Massachusetts he published *A Declaration by the representatives now met in General Congress in Philadelphia setting forth the causes and necessity of taking up arms*. This still placed the blame for the crisis on 'the tyranny of irritated ministers.'

THE OLIVE BRANCH PETITION

Thus, far from blaming the king for the descent into open conflict, the congress sent him the 'Olive Branch Petition' on 8 July. The petition was drawn up by John Dickinson, now in a more conciliatory mood than he had been when he wrote the *Letters from a Farmer*.

I would like you now to read the Olive Branch Petition (Primary Source 17.4). As you read, consider the following two questions. Why did the colonists appeal to the king? What does the petition reveal about their views of George III and his ministers?

The petition places the responsibility for the resort to arms squarely on the shoulders of the king's ministers rather than on the king himself. On the contrary, it declares in extravagant terms the loyalty of the colonists to George III. Those who supported the appeal still held out hopes that the monarch would act as an impartial judge between them and his wicked counsellors.

When the petition arrived in England, the king initially refused to acknowledge it. Instead, on 23 August he issued a proclamation declaring the colonies to be in rebellion. Although he did acknowledge the petition on 1 September, he refused to accept it while seated on the throne and declined to give it a formal answer. The proclamation was not only aimed at the rebellious colonies but also at 'diverse wicked and desperate persons within this realm' i.e. the so-called 'friends of America'. All the king's subjects were therefore 'bound by law to be aiding and assisting in the suppression of such rebellion' (cited in Greene, 1975, pp. 259–60). This effectively silenced any expressions of sympathy for the colonists since they would be taken to be aiding and abetting the king's enemies.

For their part, Congress rejected an overture of conciliation from Lord North himself. In February 1775, the prime minister offered not to levy parliamentary taxes on the colonies for defence, administration or any other purpose, apart from the regulation of commerce, if they undertook to raise revenues for those purposes themselves through their assemblies. It was sent to individual colonies and not to Congress, since Lord North did not recognise it. Congress nevertheless took it into consideration only to reject it, ostensibly because it interfered with the independence of the assemblies. Moreover, North had reaffirmed the theoretical right of parliament to tax the colonies. In reality, the dispute, as far as those represented in Congress were concerned, had gone far beyond that and was moving rapidly towards a bid for independence.

COMMON SENSE

George III saw the way the wind was blowing when he opened parliament in October. In the speech from the throne he informed the Houses of Lords and Commons that the 'rebellious war' in America was 'manifestly carried on for the purpose of establishing an independent empire' (cited in Geiter and Speck, 2002, p. 205). Most colonies were still reluctant to admit this. Even a majority of Congress shrank from the final separation with the mother country. Many minds were changed by reading a pamphlet published in January 1776 with the title *Common Sense*. It was written by Thomas Paine, who, after his dismissal from the excise service and the failure of his marriage and his business in England, had gone to Philadelphia in 1774, where he had set up as a journalist. (See Figure 17.7.)

Figure 17.7   'Poor old England endeavouring to reclaim his wicked American children', 1777, etching on paper, 24.9 × 35.4 cm. British Museum, London, Prints & Drawings, 1865,0610.1124. Photo: © The Trustees of the British Museum. There are two versions of this print. In the other, the child shown here 'mooning' is fully breeched. Britain here is depicted not as the mother country but as a sullen father (cf. Paine's criticism of George III). There is a quote from Shakespeare in the print's original caption 'and therefore is England maim'd and forced to go with a staff'. Presumably the British were held to be crippled by the colonial conflict. The size of the 'wicked children' implies that the father's attempt to hold them by the strings hooked to their noses will in the end prove to be futile.

EXERCISE	Read the extract from Thomas Paine's *Common Sense* that is provided as Primary Source 17.5. What was the 'common sense' in *Common Sense*? How do you account for the popular appeal of Paine's pamphlet?
SPECIMEN ANSWER	Much of *Common Sense* is concerned with political theory, as Paine tried to demonstrate that government is no more than a necessary evil, while hereditary monarchy was absurd. In his attack on George III, however, he articulated ideas which many Americans were thinking but which few dared utter. Thus he called him 'the Royal Brute of Britain' and 'the hardened sullen-tempered Pharaoh of England'. He thereby paved the way for the attack on the king in the Declaration of Independence. Its advocacy of independence as the only cause worth fighting for was seen by many Americans as 'common sense'.

THE DECLARATION OF INDEPENDENCE

The imperial crisis had led to the collapse of the system of colonial representation established by the charters granted to individual colonies, since their governors refused to convene the assemblies. The colonists then asked Congress how to fill the legislative vacuum thus created. After dealing with the problem piecemeal, in May 1776 it advised all colonies to form their own governments independent of any royal authority. The newly constituted representative conventions, dismissed as totally illegal by the British government, came out in favour of independence. On 7 June, a delegate from Virginia to the Second Continental Congress introduced a proposal that 'these United Colonies are, and of right ought to be, free and independent States, that they are absolved from all allegiance to the British Crown, and that all political connection between them and the state of Great Britain is, and ought to be, totally dissolved' (cited in Greene, 1975, pp. 284–5). Because some colonies were still reluctant to take the plunge, debate on the motion was postponed to 1 July. Meanwhile a committee had been appointed to draft a declaration justifying the proposal that delegated the task to Thomas Jefferson. The preamble appealing to a candid world in justification of the American cause is rightly celebrated. Previously colonists opposed to Britain had appealed to history to justify their stance, citing the liberties of Englishmen that their forebears had taken with them across the Atlantic. With the Declaration of Independence's appeal to natural rather than to historical rights they leapt out of history (see Figure 17.8).

When the motion for independence was passed on 2 July, Congress discussed Jefferson's draft declaration in committee. Some amendments were made, the most notable being the deletion of a clause accusing George III of promoting the slave trade. The committee then reported the declaration to Congress on 4 July, when it was adopted *nem con* (without objection). It was still not unanimous as New York's delegation had yet to agree. When it did so Congress added the word 'unanimous' to the title, after which it was signed.

the political will

EXERCISE

Read the Declaration of Independence (Primary Source 17.1). In the light of your reading so far for this unit, does it make a convincing case that George III was a tyrant?

SPECIMEN ANSWER

The Declaration accused George III of 'having in direct object the establishment of an absolute Tyranny over these States' and listed eighteen indictments against him to prove their charge 'to a candid world'. Read candidly, however, none demonstrate that he was a tyrant in the sense of acting cruelly and oppressively. Although each indictment begins 'he has' the thirteenth concedes that he had 'combined with others' to pass the Coercive Acts. This recognised that he had not acted alone but with the advice of his ministers. Indeed, several of the charges made against him could with more justice have been made against his ministers, since before the Boston Tea Party the king took relatively little interest in

Figure 17.8 'The horse America, throwing his master', 1 August 1779, etching on paper, 18.3 × 27.7 cm, published by William White, London. British Museum, London, Prints & Drawings 1868,0808.4599. Photo: © The Trustees of the British Museum. The rider, identified by Thomas (1986) as George III (though there is a blue ribbon in the picture, which suggests Lord North), depicts Britain. Note the fearsome flails whose use has led to the horse throwing the rider. A French officer on the right is advancing to take the horse.

colonial policy. However, he did take control of it after 1773, so the final charges that he had taken measures to suppress the rebellious colonies were valid. To blame George for that, however, was to disclaim any responsibility for the violent events that had led him to resort to repression.

CONCLUSION

The Declaration of Independence had to lay the blame for the war on the king as a final cutting of the tie with the mother country. It was a symbolic act of tyrannicide. All over the former colonies, symbols of the crown's authority, such as the royal coat of arms, were destroyed. An equestrian statue of the king erected in New York City as recently as 1770 was pulled down and destroyed on 9 July 1776.

The course of the ensuing conflict lies outside the scope of this unit, which has been concerned more with the causes precipitating the breakaway of the colonies. The American War of Independence can be seen as a war of settler decolonisation. It would be a mistake, however, to characterise it simply as one between 'the Americans' and 'the British'. That is to overlook the fact that possibly as many as a third of the colonists were Loyalists, who retained their allegiance to Britain. From their point of view it was a civil war between British subjects. Although at the start of the conflict the colonists who took arms against Britain saw it in very much the same terms, after the Declaration of Independence they saw themselves no longer as British but as Americans.

This examination of the move towards independence has been very much from the top down. It is of course possible to examine it from the bottom up, for many colonists below the social elite participated in demonstrations against British measures. The crisis of the years between the Boston Tea Party of 1773 and the Constitutional Convention, which met in Philadelphia in 1787, has been seen as one which not only posed the question of home rule but also that of who should rule at home. The first, the achievement of independence, was answered by the elite, who harnessed the discontent of the lower orders to their cause. At times it was like riding a tiger, though they successfully rode it until independence was achieved. Thereafter the second question came to the fore. Then control over the forms of government that were to replace the British proved to be much more difficult. The War of Independence and the American Revolution, though they overlapped, were two distinct phenomena. Gary B. Nash's book *The Unknown American Revolution* provides a fuller introduction to the bottom-up way of examining the events of this period of American history (Nash, 2005).

REFERENCES

Black, J. (2006) *George III: America's Last King*, New Haven, Yale University Press.

Boorstin, D. (1988 [1958]) *The Americans: The Colonial Experience*, New York, Vintage.

Bumstead, J.M. (1974) '"Things in the womb of time": ideas of American independence 1633–1763', *William and Mary Quarterly*, vol. 31, pp. 533–64.

Dickinson, J. (1774) *Letters from a Farmer in Pennsylvania: To the Inhabitants of the British Colonies*, Philadelphia.

Fischer, D.H. (1991) *Albion's Seed: Four British Folkways in America*, New York, Oxford University Press.

Franklin, B. (1751) *Observations Concerning the Increase of Mankind*.

Geiter, M.K. and Speck, W.A. (2002) *Colonial America: From Jamestown to Yorktown*, Basingstoke, Macmillan.

Greene, J.P. (ed.) (1975) *Colonies to Nation: A Documentary History of the American Revolution*, New York, W.W. Norton.

Greene, J.P. and Pole, J.R. (eds) (1991) *The Blackwell Encyclopaedia of the American Revolution*, Cambridge, MA, and Oxford, Blackwell.

Johnson, S. (1775) *Taxation no Tyranny: An Answer to the Resolutions and Address of the American Congress*, London. Available from Eighteenth Century Collections Online.

Journals of the Continental Congress (1774) [online] Library of Congress, http://lcweb2.loc.gov/cgi-bin/query (accessed 26 November 2008). Selections also available from the Avalon Project at Yale Law School, http://avalon.law.yale.edu/default.asp (accessed 14 November 2008).

Marshall, P.J. (2005) *The Making and Unmaking of Empires: Britain, India and America c.1750–1783*, Oxford, Oxford University Press.

Nash, G.B. (2005) *The Unknown American Revolution: The Unruly Birth of Democracy and the Struggle to Create America*, London, Penguin.

Thomas, P.D.G. (1986) *The American Revolution: The English Satirical Print 1600–1832*, 7 vols, Cambridge, Chadwyck-Healey.

Thomas, P.D.G. (1987) *The Townshend Duties Crisis: The Second Stage of the American Revolution 1767–1773*, Oxford, Clarendon Press.

UNIT 18
THE END OF THE AUSTRO-HUNGARIAN EMPIRE

Annika Mombauer

AIMS

- To study the end of the Austro-Hungarian empire as an example of the end of a land empire.

- To consider the reasons for its demise.

- To encourage you to use a range of primary sources, from popular accounts to diplomatic records.

- To introduce you to some of the historical debates around this topic.

INTRODUCTION

Let's start our investigation of the end of the **Austro-Hungarian empire** by looking at a map (Figure 18.1) that shows the Habsburg empire at the height of its power, occupying huge land masses in central Europe. The first point to note is that this is a different empire from most of those you have studied so far. For example, it was located in Europe (although the Habsburgs were also for a time the rulers of the Spanish empire in the Americas that you studied in Unit 4), and it was a land empire. Unlike the British, French or Portuguese empires, it did not face the problem of administering colonial territories abroad. Moreover, it was a prime example of a dynastic empire, where one ruling family built up a collection of territories over time, through marriage, treaty and conquest.

Although it went through many different guises and was, by the time of its demise, much smaller than at its peak, it was essentially a vast empire that combined a large number of different territories and language groups inhabited by diverse cultural groups (many of which would eventually develop national claims). It was largely ruled without force or coercion, and it managed to exist into the twentieth century. It was 'a collection of formerly independent or potentially independent historical-political entities that came under the sway of the Habsburgs' (Wank, 1997b, p. 48). Some people, as you will see, would argue that without the First World War it would have continued to exist longer still. While you are studying this unit you might want to ask yourself how Austria-Hungary differed not just from other empires, but also from other land empires that you have studied.

Competing senses of national identity were a developing problem for the empire, not so much in the earlier period when few of its subjects felt strongly about the matter, but increasingly so when, in the later nineteenth century, most saw themselves as belonging to a particular national or ethnic group (and were regarded as such by others). This led to competing demands, particularly as populations overlapped and territorial claims clashed. Despite increasing demands for a consideration of national claims, the empire couldn't

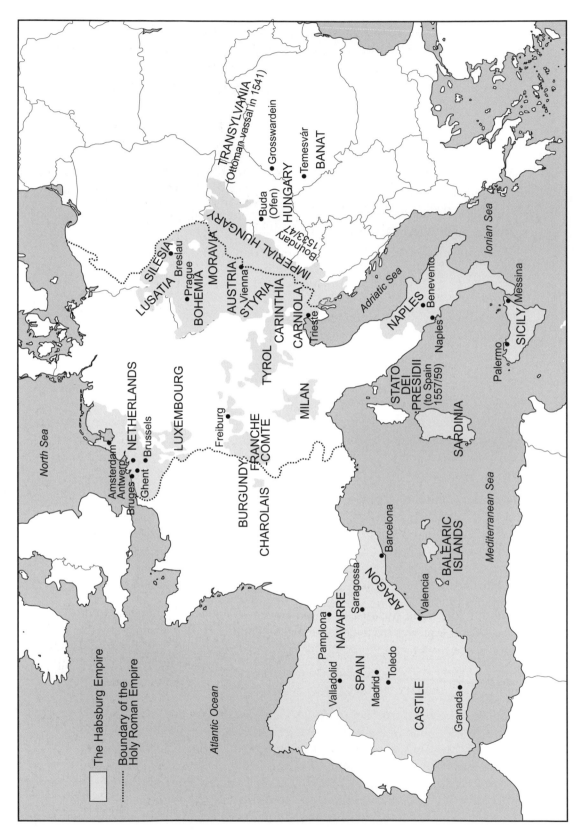

Figure 18.1   Habsburg territories in Europe in 1566, adapted from Beller, S. (2006) *A Concise History of Austria*, Cambridge, Cambridge University Press, p. 36.

easily be broken up into national blocks. Cities, in particular, had mixed populations, including large numbers of Jews. Both maintaining the empire as it was and breaking it up into separate spheres were likely to cause difficulties.

This unit will address the question 'Why do empires end?' with the example of the Austro-Hungarian empire's demise in 1918. Although the Austro-Hungarian empire itself only lasted for fifty years (from 1867 to 1918), it was part of the history of the Habsburg empire, which traced its roots back to the eleventh century. This unit will give you some background about this history and some understanding of the scale of the Habsburg empire in its heyday by providing a brief outline of the empire's history from the Holy Roman Empire to the so-called *Ausgleich* (compromise) of 1867, when the Habsburg empire became the Austro-Hungarian empire. The period of the following fifty years will be studied in more detail. The unit will also discuss the problems the empire experienced as a result of its different cultural groups and nationalities. You will also study aspects of the Austro-Hungarian empire at war and consider why the empire collapsed in November 1918 – was this due to the lost war, or was it already doomed, as some historians have argued? To answer this question, you will consider both long- and short-term causes of the end of the Austro-Hungarian empire and be introduced to some of the historiographical debates around this topic. Contemporary documents will show that while many people at the time felt that the empire was on the decline and perhaps even doomed, others were much more positive about its future.

However, before we turn to the history of the Habsburg and Austro-Hungarian empires, let's consider the empire at the beginning of the twentieth century, just a few years before the outbreak of the First World War and its final demise. As I have already said, the empire was a perfect example of a dynastic empire which depended on a ruling family. In this context, I would like us to look at the role the emperor and the Habsburg monarchy played in providing cohesion to such a diverse empire.

THE HABSBURG MONARCHY AS UNIFIER

Without doubt, the Austro-Hungarian empire in the years leading up to the First World War was troubled by domestic conflict and undermined by the large number of different and competing nationalities within it, many of whom objected to being subjected to either German rule in Austria[1] or **Magyar** rule in Hungary, and wanted to assert their independence (see Figure 18.2).

One threat to the empire was **irredentism**, which was the policy, pursued by countries such as Serbia and Italy, of trying to recover some of their former subjects and territories from the Austro-Hungarian empire and to reunite them with their own countries. In addition to irredentism, **panslavism** (the desire for

---

[1] In the context of the Austro-Hungarian empire, a person referred to as 'Austrian' was ethnically German.

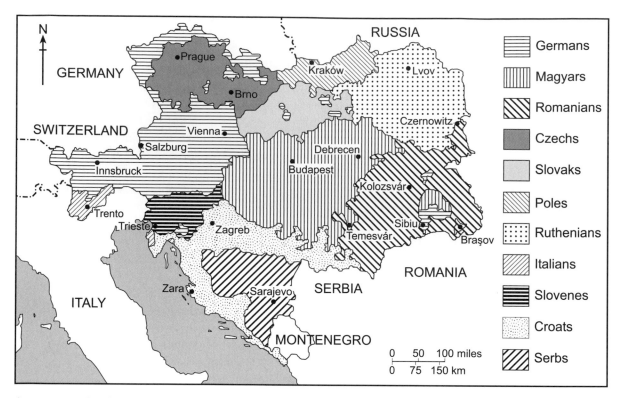

Figure 18.2   The eleven major ethnic groups of the Austro-Hungarian empire, adapted from Sked, A. (2001) *The Decline and Fall of the Habsburg Empire 1815–1918*, Harlow and New York, Longman, p. 284. © Pearson Education Limited 2001. All these ethnic groups were ruled by the Austrian emperor and Hungarian king, Franz Joseph,[2] and by the governments in Vienna and Budapest. While, as we will see later, the *Ausgleich* of 1867 had created the Austro-Hungarian empire and had given the German (Austrian) and Hungarian minorities the right to rule the empire, the other nationalities had not been accorded such privileges and, over time, this would lead to resentment. In this context, the German/Austrian minority within the empire was at times as much of an undermining factor as the other nationalities. The rise of German-speakers' sense of their own ethnic nationalism, whether within Austria or on a pan-German[3] level, threatened to destroy the very basis of the ideology of the empire: a dynasty ruling over a multinational empire not exclusively as 'Germans' but primarily as a legitimate dynasty.

the political union of all Slavs or Slavonic-speaking peoples) was a particular threat. Given the large numbers of Slavs that resided within the empire, moves by Serbia and Russia, for example, to foster a union of Slavs was a threat to the integrity of the empire. It would eventually lead to the adoption of a foreign policy that led to the outbreak of the First World War, and thus to the end of the Austro-Hungarian empire.

In 1900, the population of the empire was constituted as shown in Figure 18.3.

---

[2] In English texts, his first name is often given as Francis and his second name as Josef. The correct German spelling is Franz Joseph.

[3] Some of the German-Austrians would have preferred Austria to be part of a greater Germany and saw their future there, rather than in the multi-ethnic Austro-Hungarian empire.

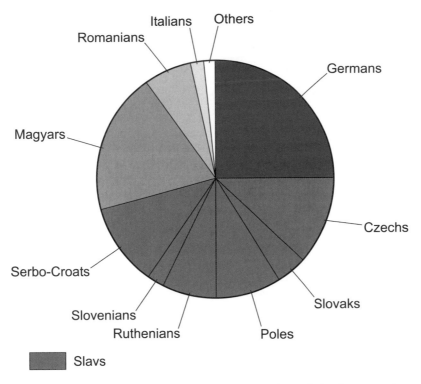

Figure 18.3   National shares in Austro-Hungary's total population in 1900, adapted from Hamann, B. (1999) *Hitler's Vienna: A Dictator's Apprenticeship*, New York and Oxford, Oxford University Press, p. 89. © 1999 by Brigitte Hamann.

There were a number of attempts to create a feeling of unity among the peoples of the empire, including Crown Prince Rudolf's idea to publish a vast encyclopaedia of the Austro-Hungarian monarchy, to instil pride in the empire in all of the nationalities that constituted it. But it was the monarch and his family, in particular, who were able to provide a unifying element for the otherwise divided empire.

The aged Emperor Franz Joseph, who had occupied the Habsburg throne since 1848, was a particular focal point for his subjects. His wife, Empress Elizabeth, had managed to heal some of the rifts between the Austrian and Hungarian parts of the empire through her love of Hungary and her public support for the country. However, after her assassination by Italian anarchist Luigi Luccheni at Lake Geneva in 1898, it was chiefly the emperor who helped to unite an otherwise fairly divided empire. His subjects were touched by his personal tragedies (the death of his small daughter, the suicide of his son, the assassination of his wife, his subsequent lonely existence in Vienna) and his diligence and hard work (rising daily at 5 a.m. and working at his desk until the evening). You can find paintings of a young Franz Joseph (Plate 5.1) and Elizabeth (Plate 5.2) in the Visual Sources Book.

This is how the Austrian writer Josef Roth[4] described the emperor's all-pervasive presence in his famous 1932 novel, *Radetzky March*:

> Carl Joseph stared at the Emperor's portrait hanging on the opposite wall. There, in the flower-white of a general's uniform stood Francis Joseph, with the wide, blood-red sash across his chest, and at his throat the Order of the Golden Fleece ... At home this very portrait hung [in] the District Commissioner's [his father's] study. It hung in the great hall of the Cadet School. It hung in the colonel's office in the barracks. The Emperor Francis Joseph was scattered a hundred-fold, throughout the length and breadth of his Empire, omnipresent among all his people as God is omnipresent in the world.'

(cited in Wheatcroft, 1996, p. 268)

In an empire that was fiercely divided among its different nationalities, this unifying figure came to play an important role. Some contemporaries, however, were concerned that this was perhaps not enough. The Habsburg army officer Ulrich Klepsch worried that any loyalty towards the emperor was to him personally, rather than to the Habsburg state: 'It seems to me as if only the love of the peoples for the person of the emperor was the bond, the *only* one, which held Austria together' (cited in Wank, 1997b, p. 46).

The extent to which the nationalities did not regard themselves as part of the Habsburg empire becomes clear if we consider that, for example, the Czechs, Poles and Slovenes insisted on independent representations 'in areas such as the Second International, the Olympic games and other international sports organizations, and in professional organizations of scholars and scientists' (Wank, 1997b, p. 47). Thus, the Czech team taking part in the 1908 Olympics marched under the name Bohemia behind its own flag.

In the words of Andrew Wheatcroft, Franz Joseph 'embodied empire', and at times this role was purposefully used to create unity (Wheatcroft, 1996, passim). One such example was the emperor's diamond jubilee of 1908, when Franz Joseph celebrated sixty years on the Habsburg throne. To commemorate his jubilee, public celebrations on an unprecedented scale were planned for Vienna, harking back to the Habsburg monarchy's glorious past, uniting the many separate nationalities that resided within the empire, and allowing each a platform on which to honour the emperor. Initially, Franz Joseph rejected any plans to commemorate his long reign, but he finally gave in to the persuasive claims of the advocates of a celebration who claimed that the festivities would not only bolster trade and tourism, but – more importantly – that they would help to foster patriotic feelings and would help to counter the animosities between the different nationalities within the empire (Hamann, 1999, p. 93).

---

[4] The German-speaking writer and journalist Josef Roth (1894–1939) was born near Lemberg (Lvov) in Galicia.

This celebration of the imperial myth was deliberately planned to be even more impressive than the diamond jubilee of Queen Victoria in 1897, which had celebrated the long reign of the queen of Britain and empress of India (as well as of the British empire). The celebrations consisted of two main events: a visit by the German Kaiser and the ruling princes of Germany's principalities and kingdoms to Vienna in May, and an elaborate parade in Vienna in June of 1908.

The visit of the German princes and the German Kaiser (see Figure 18.4) was a high-profile public event, as well as a 'political sensation' (Hamann, 1999, p. 94). There was fear of the possibility of German-national rallies, and soldiers were used to prevent any such outbursts, while thousands of people watched the unprecedented spectacle. The importance of the visit lay in part in its very public statement of unity with the German ally – the German empire was Austria-Hungary's main and most important ally since they had concluded the Dual Alliance in 1879. However, it also underlined the essential German nature of the Habsburg monarchy – the German princes honoured him as one of their own.

Figure 18.4   Franz Matsch, *Franz Joseph Receiving the Deputation of German Princes in May 1908*, 1908, oil on canvas. Museen der Stadt Wien. Photo: Museen der Stadt Wien.

Even more thrilling for the population of Vienna and the provinces was the massive parade on 12 June, which depicted a thousand years of the empire's history, and included presentations of all the empire's nationalities. Twelve thousand people and four thousand horses participated in the parade, and thousands of visitors were attracted to Vienna to witness the spectacle (see Figure 18.5).

Figure 18.5   Kaiser's *Huldigung Festzug* (celebratory parade), Vienna, June 1908. Photographed by R. Lechner, Vienna. Photo: Museen der Stadt Wien. The parade celebrated the sixtieth anniversary of Franz Joseph on the Habsburg throne.

EXERCISE

Now read Primary Source 18.1, 'Imperial and foreign intelligence: the Austrian jubilee' from *The Times*, 13 June 1908, which is a contemporary account of the event. The article will give you a sense of the general atmosphere of the day. I'd like you to look for evidence of how the *Times'* correspondent evaluated the importance of the event for the future of Austria-Hungary. (An additional report, detailing the events of the German princes' visit, is also available via the course website as the optional Primary Source 18.2.)

SPECIMEN ANSWER

There are two instances where the author refers to the difficulties of Austria-Hungary's present position. He likens the patriotic displays of the day to 'a demonstration of *Gesammt-Patriotismus*' [unified patriotism] and continues 'The ravens who croak over the impending disruption of Austria would have taken flight could they have witnessed this manifestation which sprung from the past, projected itself across coming decades [*sic*]' (p. 1). The events of the day had proven that the Austrians were, in the words of the correspondent, 'a nation without knowing it'.

Furthermore, the author refers directly to pan-Germans as one group within the empire whose attempts to undermine the status quo were challenged by the day's display of unity:

> Apostles of Pan-Germanism, were any such present to-day, must have found food for reflection in the thrill that ran through the spectators and the roar of applause that burst forth as the Emperor, with the Archdukes and the brilliant assemblage of general officers, stood at the salute while Hofer's men[5], with their uncouth weapons, shambled across the scene. (p. 3)

The overall impression was thus positive. This had been a successful public event that achieved the organisers' aim of creating, if not unity, at least the impression of it. The Viennese painter Oskar Kokoschka,[6] who had been in Vienna at the time, remembered the event in his autobiography, written after the First World War, when he bemoaned the fact that it seemed so long since June 1908

> when Franz Joseph's Diamond Jubilee had been celebrated in Vienna, and groups of all the peoples who lived in the Monarchy – Slav, Latin, Magyar and Austrian – had passed along the Ringstrasse in their colourful costumes, cheering, singing and dancing to their own music. It had been a festival of many nations, now almost unimaginable; one has only to contrast it with today's highly organised mass parades, in which human beings serve merely as stage props. But the old Emperor had been something of a father figure.
>
> (cited in Mason, 1997, p. 111)

(A longer extract from Kokoschka's memoirs is available via the course website as the optional Primary Source 18.3.)

Other contemporary commentators also had a largely positive impression of the condition of the empire around this time, particularly when compared with the time of the previous jubilee in 1898. The French historian Louis Eisenmann wrote of the empire in 1910:

> On December 2, 1908, Francis Joseph I celebrated the sixtieth anniversary of his accession to the throne. On the occasion of his [Golden] Jubilee (December, 1898), Europe had viewed with fear and distrust the future of the monarchy, which seemed inevitably doomed to dissolution at the death of Francis Joseph. But [ten] years have elapsed since then, and the prognostications are wholly different.

---

[5] In 1809, Andreas Hofer and his men had fought against the decision of the Treaty of Pressburg to give the Tyrol region to Bavaria. They fought Bavarian and French forces and ensured that the Tyrol remained part of the Austrian Empire.

[6] Oskar Kokoschka (1886–1980), Austrian (German-speaking) artist, poet and playwright, best known for his expressionistic portraits and landscapes.

The acute crisis has been dispelled solely by the internal forces of the monarchy. The external dangers, that is to say, Pangermanism and Panslavism, appear much less serious today than at that time. Pangermanism has been swept aside by universal suffrage, and the Panslavonic feeling is growing weaker ... There is still a violent struggle between the nationalities, but the inevitable solution is in sight. The union between Austria and Hungary has, in reality, been strengthened by the new Compromise, and the new Eastern policy. It seems as though all the Austrian, Hungarian, and Austro-Hungarian questions could be settled from within.

(cited in Mason, 1997, pp. 106–7)

(The whole reading is available via the course website as the optional Primary Source 18.4.)

From Eisenmann's account one would not have got the impression that within a few years the empire would collapse and be divided up into different states or subsumed within them. And yet, only six years after this event, Austria-Hungary's leaders reacted to perceived threats from outside (and to a lesser extent within) their empire by launching a war against Serbia, one of the nations that had been regarded as a particular threat. And only ten years after the jubilee celebrations, the end of the war spelt the end of the Austro-Hungarian empire. How did this happen, and why could the potential for a unity of nations as witnessed by these and others not be sustained?

For a start, it would seem that Kokoschka had a somewhat rosy view of the events of 1908, and that Eisenmann overstated the harmony that existed within the empire's borders. The celebrations had actually been marred by the animosities of the empire's different nationalities, and underlying all the celebrations was the constant threat of unrest.

In fact, the organisers had trouble filling the expensive seats of the specially constructed seating that lined the parade route along the Ringstrasse. While there was interest, particularly among the poorer provincial population of the empire, to use the opportunity to visit the capital (moderate funds were provided to enable them to travel to Vienna), tickets for the main event were unaffordable to most of them. Financially, the day was a disaster. You may have spotted the *Times'* correspondent's reference to this, too: 'Accounts may presently prove hard to balance, but miserable considerations of cash were forgotten to-day' (Primary Source 18.1). Moreover, the event attracted large numbers of people to the capital that the authorities regarded as 'undesirable', while Hungarians, Czechs and Italians decided to stay away for reasons of national pride, feeling that they had been slighted in one way or another.

EXERCISE

Read the sections from Brigitte Hamann's *Hitler's Vienna: A Dictator's Apprenticeship* entitled 'The "Reich German" princes pay their respect' and 'The anniversary parade as a symbol of the era' in Secondary Source 18.1, and summarise some of the problems with the two different celebrations of 1908.

SPECIMEN ANSWER

The visit of the German princes, paying respect to Franz Joseph as the oldest of the German princes, had been the German Kaiser Wilhelm II's idea. They had needed convincing, for Franz Joseph was not considered a German prince, given that Austria-Hungary was a multi-ethnic empire. Moreover, within Austria-Hungary, there was continuing resentment over the German defeat of Austria in 1866. An additional problem was posed by the fact that there were those within the empire who would have favoured a union (*Anschluss*) with Germany, and they planned to pay their respects to the German Kaiser, despite the fact that Franz Joseph detested any pan-German displays and sentiments.

The arrival of the German Kaiser and the German princes had to be heavily policed with the help of soldiers to avoid such pan-German demonstrations. While Wilhelm II emphasised the emperor's German-ness, the latter in turn chose to focus on the celebration of the monarchic principle to defuse the situation. Of course, the alliance between the two monarchies was also stressed during the event. Abroad, the spectacle raised suspicion and was regarded as a pan-German demonstration.

The anniversary parade achieved the opposite of what was intended: namely, it 'illuminated virtually all the Dual Monarchy's problems' (p. 3). There were problems financing the event when ticket sales failed to raise the required funds. Some were outraged by the involvement of Jewish businesses in the event while others resented the prominence of the nobility in the festivities. Most importantly, national conflicts continued unabated. The Hungarians announced that they would not participate in the celebrations as the beginning of Franz Joseph's reign for them was 1867, not 1848. The Czechs pulled out of the parade after a Czech language performance of *Hamlet* had been vetoed by the mayor of Vienna, to approval by the Christian-Social and German-national press. The Italians also refused to join in when their feelings were insulted by aspects of the parade referring to the revolutions of 1848, and the Croats nearly pulled out, having been insulted by some of the contents in the festival programme.

The event also enabled poor people from all regions of the empire to travel to Vienna for free, and many took advantage of this offer. This brought the Viennese face to face with their compatriots, many of whom were illiterate and unable to communicate with them – a shocking spectacle for Vienna's bourgeois inhabitants, and more likely to promote distrust and resentment than unity.

As we have seen, despite attempts at creating harmony, and despite the fact that some contemporaries regarded the event as a success, the pronounced differences between the empire's many national minorities could not actually be put aside, even for one day of celebrations, and not even for the beloved emperor. To help us understand the reasons behind this animosity, we will now go back in time and get a sense of the history of the Austro-Hungarian empire and of some of the political events that shaped it.

THE HISTORY OF THE AUSTRO-HUNGARIAN EMPIRE

It is important to remember that, although we are looking at the reasons why the empire ultimately failed, we should not presume that it was bound to do so. We are approaching the question, as always in history, with the benefit of hindsight, but just because the empire was dissolved in 1918 does not mean this outcome was inevitable. Nor should we necessarily think of the empire as ailing throughout its history. On the contrary, we are looking at an empire with a long and successful history which, after all, was still functioning and considered one of the great powers of Europe in the early twentieth century.

The main focus of this unit, chronologically, is on the period 1867 to 1918, a time, in John W. Mason's words, of 'political decay and disintegrations, but also one of economic growth and extraordinary cultural efflorescence' for the empire (Mason, 1997, p. 1), but before we focus on this shorter period, I'd like to glance briefly at the history of the empire until the so-called *Ausgleich* of 1867, when the Habsburg empire reformed itself into the Austro-Hungarian empire. A brief look at the history of the Habsburg empire will show you that it once encompassed vast territories throughout Europe (as you have observed in Figure 18.1) and the New World and even aimed at times for world domination. With this in mind, let's see if we can establish why (or when) things started to go wrong.

'It is for Austria to rule the whole world'

You may wonder why we need to go back so far in history, given that we are, after all, concerned here with the empire's end, but there is a compelling reason for this. It is crucial to have an understanding of the empire in its prime (albeit a glancing one). When things started to go wrong for the empire at the beginning of the twentieth century, its inhabitants and, in particular, its rulers and decision makers were very well aware of their empire's long and successful history, and any views they held and decisions they made were informed by their own sense of history. If, as many of them did, they considered their empire to be declining, they also considered themselves to be the heirs of a successful world empire and were comparing their current situation with the past.

The House of Habsburg and Austrian history became inseparably intertwined when the German King Rudolf of Habsburg (the name derived from the Habichtsburg or Hawk's Castle in the Aargau in today's Switzerland) defeated the king of Bohemia on the Marchfeld, northeast of Vienna, on 26 August 1278. From this moment on, the Habsburgs were the rulers of Austria and, '[f]rom then until 1918, Austrian history is inseparable from the career of this paragon of dynastic politics' (Beller, 2006, p. 26).

Between 1452 and 1806, Austria's emperors were also crowned Holy Roman emperors and, as such, Austria's emperors came to rule over the entire Christian world – or attempted to.

> The rise of the Habsburgs to world power thus began with a claim to imperial and hence divine sanction quite at variance with modern notions of political reality. Over three centuries, from Frederick's becoming family head in 1440 to the accession of Maria Theresa in 1740, the Habsburgs sought to realize their divine right to rule, and

not only to rule their own patrimony, but to preside as God's chosen
dynasty over the entire civilized (Christian) world. Their sense of a
special divine duty and hence right, the *pietas austriaca* ... was given
its most famous formulation by Frederick III in the acronym AEIOU,
in notes made before he was even crowned emperor. In German this
stood for: 'Alles erdreich ist Österreich unterthan'; in Latin: 'Austriae
est imperare omni universo.' In English: 'It is for Austria to rule the
whole world.' Remarkably, for much of the sixteenth and seventeenth
centuries, this claim to universal monarchy was almost realized.
'Austria' – the House of Austria, the Habsburg dynasty – at times
threatened to achieve in reality the hegemony in Europe to which it
felt entitled; as Holy Roman Emperors, the Habsburgs in any case
could claim a formal superiority over Western Christendom.

(Beller, 2006, pp. 37–8)

If you compare the territorial expansion of the Habsburg empire in
Figures 18.1 and 18.6, you will get a sense of the scale of the empire in its
prime. The expansion that you can trace on these maps was largely achieved

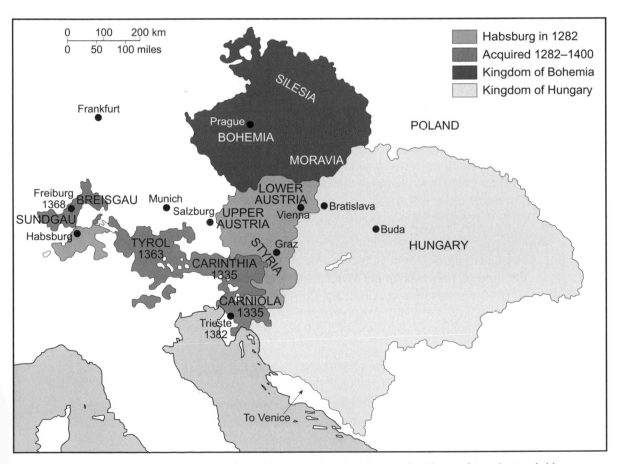

Figure 18.6   Habsburg territories, *c.*1400, adapted from Beller, S. (2006) *A Concise History of Austria*, Cambridge, Cambridge University Press, p. 32.

through marriage arrangements and success on the battlefield. Habsburg lands stretched across France and Germany (today from the Dutch coast to southern France, including the Netherlands and Burgundy). By the end of the fifteenth century, the Habsburg empire also included Spain, much of the New World, large parts of Italy and most of Central Europe (Beller, 2006, pp. 40–1).

EXERCISE

Before we begin our study of the last fifty years of the empire, I would like you to read a short extract from Mason's book *The Dissolution of the Austro-Hungarian Empire 1867–1918* (Secondary Source 18.2), which gives you a concise history of the Habsburg empire until 1867.

First, read the section entitled: 'From the origins of the house of Habsburg to 1848'. As what point, and why, does Mason identify a turning point in the development and make up of the empire?

SPECIMEN ANSWER

The turning point came with the acquisition of Bohemia and Hungary in 1526, and Croatia in 1527. Until this point, the hereditary lands that had made up the empire had been predominantly German and relatively easily integrated, whereas the new territories in the east were non-German. According to Mason, 'Just at the time when the nation-state was emerging as the primary unit in the West, the multinational empire was becoming established as the norm in eastern Europe' (p. 1). The Habsburg empire thus took a different path from that of the other countries in Europe.

EXERCISE

Mason also points to the effects of the French Revolution and the revolutionary wars on the empire. What were they?

SPECIMEN ANSWER

The empire found itself as the ideological opponent of the new order that France was advocating. Two of the main ideas of the Revolution – nationalism and political democracy – were fundamentally opposed to the Habsburg way of ruling their multinational empire. As a result of Napoleon's wars and his declaration as emperor of the French, Francis II became the emperor of Austria. The Holy Roman Empire was dissolved in 1806. The change of title signposted a shift of emphasis away from Germany. Some historians even claim that this is when modern Austria was born (p. 2).

EXERCISE

Now read the rest of the extract: 'The period of constitutional experiments: 1848–67' and answer the following questions. Why, according to Mason, did the revolutions of 1848 have more of an impact on the Habsburg empire? What were the circumstances in which Austria introduced a constitutional government, and what were the problems that constitution faced?

SPECIMEN ANSWER

The answer to the first question, once again, is nationalism. In Austria, the government faced not only a democratic, but also a nationalist challenge in 1848 (p. 3).

The constitution of 1861 pleased neither the nationalists nor the liberals of the Habsburg empire. The Magyars in particular opposed it and were eventually able, against the background of threats to Austria from Prussia and the lost war against Prussia in 1866, to force Emperor Franz Joseph to make concessions to them.

We can see how nationalism posed a long-term problem for the empire. As a result, it was lacking in internal cohesion and it was becoming an 'overstretched empire' (Okey, 2001, p. 173). Its survival had depended to a large extent on its successful alliances within the European system, but following the Crimean War, it found itself diplomatically isolated and had lost Russia as a potential ally. Worse still, the empire suffered badly on the battlefield in a number of ill-advised wars. First, in 1859, in a war against France and Sardinia-Piedmont over Piedmont territory it was defeated narrowly in the battles of Magenta and Solferino (where Franz Joseph led the troops himself). In fact, the emperor 'was largely responsible for this first great failure of his reign.' In Steven Beller's words:

> The truth was that Francis Joseph was not clever enough, or far-sighted enough, let alone tough enough, to be the absolute monarch he styled himself to be; nor was the Habsburg Monarchy strong or rich enough, 'great' enough, to perform the role he and his advisers, and Habsburg tradition, demanded of it. In their minds, Austria was a first rate, and indispensable, great power, the anchor of legitimacy and the international settlement. In reality, as Roy Bridge has put it, Austria was 'only an impecunious second-class Great Power' [Bridge, 1990, p. 135], without the wherewithal to act alone successfully on the international stage.
>
> (Beller, 1996, p. 71)

In the war against Prussia that followed, Austria was decisively beaten in the Battle of Sadowa (a Bohemian village) on 3 July 1866. In the subsequent Peace of Prague they avoided a loss of territory, but were excluded from the newly organised Germany under Prussian leadership. The defeat was a grave blow and ended Austria's 'attempt to figure simultaneously as an Italian, a German and a Balkan power' (Okey, 2001, p. 187).

The *Ausgleich* of 1867: 'deceptive stability for fifty years'

The *Ausgleich* (compromise) agreement of 1867 was a critical political turning point in the empire's history. The external defeat of the previous year had made it more difficult for Franz Joseph to resist domestic reform and he opted for the 'dualist' proposal between the Austrian and Hungarian constitutional states (Okey, 2001, p. 187). The *Ausgleich* established the state structure that would be in place until the empire collapsed in 1918. The agreement between Hungary and Austria divided the monarchy into two parts which made up the Austro-Hungarian empire or Dual Monarchy, in which the Hungarian kingdom formed a separate unit. The result was a quasi-federal structure. The elevation of the Hungarian element ruptured to some extent the principle of different territories united under one dynasty. Instead, some of the other nationalities found themselves under Hungarian control and forced to learn Magyar.

As emperor of Austria and king of Hungary (he was the last crowned king of Hungary following his coronation in June), Franz Joseph appointed the ministers for the three joint ministries that the two parts shared: the foreign office, the army and finance (though the joint finance ministry was only concerned with the funding of military and diplomatic matters). In addition, the two parliaments appointed separate delegations which discussed, independently, matters of common concern. Curiously, the two delegations communicated solely by writing to each other and would only meet in case of a deadlock (Jelavich, 1987, pp. 65–6).

Solomon Wank considers the *Ausgleich* of 1867 'the most obvious example of the empire's limited response to nationalism'. The *Ausgleich* 'gave the empire a deceptive stability for fifty years, but at the price of alienating most of the Slavs, with the exception of the Poles in the Austrian part of the empire' (Wank, 1997a, p. 104).

One of the shortcomings of the compromise agreement was that it did not properly acknowledge the rights of the many non-German or non-Magyar peoples within the empire, leading to disgruntlement and disappointment, particularly among the Czech and South Slav population. They were excluded from power although they considered themselves to be of equal importance to the Hungarians. Because of the veto that the Hungarians were able to exercise, the *Ausgleich* made it impossible to offer autonomy to any of the major nationalities within the empire (Mason, 1997, p. 8). While the government in Vienna was at times willing to make concessions to the other nationalities, it was the Hungarians who were determined to safeguard their own privileges at the expense of those of other minorities (Jelavich, 1987, p. 67). The *Ausgleich* had handed Hungary a 'virtual veto over all further efforts to remodel the empire' (Wank, 1997a, p. 104).

In 1869, Galicia was given effective autonomy, with Polish as the official language, when the Poles were rewarded for their support of the *Ausgleich* with their own compromise with the Habsburgs, although these arrangements did not stop demands for an independent Poland. On the whole, the Viennese government attempted to preserve the Austro-German independence by adopting what amounted to a strategy of divide and rule; that is to say, they attempted to play one nationality against another. However, as Wank argues, this was in the end counter-productive, for 'the concession to nationalist aspirations on which the strategy was based strengthened national elites and stoked the fires of national rivalry, which later disrupted internal tranquillity' (Wank, 1997a, p. 104).

In the long term, supporting some nationalities but not others was to have disastrous consequences. However, despite all these misgivings, the Dual Monarchy was able to survive successfully for fifty years, only to falter when the First World War was lost. Along the way, however, there were a number of junctures where, arguably, the potential problems inherent within such a multinational empire were compounded, as you will see in the next section.

The Dual Monarchy: the Austro-Hungarian empire from 1867

A number of critical junctures can be identified in trying to explain the empire's ultimate downfall, such as the following (based on Mason, 1997, p. 90):

1   the failure, in 1871, to meet Czech demands to convert the Austrian part of the empire into a federal state

2   the Austro-Hungarian occupation of Bosnia and Herzegovina in 1878

3   the Dual Alliance concluded between Germany and Austria-Hungary in 1879

4   the failure of the Badeni language decree that would have led to Czech and German languages being placed on an equal footing in Bohemia

5   Franz Joseph's failure in 1906 to impose universal suffrage on Hungary

6   the annexation of Bosnia and Herzegovina in 1908, which led to irreconcilable differences between Austria-Hungary on the one hand, and Serbia and Russia on the other.

EXERCISE

I would like you to read the extracts from Steven Beller's *A Concise History of Austria* provided as Secondary Source 18.3. This is a longer exercise than the previous ones and you should put aside a bit more time for it. Your reading will give you an overview of the history of the Dual Monarchy from 1867 onwards. When you come across the events listed above, jot down some details about them. Finally, see if you can identify an overall theme that links most of these junctures.

SPECIMEN ANSWER

1   This refers to the 'Fundamental Articles' of 1871 which could have federalised **Cisleithania** (the Austrian part of the Dual Monarchy) and would have given the Czechs more power in Bohemia. The reasons for the failure were excessive Czech demands, pressure from the new German government and objections from the Austrian German liberals. Also, the Magyars regarded the concessions as a breach of the dualist system, and Franz Joseph ultimately sided with the Hungarians, rather than risking a loss of power (p. 3).

2   Austria-Hungary's main aim at the Congress of Berlin in 1878 was the annexation or occupation of the Ottoman provinces of Bosnia and Herzegovina. Again, it was the Hungarians (or rather foreign minister Count Gyula Andrássy) who objected to an annexation, not wanting to incorporate even more Slavs into the monarchy. But there was also opposition from within Austria, from German liberals who saw both an occupation and an annexation as a 'profligate imperial adventure' and who didn't want to add more Slavs to the empire, either. In the end, Franz Joseph insisted on occupation, against the opposition of the liberals (pp. 6–7).

3   The Dual Alliance between Germany and Austria-Hungary was concluded in 1879. Bismarck's intention was to buttress the Dual Monarchy against Russia and to ensure that German influence within it was sustained. The proposed alliance was popular both with Andrássy (who wanted the support against Russia) and with Franz Joseph (who had always wanted an alliance between the two German powers) (p. 7).

4   Count Casimir Badeni's version of the compromise was to be achieved by giving Germans administrative autonomy for German Bohemia and a Bohemian Diet dominated by Czechs. His language ordinances of April 1897 were to make Czech

equal to German as an administrative language in Bohemia and Moravia, with all officials required to be proficient in both languages from 1901. This led to uproar among the German left who feared a 'Czechification' of Bohemia's administration with nothing in return for the rest of Cisleithania. The ordinances were eventually repealed in 1899, Badeni having resigned in November 1897 (pp. 12–13).

5   This was the result of the Joint Army Crisis, a struggle between the emperor and the Magyars. Franz Joseph rejected the challenge for German to be the language of command of the Habsburg army, and he opposed a division of the joint army, which had been the backbone of the monarchy. He proposed electoral reform in Hungary (which would have increased the enfranchised from 7 to 16 per cent) as a ruse to subdue the Magyars. They dropped their opposition. The emperor retained his army and powers, but in return he dropped franchise reform. However, as a result of the emperor seemingly backing electoral reform in Hungary, the franchise was soon extended in Cisleithania and universal male suffrage introduced in January 1907 (pp. 14–15).

6   The annexation of Bosnia was primarily intended to improve the empire's domestic situation with 'energetic' foreign policy. The Russians (with whom the empire usually competed for the European lands of the declining Ottoman empire) seemed interested in cooperation, but when Aehrenthal announced the annexation, he had offended the other great powers by not informing them of his intentions first, and the Russian foreign minister Isvolsky now denied having come to an informal agreement with Aehrenthal. The long-term result of the diplomatic move was disastrous. Austria-Hungary was even more dependent on Germany and relations with Russia and Serbia had severely deteriorated, while the other great powers had been offended (pp. 19–21).

As for an overall theme, almost all of these domestic and foreign problems are ultimately down to the demands and the competition between different nationalities, particularly the fears of an influx of Slavs into the empire, of an extension of Czech rights, and of an undermining of Magyar or German power, or, in the case of the annexation crisis, motivated by a desire to quell domestic discontent.

Let's look at the Bosnian annexation crisis in a little more detail. It was perhaps no coincidence that the event occurred in 1908 during the jubilee celebrations in Vienna. The policy was partly motivated by the empire's political leaders' desire to halt its perceived decline and to dispel any rumour or fears that it had ceased to be a 'great power'.

EXERCISE

Now read Secondary Source 18.4, which is another extract from Brigitte Hamann's *Hitler's Vienna: A Dictator's Apprenticeship*; this section is entitled 'The annexation of Bosnia and Herzegovina'. What was the intention behind this diplomatic move, and what were the results, both short- and long-term?

SPECIMEN ANSWER

In a sense, the annexation was intended to be a jubilee present for the emperor. It was undertaken for patriotic reasons, and to demonstrate the empire's strength and position as a great power.

The immediate results were very negative. The other European powers were surprised and irritated by the sudden move, and the German ally had not been informed in good time about Vienna's intentions. Most importantly, Russia was affronted. The Balkan states were alarmed, particularly Serbia, which considered Bosnia and Herzegovina parts of a potential Greater Serbian empire. The result of the annexation was a very real threat of war between Serbia and Austria-Hungary. Domestic conflict also resulted, as the threat of war boosted the various nationalist groups' discontent, leading to riots in a number of towns and cities, while the Social Democrats also opposed this move and spoke out against it in parliament. Rioting in Prague got so bad that martial law had to be declared on the eve of the emperor's jubilee.

The international crisis was only diffused when the German chancellor Bernhard von Bülow declared Germany's support for Austria-Hungary if a war were to result.

The long-term results were equally worrying: since 1908 a European war had become more likely and a succession of Balkan crises would further heighten the existing international tensions. Moreover, Austria-Hungary's dependence on its ally had become obvious, making it appear weaker to the outside world, while increasing anti-German feelings among the non-German citizens of the empire.

If the jubilee celebrations and the Bosnian annexation crisis had indeed been intended to create unity in the empire, the result was much the opposite, as Brigitte Hamann explains:

> Nationalism was increased rather than decreased, and those voices that perceived Austro-Hungary as outdated became louder. More and more nationalists began to view war as a solution and not only were ready to accept the collapse of the Hapsburg Empire but also desired it. This became palpable with the Czechs and Italians, and more and more so with the Southern Slavs, but also – if only within a tiny minority of the pan-Germans – with the Germans.

(p. 4)

THE END OF A GREAT POWER

From your reading so far you will have got a sense of what a formidable power the Habsburg empire once was. It really had deserved to be called a 'great power'. However, the increasing threat of competing nationalities within, and particularly of panslavism without, led to the perception, both at home and abroad, that the empire was unravelling. In the early twentieth century, the empire's declining position had become a reality that was difficult for contemporaries to ignore. As Aehrenthal exclaimed in 1911, when Austria-Hungary failed effectively to back its ally Germany during the second Moroccan crisis: 'What more can I do? We can pursue no *Weltpolitik*' (cited in Beller, 2006, p. 182). Little wonder that when its decision makers felt that their country's status was in decline, many were keen to halt (if not reverse) this process. For some, this even meant contemplating war. Among them, the chief of the general staff, Franz Conrad von Hötzendorf, advocated war on numerous occasions, for example in 1911 against Italy, and repeatedly against Serbia, who posed a particularly grave threat to the Habsburg interests and to its prestige. In Steven Beller's words: 'If the Habsburg power could not keep

even Serbia in its place, it would no longer deserve to be a great power'
(Beller, 2006, p. 183). This perfectly sums up what many contemporaries
(within and outside of the empire) felt.

Serbia had managed to extend its influence and its prestige following the
Balkan wars of 1912 and 1913[7] and the irredentist threat it posed to Austria-
Hungary was not imaginary – Serbia targeted Serb areas of the Dual Monarchy
for expansion. In addition, there were further threats to Hungarian
Transylvania from Romania, and to the South Tyrol and the Adriatic coast
from Italy (Beller, 2006, p. 183).

How the threat emanating from the newly strengthened Serbia was perceived
by contemporaries can be gauged, for example, by a famous memorandum,
drafted upon the request of foreign minister Count Leopold Berchtold in
June 1914 (before the assassination of Archduke Franz Ferdinand) by a senior
section chief in the Viennese Foreign Office, Franz von Matscheko.
The memorandum was intended to help Berchtold's negotiations with the
German ally and amounted to a 'last effort to use a diplomatic approach to
restore the Danubian monarchy's foreign policy leadership. After [the
assassination at] Sarajevo the document would be redrafted and used to justify
force, not diplomacy, as a foreign policy option' (Williamson, 1991, p. 165).
A short extract from the memorandum is reproduced below, the whole
document is available on the course website as optional Primary Source 18.5.

> **Memorandum by Sektionsrat Franz Baron von Matscheko, secret,
> undated (before 24 June 1914)**
>
> Conditions in the Balkans are now clear enough after the great
> upheavals of the last two years to permit one to assess the results of
> the crisis and to decide whether and how far the interests of the Triple
> Alliance Powers (Germany, Austria-Hungary and Italy) – especially
> the two Central Powers (Germany and Austria-Hungary) – have been
> affected by these events, and what conclusions follow for the
> European and Balkan policy of these Powers.
>
> If the present situation is compared objectively with that before the
> great crisis one must admit that the total result, from the point of view
> both of Austria-Hungary and the Triple Alliance, can by no means be
> said to be favourable. ...
>
> Serbia, whose policy has for years been motivated by tendencies
> hostile to Austria-Hungary, and who is entirely under Russian
> influence, has achieved an increase of territory and population which
> far exceeds her own expectations; the possibility of her further

---

[7] In the First Balkan War (October 1912 to May 1913), Serbia, Montenegro, Greece and Bulgaria
victoriously fought against the Ottoman empire, which lost most of its European territory. The
victors soon fell out and fought each other in the Second Balkan War (1913), when Greece and
Serbia faced Bulgaria. As a result of these wars, Serbia in particular increased her power in the
Balkans considerably.

enlargement by means of a union with Montenegro has moved markedly nearer realization as a result of her territorial proximity to Montenegro and the general strengthening of the pan-Serbian idea.

(Primary Source 18.5, pp. 1–2)

Four days after this draft was presented to the foreign minister, the Austro-Hungarian heir to the throne, Franz Joseph's nephew Archduke Franz Ferdinand, was assassinated by a young Bosnian anarchist during a visit to Sarajevo. The Austrian authorities immediately suspected Serbian forces to have been behind the assassination (they were correct in their assumption), and there was almost immediate talk of revenge and of using this act of terrorism as the reason for a reckoning with Serbia.

The Matscheko memorandum was amended against this background on 1 July with the following addition which reflects the shift from diplomacy to force in the thinking of the Austrian statesmen:

> The above memorandum had just been completed when the frightful events occurred at Sarajevo. The momentous consequences of the wicked (*ruchlos*) murder can hardly be overlooked today. But in any case it provides irrefutable evidence, if any had still been lacking, of the unbridgeable nature of the opposition between the Monarchy and Serbia, and of the dangerous character and intensity of pan-Serbian aspirations, which stop at nothing.
>
> Austria-Hungary has not been lacking in goodwill and conciliation in her efforts to establish a tolerable relationship with Serbia. But it has again been shown that these efforts were quite vain, and that the Monarchy will also have to reckon in future with the tenacious, irreconcilable, aggressive hostility of Serbia.
>
> For the Monarchy, the necessity imposes itself all the more imperatively to tear apart with a firm hand the threads which its opponents are seeking to form into a net above its head.

(Primary Source 18.5, p. 5)

Of particular concern to Vienna's statesmen was the preservation of Austria-Hungary's great power status. They even preferred to enter into a war whose outcome was uncertain, rather than to fade into a second-rate power. As Solomon Wank explains, this attitude had a lot to do with the country's history as a powerful empire:

> The relative economic backwardness of the Habsburg empire compared to the other Great Powers, made it difficult to draw subsidies from the periphery to serve the centre, and the organizational inefficiency of the imperial structure diminished its military capacity and undermined its prestige as a Great Power. From the point of view of the emperor and his advisers, the ability of the empire to play the role of a Great Power was the sole justification for its existence, even though it lacked the requisite political and economic conditions. Any other policy, such as withdrawal or

disengagement – i.e., accepting the status of a middling power which would have accorded with perceptions of it within the European Concert – was rejected because such moves would be a sign of weakness and convey the wrong signal to all of the domains under Vienna's control. It was the determination of the ruler and his advisers to preserve the shaky imperial structure and restore the empire's reputation as a Great Power that motivated them to seek salvation in war in 1914, as they had done in 1859 and 1866. In that sense the war was not an accident, of which the collapse of the Habsburg empire was an unfortunate by-product; rather, it was a symptom of the systemic crisis of the imperial structure.

(Wank, 1997b, p. 52)

Moreover, there was the fear that by appearing weak and not dealing forcefully with the Serbs, the empire would give the impression of losing its great power status, which would in turn lead to a loss of prestige vis-à-vis Germany, the only reliable ally that Austria-Hungary had. It would not want to be allied to a former great power, Vienna's statesmen feared. On its own, however, as Wank argues, the empire would not have been able to survive in the world of European power politics (Wank, 1997a, p. 111).

Vienna's decision makers chose force over diplomacy when the Common Ministerial Council met on 7 July 1914. (The abbreviated minutes of the meeting can be found in the course database as optional Primary Source 18.6.) Having first ascertained support from Germany (in the form of the famous blank cheque that the alliance partner issued by assuring Vienna of support whatever action it decided upon) the meeting concluded almost unanimously that 'a purely diplomatic success, even if it brought a striking humiliation of Serbia, would be worthless. Thus the most far-reaching demands must be made of Serbia in order to assure a rejection, which would then open the way to the radical solution of a military attack' (Primary Source 18.6, pp. 2–3).

THE END OF THE AUSTRO-HUNGARIAN EMPIRE

The empire at war

Faced with external threats, particularly from a Russian-backed Serbia, as well as internal upheaval and disquiet, and desperate to remain a great power, the 'hawks' in Vienna (i.e. those who favoured war to counter these threats) had increasingly advocated war from 1908 onwards. Their hour had come following the assassination at Sarajevo. An opportunity for war had presented itself that seemed too good to miss. With Germany's support, Austria-Hungary declared war on Serbia on 28 July 1914, unleashing the First World War, which would ultimately lead to the downfall not just of the Austro-Hungarian empire, but also of the German and Russian empires.

Now read Secondary Source 18.5, which is another extract from Beller's *A Concise History of Austria*. This is a slightly longer exercise for which you need to put aside a little more time. You will gain a brief overview of Austria-Hungary's decision to go to war and of its fate during the years 1914–18. While you are reading, jot down some notes to answer the following questions:

1   What, according to Beller, were the reasons for the Habsburg monarchy's decision to start a war against Serbia in July 1914?

2   What problems were experienced on the home front during the war?

3   How did the death of Emperor Franz Joseph, and the decisions made by his successor, affect the war effort?

1   Beller lists the need to defend the honour of the empire against Serbia's 'assault on its core values'. Crushing Serbia, it was hoped, would deter other irredentist nationalists from acting against Austria-Hungary. In addition, Germany's support had not always been reliable in the past and it had offered Austria-Hungary a 'blank cheque' on this occasion (p. 2). The emperor himself gave similar reasons when he addressed his people on 29 July, talking of the honour of his monarchy, its good name and position among the powers. Prestige played a strong role in the decision-making process. Count Berchtold later wrote in his memoirs: 'our role in world history would be over if we feebly allowed fate to do what it willed' (p. 3).

2   One of the main problems was supplying food and fuel to the population, and strict censorship led to a mistrust of the authorities, even among those who supported the war effort in general (pp. 3–4). Later in the war, the severe shortages of food and fuel led to labour unrest, strikes and growing popular unrest in the streets where the population was forced to queue ever longer for bread. There were ever-increasing demands for autonomy among the different nationalities (pp. 6–7).

3   Franz Joseph's authority and popularity had been largely based on his person alone. When his successor, Emperor Karl (Charles), came to the throne, he lacked the respect of his subjects, and did not have his predecessor's long experience of running such a complex empire. He made some decisions which, though well-intentioned, only served to undermine the war effort further. In particular, at home they led to increasing calls for virtually independent national states (p. 5).

Of course, the lack of supplies not only affected the home front, but also severely hampered the military effort of the empire's army. In August 1918

> the once venerable *k.u.k.* Army was no longer a fighting force. ...
> Dysentery, malaria, and malnutrition had reduced the Army's rank
> and file to a pathetic shadow of its former self. The Sixth Army
> reported that its soldiers on average weighed 120 lbs. ... Most soldiers
> had just one set of clothes, and these were but tattered rags. One
> regiment at the front noted that only every third man possessed a coat.
> Other units reported sentries manning their posts without underwear
> or trousers. Most soldiers went for days without meat or fat. ... A
> soldier in Dalmatia informed his officer: 'We are not heroes, but
> beggars!'

On 18 August, General Arthur Freiherr Arz von Straussenberg undertook what was to be the last formal assessment of the k.u.k. Army. His report was a strange mixture of naivety and ignorance. The Chief of the General Staff finally appreciated that the Great War had taken on 'the characteristics of an economic struggle of survival', and accepted that it had become 'a question of the Monarchy's existence'. He now understood that modern industrial warfare demanded that the economic, political, and social components of the national polity be coordinated! Yet Arz staunchly defended the right of officers to preferential rations and accommodation, and declined to follow what he called the 'German example', whereby officers and men ate the same food at the front. Such an egalitarian turn was out of the question due to the 'differences in educational levels' between officers and men. How could one expect Austrian-German officers to consume food from kitchens staffed by different nationalities? The General found the prospect 'insufferable'. And what Austrian-German officer, Arz wished to know, would agree to serve in an army where officers and men ate from the same menu?

(Herwig, 1997, p. 434)

With defeat merely a few weeks away, the general advocated adhering to social norms that had once defined military life in Austria-Hungary, but that had surely become an anachronism. This was a particularly curious juxtaposition to what ordinary citizens were experiencing on the home front.

The effects of the Allied blockade were felt very early, and the government issued advice on saving food, on frugality, and on the need to make home-front sacrifices, while stressing that the expected shortcomings were the effect of external forces (Healy, 2004, p. 36). But it wasn't long before actual shortages were experienced. Already in 1915, many shoppers would return home empty handed, 'and with little for sale at the markets, civilians began to question the meaning and limits of home-front sacrifice' (Healy, 2004, p. 40).

Civilian mortality increased during the war, as Table 18.1 demonstrates.

Table 18.1   Deaths of Viennese women during the First World War

1912	15,355
1913	15,390
1914	15,310
1915	16,305
1916	17,029
1917	20,816
1918	23,898
1919	21,223

(Source: Rosenfeld, 1920, p. 27, cited in Healy, 2004, p. 42)

By the end of the war, the population had been severely weakened by malnutrition. According to a study conducted in early 1919, between 7 and 11 per cent of wartime deaths in Vienna had been the direct result of starvation, while in 20–30 per cent of cases where a post mortem had been conducted, starvation had contributed to the cause of death, usually a disease – so even if people didn't actually starve, they suffered from acute hunger, which made them susceptible to diseases (Healy, 2004, pp. 41–2).

It is not surprising that such appalling conditions exacerbated the tensions between the different nationalities.

> In March, 1915, Vienna's Polish-language newspaper reported a disturbing incident: a fourteen-year-old Polish-speaker, Fräulein M., was attacked by two boys while window shopping. One of them shouted 'Polish pig!' as he hit her in the face. The journalist lamented that such behaviour from Viennese children was not uncommon: '[C]hildren are usually just a mirror of the attitudes of older people. I must add that I have already witnessed such behaviour from Viennese children several times before. As the "little patriots" heard that I speak Polish they ridiculed me.' ... In a more direct encounter, a Polish-speaking high-school student reported that he had been heckled and beaten, denounced as a 'Polish cow' and 'Polish pig' in a bread line 'not only by women, but also small children' who were angry that a Pole had gotten a loaf of bread.
>
> (Healy, 2004, p. 237)

In fact, such domestic tensions had been expressed as soon as war had broken out, with Czech people finding themselves the subject of racial abuse. The windows of Czech schools in Vienna were smashed in July 1914, for example, as retaliation for the murder of Franz Ferdinand by a Slav, and such animosities continued to be expressed throughout the war (Healy, 2004, p. 238). It is perhaps surprising that the army managed to function largely unhindered by such nationalist sentiments. In July 1914, the different nationalities that made up the joint army rallied behind the common cause of defending the Austro-Hungarian empire – though to what extent they were merely supporting their comrades and to what extent they really fought for the empire as a whole is impossible to gauge. Whatever unity was displayed was, however, eroded by the unsuccessful war, and in 1918 there was little willingness to continue with the outmoded empire.

Some historians have pointed to the internal conditions as the 'primary reason' why the empire collapsed in 1918.

> During the war, the Austro-Hungarian authorities lost the battle for hearts and minds to those who believed in new state structures and new forms of government. ... unresolved political and national issues from the prewar period ... festered increasingly during the war,

exacerbated by war-weariness and the critical food situation. They
formed the essential domestic basis which enabled outside forces, the
'secondary reason', to contribute to the Monarchy's dissolution.

(Cornwall, 2000, p. 443)

The break up of the Austro-Hungarian empire

The formal end of the Austro-Hungarian empire came when it had lost the
First World War following a request for an armistice by Emperor Karl on 28
October 1918. It came into effect on 4 November. On 11 November the
emperor abdicated, though he did not formally renounce his throne. The
Hungarians signed their own armistice on 13 November. This demonstrates
how the lost war proved to be the final straw for the outmoded and somewhat
artificial construction that had been the Austro-Hungarian empire. To survive,
it had seemingly depended to a large extent on the person of the old emperor,
Franz Joseph, who had died in 1916. Against the background of military
defeat, the young Emperor Karl was unable to unite his subjects and the
Austro-Hungarian empire perished at the end of the First World War, along
with the German, Russian and Ottoman empires.

It might be fair to say, however, that the Austrian empire's demise was settled
as early as July 1914, when its leaders declared war on Serbia. It was a war
that they hoped they could win, relying to a large extent on support from their
alliance partner Germany, but that they could not be certain of winning. It was
the conclusion to years of domestic strife caused by the 'nationalities problem'
in which the government in Vienna had felt threatened particularly, but not
exclusively, by Serbian nationalists who denied the Austrians' 'divine right' to
rule over the many different peoples of the Austro-Hungarian empire. Thus, it
was the assassination of the Austrian heir to the throne by a Serbian nationalist
that became for Vienna's military and political leaders the *casus belli*, the
reason for declaring war on Serbia on 28 July 1914. This action triggered
events that led to the outbreak of the First World War, which the Dual
Monarchy was not to survive.

At the end of the war, the empire was replaced by a number of national states
which represented some, though by no means all, of the nationalities that
had previously lived within its borders (see Figure 18.7). The new Austrian
Republic, which was created following the peace treaty of St Germain on
10 September 1919, consisted of a small German-speaking area around
Vienna, while Czechoslovakia, Yugoslavia, Poland and Hungary became
independent countries. In addition, territories were lost to the empire's
neighbours: Poland took Galicia, Italy took the Trentino, the South Tyrol,
Trieste, the Istrian peninsula and the Dalmatian islands. Bosnia-Herzegovina
became part of Yugoslavia. Hungary's postwar fate was settled by the Treaty
of Trianon on 4 June 1920. It lost three-quarters of its territory and two-thirds
of its subjects. Slovakia and Ruthenia were given to Czechoslovakia, Croatia-
Slavonia and the Banat of Temesvar to Yugoslavia and Transylvania to
Romania (Herwig, 1997, pp. 439–40.)

Figure 18.7   First World War postwar settlements, adapted from Goldstein, E. (2002) *The First World War Peace Settlements, 1919–1925*, London and New York, Longman, p. xv. © Pearson Education Limited 2002.

But was this outcome inevitable? With the benefit of hindsight it might seem to us today as if the empire was doomed, as if it could not possibly have survived long into the twentieth century, with or without the First World War, particularly given the volatile problem of its many competing nationalities. But historians have long debated whether this view is correct, and some would argue that the empire was not, in fact, threatened from within and could have survived longer. Of course, we can only speculate what would have happened if the war had ended with a victory of the Central Powers (or indeed if it had not happened at all), rather than with their humiliating defeat, but it is worth considering arguments for the empire's inherent stability, and those which regard the war as having been the catalyst of an inevitable decline.

There is even some debate over the importance of the nationalities question. Nobody would deny that the empire was hampered by its many nationalities, not least at a time when nation states were being established all over Europe. However, John W. Mason warns against coming to simplistic conclusions:

> There is a temptation among historians to take a Western European view towards nationalism and assume that the eleven national groups within the Austro-Hungarian Empire would sooner or later have achieved autonomous statehood. But few people living in western or eastern Europe in the late nineteenth and early twentieth centuries envisaged such an outcome

> (Mason, 1997, p. 88)

As Mason points out, even Karl Marx thought that the Slavs were better off under the rule of Germans and Magyars (with the exception of the Poles). Moreover, the different nationalities were so mixed together that it was not simply a case of drawing boundaries around some actual or assumed national territories (although maps such as Figure18.2 might give you that impression!). Furthermore, not all national minorities wanted independence. The Czechs, for example, did not favour the dissolution of the empire, and merely wanted more privileges for themselves. Such demands did not 'touch the fundamental question of the Monarchy's existence' (Mason, 1997, p. 88). In other words, the mere fact that the empire was made up of so many nationalities did not necessarily have to lead to its dissolution.

Other historians also seek to play down the nationality problem. According to Alan Sked, the empire fell because it lost the war. 'A win for Germany, on the other hand, would certainly have ensured its survival in some form or other' (Sked, 1989, p. 264). Sked speaks of 'misplaced determinism' of those who think that the empire was doomed to failure. Instead, he argues that, 'had the Central Powers actually won the First World War, the Habsburg Monarchy would have survived not merely intact, but almost certainly expanded' (Sked, 1989, p. 187). This is not, perhaps, so unlikely, given that such a victory would have boosted imperial prestige, and left Russia weakened by revolution and Serbia chastised. Moreover, Sked argues that 'it is by no means obvious that the nationality problem was the reason for its fall. Most nationalities fought for it during the First World War right up until the end.

Before 1914, if anything, the nationality problem seemed to be abating' (Sked, 1989, p. 264).

We can certainly find contemporary evidence that supports Sked's views (e.g. the fact that the various nationalities did fight for the empire during the war, and largely until the bitter end, despite their rivalries), but it is also possible to demonstrate that contemporaries regarded the nationalities issue as a serious problem. It could be argued that the reason why the empire went to war (which without doubt led to its downfall) was largely due to the pressure it felt from Slavs within and outside of its borders. Optional Primary Sources 18.5, 18.6 and 18.7 provide evidence that counters Sked's arguments.

The historian Solomon Wank disagrees with the 'rosy picture' that Sked and others (e.g. István Deák, 1994) put forward. While it might apply with regard to the empire's economic growth, he argues that it does not hold true regarding political stability or the problem of nationalities (Wank, 1997a, p. 96). As he asks elsewhere:

> Can the empire be described as politically stable and the nationality question as attenuated when the constitutions of Istria, Croatia, and Bohemia were suspended in 1910, 1912 and 1913 respectively, and the Austrian parliament (Reichsrat) was sent packing in March 1914, with no inclination on the part of the prime minister, Count Karl Stürgkh, to recall it any time soon? Is it evidence of stability to claim as many historians do, that only two things held the empire together – veneration of old emperor Francis Joseph and the loyalty and devotion of his army?
>
> (Wank, 1997b, p. 46)

He makes two main points to counter Sked's arguments: (a) that it matters what contemporaries *perceived* the situation to be – a sense of 'impending doom' in 1914 influenced their decisions – not necessarily what the situation actually might have been (Wank, 1997b, p. 47); and (b) that he does not think a victory in the war would have resulted in the survival of the empire:

> The question of the health of the Habsburg Empire in 1914 may be debatable, but it is also beside the point. Whatever its socioeconomic condition, the imperial Habsburg political elite saw its empire as bordering on dissolution – the next candidate for sick man of Europe. Four days before Austria-Hungary's declaration of war on Serbia, Count Alexander Hoyos, a highly ranked foreign ministry official and one of the architects of the war policy, declared in a tone of anguished bravado: "We are still capable of resolve! We do not want to nor ought to be a sick man. Better to be destroyed quickly." [The optional Primary Source 18.7 further illustrates this point.]
>
> ...
>
> It is worth noting that even a victory by the Central Powers in World War I probably would not have ensured the continuations of the Habsburg and Ottoman states as empires. ... [Alan Sked's argument

that the Empire would have survived a victorious war intact and probably even expanded] is belied by Sked's claim that in the event of victory the empire would have been reduced to a military and economic appendage of Germany, 'with little future as an independent state'. Survival in that condition would have been tantamount to the end of the Habsburg Empire as an imperial political construct.

(Wank, 1997a, pp. 96–7)

Of course, we won't be able to settle this dispute here, but you may have views one way or the other on whether the empire was doomed – war or no war – or whether a victorious war could have saved it, as some contemporaries hoped. Perhaps under such circumstances the empire would have proved more viable than we assume with hindsight?

CONCLUSION

Our investigation of the history and decline of the Austro-Hungarian empire has revealed that its competing nationalities were a constant and long-term problem, and that its set-up was becoming an increasing anachronism at a time when nation states were being founded in Europe. In addition, this was a time when dynasties were no longer effective as the glue for political systems and were being sidelined in favour of constitutional monarchies, and even being replaced by popular sovereignty.

You will remember reading about China in Unit 11, and that the Qing Dynasty also fell about this time, 1911, because of rising Han nationalism. And while the Ottoman empire finally collapsed as a result of the First World War, the rise of Turkish nationalism was already undermining the basis of this land empire, based on dynastic rule over multiple territories and peoples. These comparisons suggest that these empires didn't just fall apart, but that perhaps they were becoming outmoded, and that in Europe the war just helped them along. In other words, we can legitimately ask if the old basis of land empires in Eurasia was being eroded more generally at this time and might have become outmoded, war or no war. Ironically, this was happening at the same time that the European overseas empires were, despite the germ of nationalism, reaching their peak extent (the British empire's peak extent, for example, was in the interwar period).

We have also seen that great importance was attached to the (perhaps today somewhat abstract) notion of being a 'great power' and preserving great power status, almost at any cost. Could Austria-Hungary perhaps have survived as a second-rate power? Its most influential decision makers at least did not think so, preferring to risk everything in war. And could the empire have survived without its figurehead, Emperor Franz Joseph? When he was gone, the empire floundered – again, we simply do not know if his successor could have fared better in times of peace. Certainly he was not able to unite his subjects during the war.

We have seen that historians, as usual, disagree in their interpretations of why the empire collapsed. Did it experience only 'deceptive stability' while failing to address its nationalities problems, as Wank argues? Or did the history of the empire resemble a 'path to destruction', as Mason claims? Or did the empire actually do quite well and had the chance to recover, only to be hampered in this by the unsuccessful war, as Sked maintains?

These questions are specific to a discussion about the end of the Austro-Hungarian empire, but you might be able to draw some more general conclusions about this and other important land empires that you have studied in this course (China, Unit 11, and Russia, Unit 7). As we have seen, they all started to collapse at around the same time and they shared many similar characteristics. Perhaps ultimately the answer to why the Austro-Hungarian empire collapsed could at least partly be found by looking outside its immediate experience and focusing more broadly on the end of empires per se, as well as on the significance of dynasty and of nationalism in the early twentieth century.

REFERENCES

Beller, S. (1996) *Francis Joseph*, London, Longman.

Beller, S. (2006) *A Concise History of Austria*, Cambridge, Cambridge University Press.

Bridge, F.R. (1990) *The Habsburg Monarchy among the Great Powers, 1815–1918*, Berg, Oxford.

Cornwall, M. (2000) *The Undermining of Austria-Hungary: The Battle for Hearts and Minds*, New York, St. Martin's Press, 2000.

Deák, I. (1994) 'The fall of Austria-Hungary: peace, stability and legitimacy' in Lundestad, G. (ed.) *The Fall of the Great Powers: Peace, Stability and Legitimacy*, Oxford, Oxford University Press, pp. 81–101.

Hamann, B. (1999) *Hitler's Vienna. A Dictator's Apprenticeship*, Oxford, Oxford University Press.

Healy, M. (2004) *Vienna and the Fall of the Habsburg Empire: Total War and Everyday Life in World War I*, Cambridge, Cambridge University Press.

Herwig, H.H. (1997) *The First World War: Germany and Austria-Hungary 1914–1918*, New York, St. Martin's Press.

Jelavich, B. (1987) *Modern Austria: Empire and Republic, 1815–1986*, Cambridge, Cambridge University Press.

Mason, J.W. (1997) *The Dissolution of the Austro-Hungarian Empire, 1867–1918*, 2nd edn, London, Longman.

Okey, R. (2001) *The Habsburg Monarchy, c. 1765–1918*, Basingstoke, Macmillan.

Rosenfeld, S. (1920) *Die Wirkung des Krieges auf die Streblichkeit in Wien*, Vienna, Volksgesundheitsamt.

Sked, A. (1989) *The Decline and Fall of the Habsburg Empire, 1815–1918*, London, Longman.

Wank, S. (1997a) 'The disintegration of the Habsburg and Ottoman empires. A comparative analysis' in Dawisha, K. and Parrott, B. (eds) *The End of Empire? The Transformation of the USSR in Comparative Perspective*, New York, M.E. Sharpe, pp. 94–120.

Wank, S. (1997b) 'The Habsburg empire' in Barkey, K. and von Hagen, M. (eds) *After Empire: Multiethnic Societies and Nation-Building. The Soviet Union and the Russian, Ottoman and Habsburg Empires*, Boulder, Westview Press, pp. 45–57.

Wheatcroft, A. (1996) *The Habsburgs: Embodying Empire,* London, Penguin.

Williamson, S.R., Jr (1991) *Austria-Hungary and the Origins of the First World War*, Basingstoke, Macmillan.

In the (20th) Britain consciously wanted to devolve power to their former colonies, instituting 'dominion' states and allowing internal, as well as external, autonomy in certain decisions taken. Whilst the process of decolonisation was similar to America, a form of 'colonial' nationalism exhorted by Indian elites met with no war, as in America, but with firm demands from Great Britain.

UNIT 19
INDIA 1885 TO 1947

Karl Hack

AIMS

- To outline the end of empire in India, which ultimately led to four independent countries (India, Pakistan, Burma and Bangladesh[8]).

- To consider how far this represented a negotiated ending of empire.

- To allow you to analyse three areas crucial in shaping this Indian decolonisation, namely: British approaches to decolonisation; Indian nationalism; and communalism.

INTRODUCTION

The other units in this block document the American War of Independence of 1775–83 (Unit 17), the Austro-Hungarian disintegration up to 1918 (Unit 18), and the nasty insurgencies in Algeria and Angola after the Second World War (Unit 20). Even though they cover a range of solvents of empire, in each case they show independence emerged only after violent conflict. This might lead you to conclude, to paraphrase Mao Ze Dung (Mao Tse Tung), that the end of empire grows out of the barrel of a gun. By contrast, I want you to consider the possibility that decolonisation can flow more from the pen and the peaceful protest. In particular, I want you to look at the events, policies and forces that led to the 'transfer of power' in India and Pakistan on 14–15 August 1947. To some degree at least this represented not merely a retreat in the face of guns, but a 'planned' transition to independence.

Subsequent sections will trace the varied origins of this transfer of power. They will discuss:

- the international context
- the object of decolonisation: India as prize colonial possession
- British approaches to decolonisation in India
- Indian nationalism and non-violent protest
- caste and communalism.

The last three cover three narratives – British, nationalist and communalist – which threaded together to shape the timing, nature and outcome of decolonisation. As you will see, you have to tackle all three if you are to understand India's decolonisation in its full complexity.

---

[8] Burma separated from India effective from 1937, becoming fully independent in 1948. India and Pakistan achieved independence in 1947. East Pakistan separated off as Bangladesh in 1971. Ceylon, independent as Sri Lanka from 1948, had never been part of British India, despite its proximity.

THE INTERNATIONAL CONTEXT

Before we turn to India in specific, you first need to understand how Indian decolonisation was embedded within two longer-term, international, processes: first, the move to responsible self-government in British settler colonies; and secondly, the move towards modern nationalism and self-government across Asia.

First, let's take the movement towards self-government in British settler colonies. The postscript to Unit 17, on the birth of the USA, was that Britain made early concessions elsewhere, rather than risk losing the support of local settlers. Faced with demands from settler colonists in the nineteenth century, Britain therefore conceded increasing doses of 'responsible' government, notably from 1839 onwards.[9] Typically, a governor accepted more non-officials onto his executive and legislative councils to represent 'interests'. Then he would allow some legislative councillors to be elected. Finally, there would be 'responsible' government.

The latter meant that the executive – the government – would answer to (be responsible to) an assembly, and rely on votes in that council to carry its policies. The end result tended to be that the strongest groups in the legislative were allowed to choose some of their number to act as 'ministers', controlling specified government functions. Typically, defence and foreign affairs were among the last areas ceded to local control in this way, with the governor also retaining smaller and smaller areas of reserved power over time. It was also implicit that such colonies could not unilaterally change their constitutions. By 1910, the Federation of Australia, Canada, New Zealand, Newfoundland (1907–34) and the newly formed Union of South Africa had all acquired full internal self-government, and as such were referred to as 'dominions' rather than 'colonies'.

With South Africa, and from the 1920s the Irish Free State too, demanding more flexibility in foreign policy, the 1926 Balfour Report defined dominions as having full external as well as internal autonomy. This definition was subsequently formalised by the 1931 Statute of Westminster. The British assumption was that such early concessions would preserve the cooperation of white dominions, based on ties of kinship, economics and security. Since British emigration to most of these areas seemed healthy in the 1920s, and a 1932 Ottawa Agreement provided for preferential tariffs among empire countries (much valued in the depression era of the early 1930s), these assumptions seemed reasonable. Britain therefore felt it could make its world system of power work without insisting on sovereign rights over all territories (Darwin, 1980).

---

[9] In 1839, Lord Durham's report (he was a former governor-general of British territories in North America), recommended giving responsible government to settlers to encourage loyalty and constructive participation in government. Though his specific ideas were not adopted, the general approach triumphed over the next few decades.

These developments had implications for India which, between 1917 and the 1930s, came to enter a kind of twilight status, as more than a colony but less than a full dominion. India started to be admitted into gatherings of the self-governing dominions from the First World War, when its contribution of over a million troops (the bulk of empire forces in the Middle East) earned it representation at the Imperial War Cabinet from 1917. India was represented at the Versailles Peace Conference of 1919 (albeit by British and loyalists), and was a founder member of the League of Nations in 1920: the only member not fully sovereign and independent.

But even for India this acceptance as a partner of the dominions, rather than merely as autocratically governed 'non-white' colony, was partial and half-hearted. The formula remained for the moment that of 'the dominions and India', with a question mark over when, and indeed whether, this non-white territory might achieve full 'dominion status'. For the Indian experience could also be located in a very different story: that of the growing assertiveness of non-western subjects in general, and of Asian subjects in particular.

The story of the growth of 'modern' Asian nationalism is particularly important for India. Such nationalists combined elements of 'revival' (emphasising 'traditional' religion, history and identities) and reform or 'modernisation'. Hence early twentieth-century Chinese reformers emphasised self-modernisation as much as anti-western sentiment. Japan was a further encouragement: forcibly opened to western trade from 1854, in 1904–05 it defeated Russia in a war over who would have most influence in northeastern China. Some Asian nationalists now looked to Japan for inspiration.

Should the early increases in self-government in India, which gathered pace in the 1920s–30s, therefore be seen as part of a wider pattern of decolonisation in 'monsoon Asia' (Low, 1991, pp. 22–57)? True, the French in Indochina (now Vietnam, Cambodia and Laos) and the Dutch in the Netherlands East Indies (now Indonesia) proved obdurate. Partly as a result, there was a limited army mutiny in Indochina in 1930, and ferocious agrarian revolt in key regions in 1931–32, against which the French called in airstrikes. But the British feared the cost of such a violent approach could be too expensive in politically advanced colonies such as India.[10] There was a turn towards underground cell organisation and revolutionary strategy by the Indochina Communist Party. Moderates there were in danger of being tarred as collaborators and outflanked by 'extremists'. In other words, interwar imperial powers could and often did resist nationalism, but it was increasingly obvious that the short-term and long-term costs of riding roughshod over local opinion were increasing (Foster, 1995; Short, 1995).

In other parts of Asia, colonial regimes made far-reaching concessions in order to constitutionalise opposition (so blunting any turn to violence), and to maximise collaboration. Full internal self-government was granted to the

---

[10] The British did use 'air policing' themselves, but mainly in sparsely populated or underdeveloped regions, such as parts of Iraq.

American colony of the Philippines in 1935, mainly because of American politics, rather than because of any protest by a Philippine elite, which retained huge interests in exports to the USA. Two years later, a large measure of internal autonomy was granted to Burma (1937), upon its ceasing to be a province of India (which it had been from 1885). It was allowed to hold elections and a Burmese prime minister and cabinet were appointed, although the British governor retained a veto in many areas, and kept firm control of security forces, in which Burmese were heavily outnumbered by Indians and hill peoples.

In short, the 'end of empire' in India needs to be seen not simply as a short sprint for freedom from the 1930s or from 1942 to 1947, but as a case study of Asian decolonisation, and as the pivotal test case for how far Britain's 'dominion' model of self-government could make the leap from settler to non-settler empire.[11]

The Indonesian example

By the late nineteenth century, traditional rulers in the Netherlands East Indies (Indonesia) had been coopted into the colonial hierarchy. In response, a movement for 'revival' of identity and culture, and 'reform', developed by 1900. The latter included petitioning the colonial state for more access to modern education and bureaucratic appointments. The lead was taken by western-educated sons of the old elite, who achieved some autonomy because of holding posts as professionals. *Budi Utomo* ('Beautiful Endeavour') was set up in 1906 by just such professionals. It stressed renewal of Javanese culture, and petitioning the government in 'loyal protest'. A whole series of sectional movements, such as 'Young Sumatrans', were founded by the 1920s.

Sarekat Islam (Islamic Association), meanwhile, originated around 1911. Muslim merchants organised partly in response to the threat of Chinese businesses, but local farmers often joined because of its religious element. It peaked at 2 million in the First World War, then shrank quickly because of fractures and leadership fears after localised violence in 1918. Other organisations took up the mantle of Muslim leadership.

Metropolitan concessions. A Volksraad, or central council, was established in 1917, with 'inlanders' (natives) indirectly elected to it by municipal boards. By the 1930s, 'inlanders' were the majority. But they could do little more than comment on colonial legislation and there were no plans to make officials responsible to the council.

Secular nationalism. The Dutch-language educated Indies elite began to see themselves not merely as part of particular groups and islands, but additionally as 'Indonesian'. In the 1920s, Malay (known as Bahasa) became the lingua franca of newspapers. A 1928 youth conference adopted the name Indonesia, with its own national flag, anthem and language (Bahasa). Study clubs grew up, and from them the Indonesian nationalist party

[11] I am defining decolonisation as a long-term process of colonial peoples reasserting autonomy.

(Partai Nasional Indonesia – PNI). This emphasised a secular approach, helpful partly because many 'Indonesians' mixed Islam with attachment to Hindu epics and local beliefs. The PNI leader Sukarno also used classic Javanese imagery (based on Hindu epics) to attract peasant support. The PNI engineered a short-lived federation of nationalist parties from 1927. But Dutch repression of its non-cooperation from 1930 saw radical nationalists imprisoned, with those remaining resorting to cooperating. By 1941, however, most parties were frustrated enough to come together at a national conference to demand faster constitutional progress. This the Dutch denied until, after defeat by the Japanese in March 1942, they promised more autonomy at the war's end.

Finally, Japanese occupation authorities (1942–45), allowed nationalists to declare independence on 17 August 1945. By then it had already given thousands of young people paramilitary training, in the hope of encouraging resistance to the western powers. As a result, while the Dutch retook the towns in 1945–49, guerrilla bands persisted. When the USA threatened to withdraw development funding for the Dutch in Europe – fearing further resistance could help push nationalists towards communism – the Dutch finally negotiated Indonesian independence for October 1949. 'Indonesia' thus demonstrates many similar traits to India, but with Dutch policy resulting in contrasting outcomes. In particular, Dutch refusal to accommodate more quickly, after key nationalists 'collaborated' with the Japanese during the war, led to a violent independence struggle in 1945–49 (Low, 1991, pp. 120–47; Short, 1995, pp. 15–33 – Short's article is available on the course website as the optional Secondary Source 19.1).

WHAT WAS TO BE DECOLONISED? INDIA AS PRIZE COLONIAL POSSESSION

India is, then, an example of a more general Asian process of decolonisation, and the pivotal case in British decolonisation: being the first non-white area to move towards a substantive measure of self-government, if not dominionhood. More than that, in sheer scale India dwarfs other decolonisations. In 1865, it had around 200 million people. By 1938, its 389 million inhabitants constituted around 16 per cent of the world population of 2.4 billion. In the 1930s, it contained just over half the total population of all empires combined (Butler and Butler, 1986, p. 323; Etemad, 2007, p. 123; Duffet et al., 1942, p. 15). Just one province alone, Bengal, with a population of over 60 million in 1941 (Chandrasekhar, 1946, p. 15), was almost comparable in scale to the entire French empire, which had a population of 86.1 million in 1936 (Thomas, 2005, p. 1). India was not just part of an empire, but also an empire in its own right.[12]

Did its size contribute to the process. 389 million inhabitants?

---

[12] Alternatively, we can think of the British empire as having a number of sub-imperialisms, with India, Australia and other territories controlling local and regional dependencies themselves.

[handwritten margin note: Was this difficult to give up? or a border on G.B.?]

India supported an entire military superstructure of British imperialism stretching across the Indian Ocean and away to China. From the time that Britain had become a land power in India, in the 1750s (Unit 8), Indian troops had served in regions as far apart as China and the Middle East. Singapore (until 1867) and Aden (until 1937) had come directly under Indian control, as bookends to the Indian Ocean. By the 1920s, this meant, in peacetime, that it had an army set at around 218,000: a third of these British battalions, two-thirds Indian sepoys, and all paid for by Indian funds (Jeffrey, 1981).

Finally, India played an important part in Britain's international trade. India enjoyed vast British investments, notably in railways, accounting for as much as 10 per cent of British foreign investment. Britain also ran a sizeable surplus on its trading account with India, with notable exports including finished cotton and machinery. This was further boosted by profits in 'invisibles' such as shipping. India, in turn, ran a sizeable surplus with areas Britain ran a deficit with, such as North America. So India helped to balance Britain's overall trade.

By 1938, then, India was an empire within an empire; a subcontinent just short of 389 million souls, occupying an area more than a third of the size of the USA, and vital to Britain's eastern military power and its balance of trade.[13] Now, before you go any further, I want you to make sure you have a clear notion of India's main provinces and cities.

EXERCISE

Using Figure 19.1:

1   Familiarise yourself with the locations of Delhi, Bombay, Madras and Calcutta. How do the locations of the three presidencies (as Bombay, Madras and Calcutta were called) contrast to that of Delhi?

2   Note the extent of the princely states. Do you remember from Unit 10 how much of India they took up?

3   Familiarise yourself with the names and positions of the eleven provinces (shaded darker grey) of post-1937 India.

SPECIMEN ANSWER

1   The three presidencies are all on or near the coast, as befits their origins as East India Company trading posts. Delhi is inland and to the north, as befits the capital of the mainly inland Mughal empire, which had technically ended in 1858, after the Indian Mutiny-Rebellion of 1857.[14]

2   By the 1930s, about one-third of the territory consisted of semi-autonomous, indirectly ruled Indian princely states. [What is not obvious from the map is that these territories contained about 25 per cent of the population.]

3   The eleven provinces by 1937 were: (in the north) Sind, North West Frontier Province, Punjab, United Provinces; Bihar; (in the east) Bengal, Assam, Orissa; (in the centre) Central Provinces; (in the south) Madras; and (in the west) Bombay [for their populations, see Table 19.1 below].

---

[13] In 1938, the area of India was more than 40 per cent of that of the USA. The area of post-partition India was about one-third.

[14] British India's capital transferred from Calcutta to Delhi in 1911, with the government decamping to Simla each summer to avoid the heat of the plains.

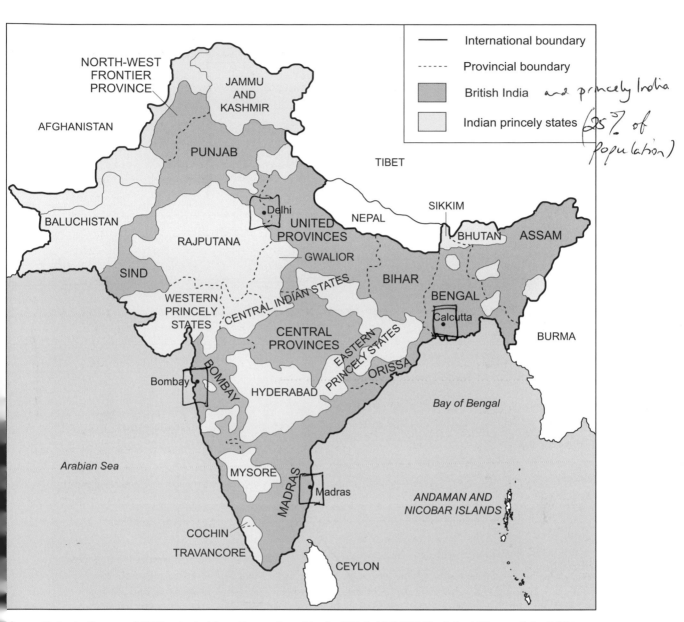

Figure 19.1   India around 1937, adapted from Brown, J. and Louis, W.R. (eds) (1999) *The Oxford History of the British Empire: Volume IV: The Twentieth Century*, Oxford, Oxford University Press, p. 432. 1937 was the year Burma was officially separated as a colony in its own right, and a year after the single state of Bihar and Orissa was split in two (see Figure 19.7).

DISCUSSION

It is worth doing this basic exercise, if only to reinforce how difficult it was likely to be to manage decolonisation over such a vast, complex area. 'India' was made up of 'British India', comprising eleven provinces by 1937, and 'princely India'. The latter was made up of several large and several hundred small sovereign states over which Britain enjoyed some suzerainty (an ability to control some portion of their sovereignty, especially foreign affairs). See, for instance, Figure 19.2 for the ruler of the princely state of Nawangar. As you will see below, this division caused tensions. How could semi-autonomous princes be reconciled with increasing democracy in British India?

Figure 19.2   Kumar Shri Ranjitsinhji – who later became H.H. Shri Sir Ranjitsinhji, Jam Sahib of Nawangar – in ceremonial dress, c.1910. Photographed by Bob Thomas. Photo: Popperfoto/ Getty Images.

You should also note that provinces changed over time. Burma ceased to be a province effective from 1937. Bengal was, until 1905, one big province, with a lingua franca, Bengali. Its separation and then reunification (1905–11) played a major part in the growth of Indian nationalism. Separation enraged nationalists, reunification disappointed many Muslims who had seen a mainly Muslim East Bengal appear and disappear.

Table 19.1   Provincial population (millions)

Province	1931	1941	Per cent increase
Madras	44.21	49.34	11.6
Bombay	17.99	20.85	15.9
Bengal	50.11	60.31	20.3
United Provinces	48.41	55.02	13.6
Punjab	23.58	28.42	20.5
Bihar	27.73	28.82	3.9
Central Provinces	15.32	16.82	9.8
Assam	8.62	10.20	18.2
North West Frontier Province	2.43	3.04	25.2
Orissa	8.03	8.72	8.6
Sind	3.89	4.54	16.7
United Kingdom	46.038	48.216	4.7

(Sources: adapted from Chandrasekhar, 1946, p. 15 (Indian provinces) and Butler and Butler, 1986, p. 323)

BRITISH APPROACHES TO DECOLONISATION IN INDIA

So much for geography. We now need to get an overview of two more things. First, what was the 'system' to be decolonised? In other words, how was India governed? Secondly, so we have a skeleton to hang our more detailed themes on, what were the main stages by which Britain ceded Indians more self-government?

EXERCISE

Read the extract from Fieldhouse's *The Colonial Empires* provided as Secondary Source 19.2. Read it through once to get the feel of it, and then refer to the more precise pages given below for each question. You should spend most time on question 2.

1   What were the main supports for British power in India (pp. 1, 4)?

2   Outline the stages by which central councils were reformed in India between the 1890s and 1935 (pp. 2–3 and 9–10).

1   As buttresses of British power, Fieldhouse mentions the Indian Civil Service (ICS), brute force, law, the fiscal and economic system, and 'passive or positive acceptance of alien rule by Indians' (p. 4). The ICS, never much more than 1000, was the glue for the system. The first Indian was admitted in 1864, and just 5 per cent were Indian by 1915. The security forces, meanwhile, included an army of around 73,000 British and 154,000 Indians in 1885, with the ratio set at about 2:1 after the Mutiny-Rebellion of 1857. But Fieldhouse points out that these numbers of ICS, army and police could never had compelled 200 million (1865). So he suggests that Indian passivity, and involvement as collaborators, was vital at every level bar the very top. For every European ICS member, there were many more Indians in subordinate services who put policy into action.

2   The governor-general or viceroy at first ruled autocratically with the advice of a small executive council, assisted by a legislative council. Initially the latter was made up almost entirely of officials (those holding government office), but by the 1890s they included small number of unofficials. From 1892, some of the latter were to be elected (indirectly, by local corporate bodies). In 1909, the 'Morley–Minto' reforms allowed some members to be directly elected. Secretary of State for India Edwin Montagu then announced in 1917 that the new goal for India was 'the gradual development of self-governing institutions with a view to the progressive realisation of *responsible government* [my emphasis] in India as an integral part of the British Empire'. The 1935 Government of India Act promised to give Indian ministers or their equivalent control of some aspects of central government. But this central diarchy (dual power) never became operative, because not enough princely states signed up to bring the proposed federal structure into being. Finally, British entry into the Second World War, and defeat in Singapore by the Japanese, resulted in the Cripps offer of March 1942 [this is provided as the optional Primary Source 19.1]. Sir Stafford Cripps [then a Labour member of the British cabinet] offered India full dominion status to be made effective soon after the end of the war.

Was the war the prompt? (handwritten marginal note)

While progress at the centre stalled between the wars, the British attempted to divert Indians' energies into the provinces. The 1919 Government of India Act gave Indians substantive powers in the latter. Though the British retained control of the most important functions, areas such as education were transferred to the control of Indian ministers who were responsible to the assemblies. This came to be known as diarchy. The 1935 Government of India Act then gave Indians full ministerial responsibility in the provinces, subject only to the governor's reserved and emergency powers. These provisions became effective with the 1937 elections, after which Indians enjoyed a considerable measure of internal self-government in the provinces. Table 19.2 shows the milestones in constitutional reform.

Table 19.2   Milestones in constitutional reform

Date	Event
1870s–80s	Elections introduced for local and municipal boards
1885	Indian National Congress formed
1892	Indian Councils Act. More Indians and unofficials included
1905–11	Bengal province divided by Lord Curzon and then reunited
1906	Muslim League formed. Muslims promised separate electorates
1909	Morley–Minto Reforms. Indirect elections of Indians to central legislature by district and municipal boards. Separate electoral rolls for Muslims
1917	Montagu announcement that the aim for India is 'responsible government as an integral part of the British Empire'. Montagu–Chelmsford Report of 1918 recommends changes
1919	Government of India Act 1919: diarchy in the provinces, with Indian ministers in eight of nine provinces (later eleven). Review to be undertaken within ten years. Indians were now the majority in the central legislature, but with few powers there
1926	Balfour definition of dominions following the Imperial Conference
1927	Simon Commission appointed (all-white under Liberal Sir John Simon) to review the Government of India Act of 1919. Recommends full provincial autonomy, diarchy at a centre, and federalism to include the princes in central councils, but with Britain retaining defence, external affairs, and far-reaching safeguards
31 October 1929	Lord Irwin statement, as viceroy, that 'the attainment of Dominion status' was the 'natural issue' of India's progress. Considerable opposition, notably in the UK Conservative Party
November 1930 to January 1931	First Roundtable Conference to discuss a new constitution. Princes endorse federal principle
September–December 1931	Second Roundtable Conference. Congress joins with Gandhi as sole representative after Gandhi–Irwin Pact of March 1931

[handwritten margin notes:] concerted effort to 'decolonise' but to keep control — obvious contrast with U.S.A.

Date	Event
1932–34	British parliament refines proposals via debate and committee
November–December 1932	Third Roundtable Conference. Few main political leaders attend, as civil disobedience has recommenced
1935	Government of India Act. Full responsible government in the provinces. Diarchy to come into force in the centre when enough princely states accede. India to be federal, with increased flexibility for provinces
March 1942	Cripps offer of full self-government at the war's end
1946	Indian interim government formed in September. Muslim League joins in October
20 February 1947	British prime minister Clement Attlee announces Britain will leave by 1948 at the latest, after Congress and League negotiations stall
14–15 August 1947	Independence for India and Pakistan

[handwritten margin notes: "War became the prompt for the British move to the / government self-..."]

[handwritten margin notes: "Was there any need for Indian 'colonial' nationalism? Yes. Britain was intent on a move to self-government but with or an empire. C.W. broke the link with empire. Fuel! important act in the process."]

[handwritten annotation beside 1935 row: "Stalemate" (Darwin)]

This is, of course, a summary mainly from the British side. Indeed, the Fieldhouse extract you have read comes close to a 'liberal' interpretation of empire – that the genius of British imperialism was its provision of law, peace, and willingness to make concessions as local populations progressed. The logic of this would be that the British always intended, indeed needed, to develop what Macaulay's famous 1835 Minute on Education described as 'a class who may be interpreters between us and the millions whom we govern; a class of persons, Indian in blood and colour, but English in taste, in opinions, in morals, and in intellect'. As this class had developed the British had gradually associated it with councils, and, as Macaulay had envisaged, there was always the possibility that such a class might eventually merit self-government (cited in Burton, 2001, pp. 18–20).[15]

Fieldhouse would never put it that crudely. But of the Montagu Declaration of 1917 he suggests that, 'This ... immediately transferred India from a permanent dependency to a future Dominion. It remained only to phase the transfer of power' (Secondary Source 19.2, pp. 9–10). Compare that to Edwin Montagu's words in the House of Commons on 20 August 1917:

> The policy of His Majesty's Government ... is that of the increasing association of Indians in every branch of the administration and the gradual development of self-governing institutions with a view to the

---

[15] Macaulay's minute was most concerned with directing funds away from local learning, and towards encouraging English-language education. After the Mutiny-Rebellion of 1857 Britain was much more solicitous of Indian traditions, and ambivalent about the English-educated, but needed them nonetheless.

1917 ?

progressive realisation of responsible government in India as an integral part of the British Empire. They have decided that substantial steps in this direction should be taken as soon as possible ...

I would add that progress in this policy can only be achieved by successive stages. The British Government and the Government of India ... must be judges of the time and measure of each advance, and they must be guided by the co-operation received from those upon whom new opportunities of service will thus be conferred and by the extent to which it is found that confidence can be reposed in their sense of responsibility.

(cited in Madden and Darwin, 1993, p. 678)

(If you wish, see optional Primary Sources 19.2–19.4 for further debate over this.)

There was ambiguity about when and whether the final destination was full dominion status.[16] Meanwhile, in Fieldhouse's account, the 1935 Government of India Act's provisions for diarchy at the centre are delayed mainly because of the princes not signing up. Yet even here we see hints of a very different story, in which British resistance to change is greater, and nationalist pressure more necessary. He notes that early Indian nationalists developed a 'drain theory' critique, which held that India's economic strength was drained by civil service pensions and salaries, by military expenditure, and by the destruction of Indian crafts by Manchester cottons.

The approach implicit in Fieldhouse's summary goes to the heart of this unit. I would like to suggest, for argument's sake, two opposed interpretations:

1   Indian decolonisation was oiled by the growth of an English-educated Indian elite, combined with the application to India of the settler, later dominion, model of progress to self-government within the empire. Only the phasing was at issue by the 1920s–30s, even if Britain put the emphasis on slow progress in reward for demonstrated responsibility.

2   That the reverse is true. The British retained control of the army and security apparatus, and made concessions in areas less critical to protecting their overall control. A significant part of the British establishment, notably in the ICS and in the UK Conservative Party, wanted to delay, perhaps indefinitely, any Indian move to full dominion status. So there was a need for compelling 'push' factors, which might include international forces, nationalist campaigns and changes in Indian society.

If the second proposition were true, it would raise the question: what cleared the path? In the next section, we will ask how far Indian nationalism and 'non-violent' protest were crucial in helping to change British plans. But for

the push .

---

[16] The ambiguity was deliberate. In 1917, the Conservatives were prominent in the Lloyd George coalition, and much of the party wanted concessions limited. Similarly, Conservative reticence about concessions contributed to the innumerable safeguards added to the 1935 Government of India Act.

now let us look at another possibility: that war and war's aftershocks played a predominant role.

WAR

We have already seen that critical concessions were made in wartime. The 1917 Montagu Declaration came when there were only a handful of British battalions left in wartime India, when inflation and shortage ravaged the country, and when many Muslims were angry that Britain was at war with Ottoman Turkey, whose sultan was recognised as khalifa (Islamic leader), and guardian of the holy places of Mecca, Medina and Jerusalem. In the same year, India, which took on considerable loans and expenditure helping London in the war (including an outright gift of £100 million), was allowed to levy a charge of 7.5 per cent on the import of Lancashire cottons. Together with the growth of wartime Indian industry to make up for the diversion of British exports to war production, this signalled the postwar withering of India's role in balancing Britain's international balance of payments (Gallagher and Seal, 1981, pp. 399, 403; Tomlinson, 1979). From the 1920s, India gained the right to use tariff protection, and from the 1930s, control over currency and exchange policies.

Did the Second World War also help to remove British roadblocks, and reshape decolonisation?

EXERCISE

Read the extract from Darwin's 'Imperialism in decline?' (Secondary Source 19.3). Outline Darwin's explanation for the significance of the 1935 Government of India Act, and its place in imperial policy.

SPECIMEN ANSWER

Darwin sees the Government of India Act of 1935 as a stalemating action. Even if the new central legislature did ever come into being, it was so structured that the princely states and Muslims, in separate electorates, would ring-fence Congress power. The princely states were in no mood to cooperate anyway, and so not enough signed up to trigger the new central legislature. Meanwhile, full self-government in the provinces was aimed at embedding Congress and other politicians in government, making it difficult for them to withdraw cooperation. Beyond this, the 1935 constitution reserved to the governor and his appointees far-reaching powers over defence and external affairs, and removed from Indian control huge swathes of revenue.[17]

DISCUSSION

For Darwin, 1935 was a carefully constructed stalemate, and it was the war that saved the Indian National Congress from stagnation if not fragmentation. War provided the central Congress leadership an excuse (India was declared at war by the viceroy without consultation in September 1939) and an opportunity (a Britain at war might make concessions) to abandon provincial government. Congress members were withdrawn from provincial ministries by November 1939. The viceroy did make an offer on 18 October 1940, confirming that the aim was dominion status after the war, to be effected by constitutional negotiations then. But no date was specified for independence, there was a caveat that minority concerns must be addressed, and for the war's duration Indians were only promised

---

[17] For instance, civil service salaries and pensions, the military budget, and debt financing.

consultative roles. Congress launched individual acts of civil disobedience in 1940, and from August 1942 issued a 'Quit India' order, encouraging the withdrawal of all cooperation.[18]

Darwin is fitting Indian developments into a bigger imperial canvas. He argues that, after the First World War, Britain returned to a position of relative strength. Yes, the empire faced postwar ferment, and made concessions in Egypt (independent 1922), Ireland (an Irish Free State partitioned off from Ulster in 1921–22), Iraq and elsewhere. But British financial muscle and military protection, and white settler ties in the case of the dominions, meant it was confident concessions would reinforce rather than disintegrate its system of international power. Britain hoped to rid itself of much of the headache of day-to-day management, while retaining the dividends. Britain tried to structure 'decolonisation' as tactical adjustments that would maintain control over areas key to its worldwide system of power, such as military bases in Egypt and Iraq. Britain's empire now reached its maximum extent, as it gained ex-German colonies (German East Africa as Tanganyika, now Tanzania), and areas from the now defunct Ottoman empire (Palestine, Iraq), as mandates.

Some caveats must be registered. India's value to Britain was declining in both financial and manpower terms. Wartime debt combined with the need to provide Indian politicians in the provinces with funds saw the Indian army underfunded after 1919. When it was deployed, as to Shanghai in 1927, the British increasingly found themselves picking up the bill. When its modernisation was planned from 1939, Britain again loosened its purse-strings. It was still Britain's emergency fighting force, but now it had to be paid for. Furthermore, by the 1930s, British exports to and investment in India were greatly reduced in significance. Indian tariffs rose, including on iron and steel from 1924, Japanese competition increased, and domestic Indian manufacturers boomed (Gallagher and Seal, 1981, pp. 403–4). That is even without reckoning on the impact of nationalist campaigns against foreign cloth. By 1945, a Britain burdened by wartime debt (including £1 billion to India) could scarcely afford what once had been free.

Nevertheless, in Darwin's model some in the ICS, and some politicians in the UK, were in 1935–39 hoping that provincial government would limit all-India organisation, throwing into relief provincial, social and economic divisions. If you bear in mind that most of the eleven provinces would have made a decent-sized colony individually (and some princely states, such as Hyderabad, too), you can see the potential. In the 1920s–30s, two large provinces did indeed resist Congress and Muslim League dominance: in the Punjab a Unionist Party joined Muslim, Hindu and Sikh elites and landowners; and in

---

[18] It is not clear how far Indian National Congress doubts about Britain's coalition government motivated them. Prime Minister Churchill had opposed the 1935 constitution. He had argued the August 1941 Atlantic Charter – an Anglo-American agreement of war aims including 'self-determination' for all peoples – did not apply to colonies. Yet his government included Labour ministers more sympathetic to Indian ambitions, such as Clement Attlee, who would be elected prime minister in July 1945.

Madras a non-Brahmin Justice Party briefly flourished (the **Brahmins** and caste are discussed later).

This suggests that the key unblocking force was not to be Indian nationalism alone, but its combination with war, and the changes in the international system and in India that war stirred (Darwin, 1988, pp. 79–100; Gallagher and Seal, 1981, pp. 406–7). Even then, little happened at first. Congress withdrew from government in 1939, but to what effect? Congress's 1940 call for individual civil disobedience was ineffective. The Indian army, relying on volunteers, ballooned from 150,000 to over 2 million. It was only when war brought humiliating British defeat, with the fall of Singapore on 15 February 1942 and the loss of over 100,000 men, half of them Indian, that further concessions were forthcoming. As in the First World War, so in the Second – British weakness (by March, Japanese troops were pouring into Burma and its aircraft carriers had entered the Indian Ocean) and British need to confirm the loyalty of Indian collaborators and troops led to concessions. War, not Congress, was the immediate trigger.

linked

The concessions came in the form of the Cripps offer of March 1942. When Britain refused to give Indians more substantive power in an interim government as well, Congress called forth the 'Quit India' movement from August (Congress's resolution is given in optional Primary Source 19.5). But again nationalist pressure after the concessions failed to leverage more from Britain. There was a deterioration into widespread violence following the mass arrest of Congress leaders. In places, notably for instance in Bihar, railway track was damaged and police stations burned, but without extracting any further concessions. Arguably Congress actions weakened its hand, since the Muslim League, which offered continued support to the government, increased its influence (Darwin, 1988, p. 87).

Lord Linlithgow (viceroy from 1936 to 1943) took heart from this continuing support from the Muslim League, many princes, and sectional groups such as the **Hindu Mahasabha** (a conservative Hindu group). Was this cementing the obstacles to all-India agreements, and making further advance to self-government more difficult? On 19 October 1943, Linlithgow wrote to Lord Wavell, the military man about to replace him as viceroy, that he thought the Raj might survive another thirty years (Moon, 1977, p. 19).

But before you get carried away by Linlithgow's imperialist optimism, bear in mind the longer term undercurrent. Even without the war, increasing Indianisation of the ICS and, belatedly, of army officers, was going to erode Britain's power more quickly. War accelerated these trends. With British rank and file and officers alike badly needed for other theatres, Indian army expansion necessitated many more Indian officers. Indianisation rates in the ICS increased from around 25 to 50 per cent in 1941–46. Indian officers went from a small cohort to being ubiquitous (Epstein, 1982; Potter, 1973). By early 1946, Wavell knew that Europeans who had delayed retirement because of war would soon leave, further vitiating British control of the ICS and police, while Indian ICS officers were now looking over their shoulder for who would succeed the British. In February 1946, a large section of the Indian navy mutinied over conditions. In August, communal violence peaked in Calcutta, where clashes left several thousand dead. Together these changes meant that, come 1946, Britain was in the business of getting out with minimum damage, preferably keeping India intact as a potential regional associate for defence purposes.

Hence, in September 1946, Britain granted an interim Indian government dominated by Indians (the Muslim League joined in October). With the League and Congress then becoming deadlocked in and beyond this, the British finally calculated that they needed to get out before they lost control. When Lord Mountbatten arrived as governor-general in March 1947, he did so having secured an announcement by Labour prime minister Clement Attlee. On 20 February, Attlee had declared that Britain would be out come what may by June 1948 (Attlee's statement is given in the optional Primary Source 19.6). In reality, Mountbatten soon decided that the date should be brought forward to August 1947. British strategy swung from slowing progress towards fuller self-government by playing on Indian division in the 1930s, to announcing they would go in the hope that would force Indians to come to terms with each other. As we will see in the last section, on class and communalism, the new policy did not avert a final bloodshed.

NATIONALISM

Thus far decolonisation has been discussed mainly as a function of British needs and approaches, combined with the impact of international changes. So what role did Indian nationalists play? According to the authors of *India's Struggle for Independence* (an extract from which is provided as Secondary Source 19.4):

> The Indian nationalist movement was undoubtedly one of the biggest mass movements modern society has ever seen. It was a movement which galvanized millions of people of all classes and ideologies into political action and brought to its knees a mighty colonial empire.
>
> ...
>
> [S]tate power was not seized in a single historical moment of revolution, but through prolonged popular struggle on a moral, political and ideological level.

(p. 1)

This is the struggle Gandhi (see Figure 19.3) epitomised, with his use of **satyagraha** (soul force or moral struggle), **ahimsa** (non-violence), and his abandonment of western clothes for an Indian loincloth made of **khadi** (home-spun cotton).

Figure 19.3   Mohandas Gandhi (1869–1948) next to his spinning wheel, 1946. Photographed by Margaret Bourke-White. Photo: Time Life Pictures/Getty Images.

Mohandas Gandhi's family had been anything but poor. They had provided prime ministers for a princely state near Gujarat and Bombay. He himself trained in London as a lawyer. Going to South Africa to act for an Indian commercial family, he petitioned for Indian rights, using non-violent protest and breaking of immigration and other laws to win concessions. Initially he was loyalist, and raised an ambulance corps in the Boer War of 1899–1901. After returning to India, he wore *khadi*, and also a peasant Indian style of clothing. He did practical work among peasants in between leading mass campaigns, and insisted on attending meetings with the viceroy dressed, as Churchill put it, as 'a half-naked fakir'. He thus took elements of earlier campaigns (boycotts, including of British cloth and spinning) and turned these from mere self-reliance (*swadeshi*) and urban and educated protest, into symbols of a nationalism at one with India's peasant majority.

Gandhi returned to India in 1915 with a reputation as a man who could force concessions from British authorities. After a year building up networks, he worked from 1917 to make Congress *the* representative of all India, of peasant as much as middle class, and to conciliate the Muslim League.

But British officials had long questioned the very notion of 'India'. In 1888, just three years after the formation of Congress in 1885, Sir John Strachey had assured Cambridge undergraduates that 'there is not, and never was an India ... no "Indian nation" ... that men of the Punjab, Bengal, the North-West Provinces and Madras, should ever feel that they belong to one great Indian nation, is impossible' (cited in Sarkar, 1989, p. 2). This 'Imperial' school of interpretation persisted in depicting Indian nationalists as a microscopic elite perched on top of a kaleidoscopic and mainly illiterate peasant society.[19] As the next exercise shows, this view has echoes even in modern scholarship.

EXERCISE

Read the extract from Chandra et al.'s *India's Struggle for Independence 1857–1947* (Secondary Source 19.4).

1   Briefly summarise Chandra's explanation of the Cambridge School's way of thinking (pp. 4–6).[20] What sort of power brokers does the Cambridge School argue underpinned nationalist politics?

2   Outline Chandra's argument for Congress being a powerful, mass nationalist movement, paying particular attention to the contribution of its 'counter-hegemony' to the 'nation-in-the-making' (pp. 7–14).

SPECIMEN ANSWER

1   The Cambridge School (whose foremost proponents included Anil Seal and John Gallagher [if you wish, you can read the article by Seal that is provided as the optional Secondary Source 19.5]) argued that what predominated in nationalism was disparate local elites, competing to secure patronage, power, resources and concessions for their particular locations. The result was a patron–client system in which local men delivered support for provincial power brokers who could help them. Some provincial power brokers became brokers at the national level. National-level brokers, which was in effect what Congress leaders such as Gandhi were, were necessary to parallel the Raj's own top-down structure.

2   Chandra et al. accept that there were diverse groups and interests, but reject a dichotomy between local interests and some larger commitment to nationalism. They argue that local interests did converge on the idea of Indian nationalism for its own sake. They also argue that Indian nationalism did work on moral and ideological levels to develop the notion of an Indian 'nation-in-the-making'. Congress was key in the process of realising such a nation, through oppositional campaigns but also through propaganda, and building practical links and organisation from the 1920s. These helped to build up 'reserves of

---

[19] In 1921, literacy amongst Indian males was at 14.2 per cent, of whom 12.9 per cent were literate in English. By 1941, these figures had risen to 27.4 and 18.9 per cent. In other words, as late as 1941 the INC elite were drawn from the less than 5 per cent of the male population (1 in 20) literate in English. Female education lagged behind (Brown, 1985, p. 250).

[20] In the 1970s, Anil Seal at Cambridge and his students published a series of books with a focus on locality and nationalism (Spodek, 1979).

counter-hegemony' to oppose to the Raj's 'hegemony'. By hegemony they mean an acceptance of the legitimacy of Congress leadership, and willingness to consent to, or support, its initiatives.[21]

DISCUSSION

Chandra et al. directly contradict the suggestion that Congress was not entirely nationalist, so much as an elitist organisation bringing together local power brokers, more a 'ramshackle' and shifting coalition than a movement.

For Anil Seal and the Cambridge School, by contrast, both the Raj and Indian nationalism were much weaker than previously thought, as both relied on local collaborators who acted for their own reasons (Seal, 1973), and who had to be given concessions in order to win their support. Hence, for instance, the implication is that nationalist politics was only really powerful when conditions allowed all-India power brokers to coordinate with many local issues, often in response to British imperialist structures and initiatives. Hence major campaigns usually followed British initiatives such as those of 1917–19.

Chandra et al., while not denying the power of local brokers, argue that Congress nevertheless proved capable of absorbing the energies, and at times adopting the causes of, localities and disparate nationalists. For instance, it took on issues of women, youth and **Untouchables**. They argue that it gradually became a kind of focal point for many groups, achieving a hegemonic position, by which they looked to it for leadership in nationalist causes. In this, Chandra et al. echo other Indian historians such as Sarkar (1989, pp. 6–11). Chandra and Sarkar also resist the idea that leaders can simply be reduced to power brokers. For them, idealism and sacrifice must be taken seriously as well. Thousands went to jail, and leaders such as Jawaharlal Nehru (later independent India's first prime minister) gave up lucrative positions and property, and went to jail repeatedly. For such Indian authors, then, the 'movement' advanced like a series of waves (the campaigns of 1905–08, 1919, 1920–22, 1930–32, 1940, 1942), with successive waves rising higher until their force was all but irresistible.

It did this by a combination of active phases of 'mass struggle which broke existing laws' and passive phases of 'intense political-agitational work within the legal framework'. The former included Gandhi's 'non-violent' mass tactics of civil disobedience of 1919–22 and non-cooperation in 1930–32. Since the Raj worked within a political and legal framework, it could be opposed by defying laws and withdrawing cooperation. The latter, passive phase included continuing emphasis on, for instance, boycott of foreign cloth and alcohol, the symbolic wearing of *khadi*, Gandhi's **ashrams** (model communities), and struggles to improve the lot of, and to integrate the leaders of, Untouchables and other oppressed or minority groups.

I now want to show how individual leaders, and Congress actions, worked on the ground. This should enable you to make judgements for yourself about the role of Indian nationalism. You have already come across one of its founders, namely Dadabhai Naoroji (1825–1917, see Units 3 and 10). Naoroji, you may

---

[21] The notion of 'hegemony' originates from Gramsci. Chandra et al. define the term as: 'exercise of leadership as opposed to pure domination ... the capacity of, as also the strategy through which, the rulers or dominant classes or leadership of popular movements organize consent among the ruled or the followers and exercise moral and ideological leadership over them (p. 9, note 2).

recall, did very well out of British imperialism. English-educated, he rose to become the first Indian professor in Bombay, professor of Gujerati at University College London, and from 1892 the Liberal member of parliament for Central Finsbury. You were asked to read a 1901 speech of his (Primary Source 3.7), in which he praised the benefits of British imperialism. Like many other early Congress members (see Figure 19.4), he was at pains to praise British law, order and education.

Figure 19.4   Gathering at the First Indian National Congress, 1885, from Mody, H. (1963 [1921]) *Sir Pherozeshah Mehta: A Political Biography*, London, Asia Publishing House, between pp. 128 and 129. The Indian National Congress was formed by a group of educated Indians with the support of retired British civil servant Allan Octavian Hume. The opening meeting in December 1885 at Bombay was attended by seventy-two representatives from various provinces of India.

Organisations elsewhere in Asia, such as *Budi Utomo* (see above), also practiced this 'loyal petitioning' style in the early stages of modern nationalism. Naoroji helped to found the Indian National Congress in 1885, and was elected its president in 1886, 1893 and 1906. He persuaded Indian princes to fund the East India Association, which campaigned to open the Indian Civil Service (ICS) to Indians. Like *Budi Utomo* again, early nationalism in India stressed self-reform and development by increasing access to 'modern' institutions such as the civil service and colleges.

Yet Naoroji's generation also laid the intellectual foundations for nationalism as opposed to Britain. In *Poverty and Un-British Rule in India* (1901), he argued that British rule was a drain on India's finances, diverting civil service pensions and resources, destroying Indian handicrafts by free trade and Manchester manufactured cottons, and spending disproportionately on an army that was the empire's plaything.

Naoroji straddled two worlds. He represented loyalism. In this period Congress consisted largely of professionals and merchants meeting once a year to draw up speeches and petitions. What these men sought, in between praising the British for bringing law and progress, was more access to posts and to the benefits of modernity. They were easily dismissed by the British as the chattering classes – brown Englishmen whose very education had separated them from the peasant masses the Raj claimed to defend. On the other hand, Naoroji did provide an intellectual case that Indian and British interests might be fundamentally opposed. He saw this as something surmountable, but later nationalists would interpret it as an irreconcilable difference, and decide that the best way of hurting the Raj was to hit its pocket.

The opportunity to turn theory into practice came around 1905, when the viceroy Lord Curzon split Bengal Province into two, partly to weaken its vocal nationalists, partly for administrative convenience, and conveniently creating a new, Muslim-majority East Bengal. Indians launched a mass protest movement based on *swadeshi* (self-reliance). This involved withdrawing the cooperation on which the Raj was based, by **hartals** (strikes), boycotts of British goods, particularly cloth, avoiding government courts and resigning posts. Though it eventually tapered off, had more support and impact among the middle classes in cities, and did not prevent partition, it nevertheless created a repertoire of ideas and methods, and gave Congress the credibility of having campaigned.

This first wave receded dramatically, in part because Congress split in 1907, expelling radicals such as Bengal's B. G. Tilak, who favoured more direct action. With Tilak and other radicals jailed, and the 1909 Government of India Act increasing Indian representation at the centre, Congress simmered down until the war.

"divide and conquer"

Terrorism and violence

Between 1906 and 1935, over 500 'revolutionary' crimes were registered, including many assassinations – one victim being an inspector general of the Bengal police. In 1930, a year of Congress civil disobedience, thirty-four people were assassinated, among them nine British officials (Silvestri, 2000). During the First World War, the British worried that Muslim organisations such as the tiny revolutionary Ghadr group might expand.

There was also the danger that peasants might resort to violence against landlords or the state. In March 1922, for instance, Gandhi called off non-cooperation because of events at Chauri Chaura. Peasants there, goaded by police actions, attacked and burned the police station, killing twenty-two police.

More worrying was the idea that 'extremists' would gather more support within nationalism and Congress. In Bengal, in particular, there was a tradition of violent protest, from individual terrorist acts of the 1890s, through Tilak favouring more direct action, to Subhas Chandra Bose – dubbed the Netaji (Respected Leader). Arrested eleven times by the British, Bose slipped out of the country, broadcast from Berlin, then made his way to Tokyo. He helped organise the southeast-Asia-based, Japanese-backed 'Indian National Army' (INA) from Indian troops captured in Malaya and Singapore in 1941–42. This even entered the fringes of India in early 1944 along with an invading Japanese army, before being turned back at Imphal and Kohima. He also headed a 'Free India' government. Though he died in an air crash on 18 August 1945, the INA continued to be a problem. Trials of its officers in 1945 led to widespread anger, and the eventual commuting of sentences.

Meanwhile, in 1942, Congress's 'Quit India' campaign spawned sporadic, and in places intense, violence and sabotage after its top leadership was imprisoned. All of which leaves the question: how far were British concessions to 'moderates' – and tempering of the use of coercion – motivated by fear that the alternative was increasing radicalisation and violence?

The next exercise provides a link between the events of 1907, and the development of a more mass-based nationalism from the First World War. To complete it, you will need to read parts of Gandhi's *Hind Swaraj* (Primary Source 19.7). This was published in 1908 in the newspaper the *Indian Opinion*, and as a book in 1909. Gandhi's text makes it clear that he felt the *swadeshi* movement against Bengal partition had radically changed nationalism (Gandhi, *Hind Swaraj*, pp. 22–3). The old emphasis on petitioning alone was now dead, replaced by a realisation that petition must be backed by force or suffering. The question of how much force had helped to split Congress in 1907. Hence the book is written as a dialogue between Gandhi ('The Editor') and an 'Extremist' ('The Reader').

EXERCISE

Primary Source 19.7 provides the complete text of Gandhi's *Hind Swaraj*. You only need to read the specific sections listed to answer the questions below, but you might also wish to dip into other parts of the book as well, to get a sense of the whole.

1   What does Gandhi think the cause of the British ability to hold India is (Sections VII, XI, XIX)?

2   What is Gandhi's view of India's true civilisation (Sections XIII, XIX)?

3   What methods does Gandhi prescribe for attaining '***swaraj***' (Sections XIV, XVII, XX)?

Keep your answers to one paragraph, incorporating the key terms or very short quotations from *Hind Swaraj*.

SPECIMEN ANSWER

1   Gandhi believes that the English were able to hold India because of Indian subservience. He states that 'We alone keep them', especially since 'money is their God' (p. 20). Indian division and participation in trade, tax and as servants of the state such as lawyers makes British rule possible. The implication was the continuing value of *swadeshi*-style tactics of boycotting foreign goods and posts, and producing more Indian goods such as home-spun cotton (*khadi*).

2   Gandhi's view of 'civilisation' is startlingly anti-modern, emphasising that India's superiority in civilisation lay in its morality, in a 'mode of conduct which points out to man the path of duty', and in which 'Each followed his own occupation or trade' (p. 31). He sees the ideal as an India of villages, and is profoundly opposed to cities, machinery, railways and other aspects of modernity.

3   Gandhi proposes attaining *swaraj* not just as 'home rule' but also as 'self-rule'. This can only be attained by mass campaigns that educate as much as agitate, and are based on *satyagraha*, meaning 'soul force' or truth force (p. 39). This soul force manifests as 'passive resistance', defined as 'a method of securing rights by personal suffering' (pp. 39–40), which builds support without alienating others. It requires fearlessness and strict discipline, with Gandhi identifying the latter with training by poverty, by abstinence from sex, and by taking up the handloom.

self-determination

DISCUSSION

Gandhi was adapting the tactics of civil disobedience (deliberate breaking of unjust laws) that he had used in South Africa. He was also drawing on elements already seared into nationalist Congress by the anti-Bengal partition *swadeshi*, such as boycotting British goods and institutions, and wearing Indian not foreign cloth. But beyond that not everyone approved of his anti-modernism. In a 1921 preface to the book he admitted he only aimed at 'parliamentary *swaraj*' to start with. India's first post-independence prime minister, Jawaharlal Nehru, actually lent towards state-directed development as a way of avoiding foreign dependence, and in economics it was Nehru's vision that would shape post-independence India (see box).

Jawaharlal Nehru

Jawaharlal Nehru (1889–1964) was educated at Cambridge and the Bar, and emerged as a major Congress leader in the 1920s, building on his father Motilal's political reputation, and the family base in Allahabad. Both father and son had terms as INC president in the 1920s. You can find more about Jawaharlal Nehru by looking him up in the *Oxford Dictionary of National Biography*. His daughter Indira and grandson Rajiv later became prime ministers of India as well.

But Gandhi's vision of *satyagraha* was influential. He had obtained results in South Africa. He built on Naoroji's belief that British power rested on draining India's wealth, adding that it also rested on Indian collaboration. Passive resistance would erode the very foundations of the Raj, while avoiding triggering the violent response the British were capable of. His non-violent approach also gave the British a motive to make concessions, in order to avoid fuelling more 'extremist' positions. Finally, his image of 'India' and by implication an 'Indian nation' resting on its religious spirit and 'soul force', and rooted in tradition, could appeal to a peasant mass. Gandhi was as active in establishing *ashrams*, communities experimenting in pure lives, and in supporting local campaigns by peasants and workers, as he was in his more famous campaigns. Over and above that, his appeal for use of Hindi, and his very style, reminiscent of Hindu holy men and ascetics, could appeal to non-literate groups.[22]

Gandhi rejoined a Congress already in ferment in 1916. Tilak had recently set up a Home Rule League in echo of Ireland, as also had an Irishwoman, Annie Besant. The example of Ireland, from its Easter Rebellion of 1916, through guerrilla warfare in 1918–21, to the creation of the Irish Free State as a new dominion (1921–22), suggested resistance was far from futile.

When the British tried to institutionalise India's wartime controls in the infamous Rowlatt Acts of 1919, Gandhi's moment had arrived. The controls – for instance the right to arrest without trial – were aimed at countering extremism, notably in Bengal. But Indian opinion felt they were a rejection of the spirit of the 1917 Montagu Declaration and the 1919 Government of India Act.

In March to April 1919, Gandhi led Congress in a 'Rowlatt *satyagraha*', with the resignation of posts, mass protests and the slogan of '*swaraj* in one year'. But he ended the campaign abruptly in April, after General Dyer opened fire at a peaceful Indian crowd in the Jallianwala Bagh – an enclosed public space – in Amritsar, Punjab, on 13 April. At least 369 were killed. The Punjab, reeling from wartime recruitment and shortages, had suffered simmering violence. Dyer hoped to crush this by his demonstration of calculated, lethal force against illegal protesters. It should be noted that Dyer's actions, and the repression in Punjab more generally, were double edged. On the one hand, Gandhi did call off the Rowlatt *satyagraha*. Dyer's actions had forcefully reminded nationalists of British willingness to use the **lathi** (a police cane not infrequently used when controlling crowds) freely, emergency powers where they felt necessary, and the gun too *in extremis*. Despite having to retire to England in 1920, Dyer was applauded by sections of British society and press (you might look up Dyer in the *ODNB* for more detail).

On the other hand, the Indian outrage that followed the Amritsar massacre made the high costs of excessive violence apparent to the British. Gandhi's tactics of non-violence also showed Indians a way of minimising the justification for violent repression, while maximising the moral force of the protester. Going forward, both Congress and British elites would have strong reasons to calibrate their actions.

Next year Congress returned to the fray, this time in combination with the Khalifat movement. In the 1916 Lucknow Pact, Congress had agreed to the continuation of separate electorates for Muslims, and both sides agreed to cooperate. In 1920, Britain was party to a harsh treaty with Turkey, whose sultan was recognised by Muslims as the khalifa. The Khalifat movement

---

[22] Hindi (in predominantly Hindu areas) and Urdu (in predominantly Muslim areas) are virtually identical at the everyday level, but are written in different scripts. Hindi was one of the most widely understood of India's many languages.

and Congress cooperated in non-cooperation from 1920 to 1922, until the Chauri Chaura incident (outlined in the box on terrorism above) again resulted in the movement being called off. But what exactly did such campaigns entail?

Read the extract from Sumit Sarkar's *Modern India 1885–1947* (Secondary Source 19.6).

1   In what ways did direct support for nationalism *per se* contribute to non-cooperation in 1920–22, and what evidence is there for this?

2   In what ways did particularist interests and campaigns contribute?

In each case give a few examples only. The point is to see how a complex, multilayered campaign like this worked, not to be comprehensive. I want you to get a flavour of the intricate interactions between all-India, regional and sectional interests.

1   Boycotts of council elections and posts clearly come under the heading of nationalist-inspired acts, as do boycotts of educational institutions, especially at college level, and establishment of national schools and colleges. Other examples include the establishment of **panchayats** (arbitration councils) to bypass official courts.

2   Particularistic interests included mill workers striking against cuts in jobs and salaries. Regional campaigns often involved local groups, such as the Akali movement, which challenged corrupt elites' stranglehold on Sikh shrines, called gurudwaras. The Khalifatists meanwhile were religiously motivated – by the defence of the khalifa – but in a way that did not necessarily see a unity of interest between Hindu and Muslim.

While in some cases protests may have been largely locally motivated, a simple 'nationalist' versus 'particularist' dichotomy would be naïve. The context of non-cooperation gave encouragement to local groups, but equally local groups may sometimes have expressed nationalist discontent in *satyagraha* by focusing on issues they already felt strongly about. Hence while some historians have tried to present protests in Andhra (an area south of Hyderabad) as concerning cattle fees, Sarkar pictures a broad enthusiasm for Gandhi in the area, manifesting in numerous small ways that peasants identified with, such as breaking forest regulations, avoiding fees, and attacking police parties, as well as the spread of Gandhi-centred rumours. So mobilisation on local issues may still have increased support for nationalism, and potential for future mobilisation in times of crisis. Crisis is a key word here, since *satyagraha*, with its risk of confiscation of property, fines and jail, was not sustainable indefinitely.

Campaigning also prompted the development of Congress structures. Congress set up a permanent working committee in 1920: the beginning of a gradual extension of organisation down to the local level. After campaigns it also tried to get confiscated land restored, and help people in distress. It is also true that non-violence fitted the interests of small proprietors, who did not want to see peasant or tribal unrest turning into no-rent or land campaigns. Finally, though non-violence was an aim, there were riots in places like Bombay. Ironically, some of the power of mass non-cooperation now, and civil disobedience in 1930–32, was that it kept the threat of violence simmering through its barely controlled nature. It threatened spontaneous local violence, while holding out the promise to the British that compromises by them would help avoid that violence now and in the future.

There were to be three more major bouts of nationalist campaigning in the next few years. The pattern each time was similar: British action, nationalist reaction, British concessions, further nationalist action, final repression. In between each bout, nationalists wrestled with what to do with British concessions and councils.

In the 1920s, the debate was between Congress 'no-changers', who wanted to boycott the 1919 councils, and 'entry *swarajists*', who argued for competing in elections and then making the reformed provincial councils unworkable. Congress managed to accommodate both trends.

The first major reoccurrence of mass campaigning was the civil disobedience of 1930–32. The British action was the early establishment of a review of the 1919 reforms, but by an all-white 'Simon Commission'. The nationalist reaction was to boycott that commission and a royal visit, and then in December 1929 to declare they wanted dominion status within a year, or would declare '**purna swaraj**' (complete independence). Viceroy Lord Irwin publicly promised the end aim was dominion status, but with no date or details, so Congress duly celebrated 1 January 1930 as 'Independence Day'. Gandhi began 'civil disobedience' by walking to Dandi, on the coast, where he made salt. Salt making (targeting a tax that affected the poor) then formed one plank of the campaign. The British concession came in the form of a Gandhi–Irwin pact of March 1931, whereby the campaign halted, prisoners were released, and it was agreed that Gandhi would attend the second Roundtable Conference in London as sole Congress representative. This was one of three such conferences in 1930–32, which achieved little more than suggesting a federal framework at the centre, whereby the princely states as well as British India should send representatives. It probably did not help that a British Labour government transmuted into a National Government with strong Conservative presence in late 1931, as a result of financial crisis. Far less was expected of the Conservatives. The campaign recommenced in 1932 but ultimately petered out under the impact of arrests, confiscation of property and the hope the British would anyway make concessions in parliamentary committee in 1933–34.

The resulting Government of India Act gave full provincial autonomy, with diarchy to commence at the centre when enough princely states joined, which of course they never did. This time Congress fought the elections whole-heartedly. It took enough seats in January to February 1937 elections to take control in seven provinces by July. Table 19.3 shows the milestones in Indian nationalism.

Table 19.3   Milestones in Indian nationalism (major campaigns highlighted)

Date	Event
1870s	Municipal and local district boards given elections and later Indian chairmen. Local politics boosted
1885	Indian National Congress (INC) formed
1905–07	*Swadeshi*
1907	Congress split between 'moderates' and 'extremists'
1916	Home rule leagues formed. Lucknow pact between INC and Muslim League
1919	Government of India Act for provincial diarchy. 'Rowlatt' Acts perpetuate rights such as arrest without trial, in order to deal with sedition in areas such as Bengal
1919	Rowlatt *satyagraha*
1920–22	Non-cooperation
1929	Congress demands dominion status now, or it will declare *purna swaraj* (complete independence) in a year
1930–32	Civil disobedience
1935	Government of India Act
1940	Individual civil disobedience from October
March 1942	Cripps Mission and offer after fall of Rangoon (8 March). An elected body after war to frame a constitution, no part of India to be forced to join, immediate entry of Indians to viceroy's executive
August 1942	Quit India Resolution of 8 August

Again, a lull was broken by British initiative, the viceroy declaring India to be at war in September 1939. Congress withdrew from provincial governments by October, and launched individual *satyagraha* the next year. But the real break came after the rejection of the March 1942 Cripps offer. With Japanese forces rampaging through Burma, Congress wanted real influence over the campaign, and to be in a position to treat with the Japanese if the worst happened. Britain would only offer consultative roles on the viceroy's committee now and a postwar assembly to draw up a constitution for dominion status. Hence the Congress order to 'Quit India' given in August 1942 was based as much on the nuances of war, as on what was on offer for later.

Was Quit India the height of nationalist revolt, or of futility? Maria Misra's *Vishnu's Crowded Temple: India since the Great Rebellion* describes it as:

> by British admission, the greatest rebellion since 1857. The nationalist leadership was immediately arrested, but Gandhi ... in his speech of 8 August ... declared that everyone who desired freedom would have to be his own guide, even (he implied) if it meant violence, guided only by his mantra 'Do or Die' ... the real leadership of the movement swiftly passed to spontaneous, rudimentary underground organizations ...

> The Quit India campaign was a drama in three acts. It began with massive strikes ... From mid-August the action moved to the countryside, and though this had been more or less suppressed by September 1942, a third act, now largely an underground terrorist movement, opened and played on until early 1944.
>
> (Misra, 2007, p. 220)

In Bihar, a parallel government using the Congress name emerged. Pamphlets proliferated, and 332 railway stations and 945 post offices were attacked. The British made mass arrests, torched recalcitrant villages, and even tried aerial bombardment: 66,000 were detained and 2500 killed. The British showed they could repress almost anything, but Congress proved that they could impose a terrible price. The British could pay this price in war, but would they be willing to pay it after the war?

As it was, by August 1945 the main British aim was no longer to construct elaborate mechanisms that would leave them controlling the army and external affairs: but to bring Indians together so they could exit a friendly, united India that might still be an ally and (hopefully) Commonwealth member. A large part of the reason for these diminished ambitions was communalism. Indeed, by the 1940s, 'decolonisation' was becoming as much a competition between Indians to define what India should become, as it was a clash between Indians and imperialists (see Figure 19.5 for communal riots).

COMMUNALISM AND CASTE

Would one 'India' be the result of decolonisation, and if so what would be the position in it of Muslims and oppressed classes? Such questions played a crucial role in shaping decolonisation, and especially in determining the nature of the post-independence state. This means that 'decolonisation' was not merely a matter of nationalism versus imperialism, but of Indians struggling among themselves to define what the outcome of decolonisation should be: the nature of the postcolonial state and nation.

But this does not mean that the final outcome, the partition of India externally and the entrenchment of 'Untouchable' rights internally, was a foregone conclusion. Far from it. When Choudhary Rahmat Ali coined the word 'Pakstan' in 1933 (the 'i' was added later), his image of a Muslim state in northern India was dismissed as the fantasy of a Cambridge-based pamphleteer (see Figure 19.6 for one of his later pamphlets).

This was despite prior events that suggested Muslims might already be coming to see themselves as a separate 'nation' within India. The British had granted Muslims separate electoral roles from 1909. Congress confirmed these in the 1916 Lucknow Pact. The subsequent Congress–Khalifat alliance of 1920–22 had proven temporary, as the secularisation of Turkey under Kemal Ataturk subsequently removed the Khalifat issue. In 1920, the Muslim League separated from Congress. Some elements of Indian nationalism also increased Muslim anxieties. Hindu revivalism had led to recurrent communal violence

Figure 19.5   Dead Hindu man, Calcutta, 1946. Unknown photographer. Photo: Keystone/Getty Images. The death toll during communal riots in Calcutta rose to over 2000, with 4000 people injured. Here a Hindu corpse is surrounded by Muslims armed with lathis, a lethal weapon in trained hands.

from the 1890s' cow protection campaigns. The Hindu Mahsabha (founded 1915) was perhaps not too threatening, but in 1925 the **Rashtriya Swayamsevak Sangh (RSS)** was formed following communal riots. Adherents were variously seen as Indian-style Boy Scouts or potential Nazi-style paramilitaries. Either way, their leaders espoused militant Hinduism, their anthem was tinged with anti-Muslim sentiment, and they had 100,000 members by 1940 (Misra, 2007, pp. 167–9).

Against the idea of physical separation, however, was the reality that as many Muslims lived as minorities in provinces such as United Provinces, as in provinces with large Muslim majorities (Sind, North West Frontier Province, Baluchistan) or narrow majorities (Punjab and Bengal). Figure 19.7 gives the breakdown.

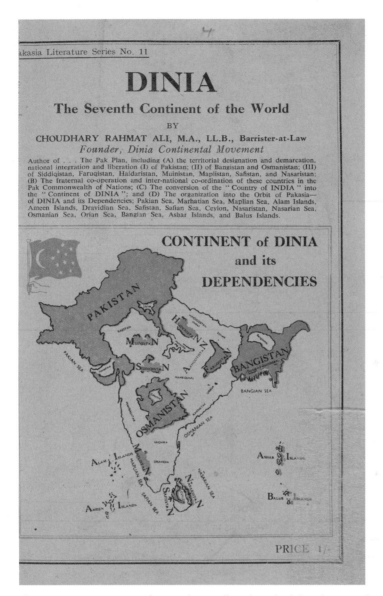

Figure 19.6   Front cover from Rahmat Ali, C. (1946) *Dinia: The Seventh Continent of the World*, Cambridge, Dinia Continental Movement. The British Library, T 50329 (a). Photo: © British Library Board. All rights reserved.

So Choudhary's idea of physical separation was tempered by the Muslim League's members from minority provinces, who tended to be disproportionately influential in the early Muslim League. Hence the League's priorities were then the preservation of separate electorates, and winning of assured percentages of representation in councils in the provinces where they were minorities. The Lucknow Pact of 1916, for instance, gave Muslims greater percentage representation in councils than their population warranted in states such as United Provinces (for Muslim percentages by area, see Figure 19.7).

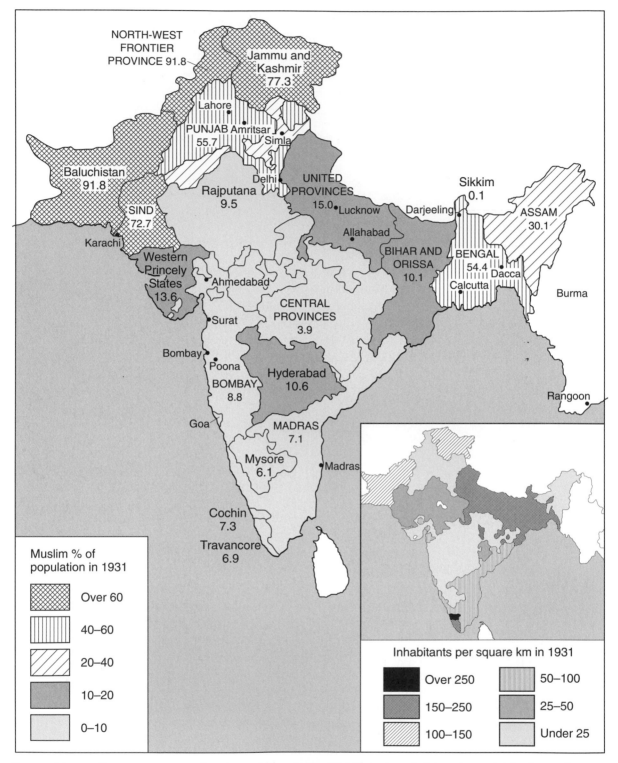

NORTH-WEST FRONTIER PROVINCE 91.8

Jammu and Kashmir 77.3

Lahore

PUNJAB 55.7 Amritsar
Simla

Baluchistan 91.8

SIND 72.7

Karachi

Rajputana 9.5

Delhi

UNITED PROVINCES 15.0
Lucknow

Allahabad

Sikkim 0.1

Darjeeling

ASSAM 30.1

Western Princely States 13.6

Ahmedabad

BIHAR AND ORISSA 10.1

BENGAL 54.4
Dacca
Calcutta

Burma

CENTRAL PROVINCES 3.9

Surat

Bombay

Poona

BOMBAY 8.8

Hyderabad 10.6

Rangoon

Goa

MADRAS 7.1

Mysore 6.1

Madras

Cochin 7.3

Travancore 6.9

Muslim % of population in 1931

	Over 60
	40–60
	20–40
	10–20
	0–10

Inhabitants per square km in 1931

Over 250	50–100
150–250	25–50
100–150	Under 25

Figure 19.7   Muslims as percentage of total population, India, 1931 (by major administrative regions), adapted from Porter, A.N. (1991) *Atlas of British Overseas Expansion*, London, Routledge, p. 169. Note that at this time, Bihar and Orissa were still a single state (see Figure 19.1).

Read 'Mahomed Ali Jinnah's Fourteen Points, March 1929' (Primary Source 19.8) – these were fourteen demands made by the Muslim League to Congress in 1929. How did these try to balance the needs of Muslims from different provinces?

Muslim majorities in the Punjab and Bengal would be entrenched by reserving seats there. Muslims in provinces where they were minorities would be guaranteed a third of seats. All Muslims would be guarded both by specific proscription of freedoms, including of worship, and by rights in the central legislative assembly. The latter would include having one-third of the seats, and the right for any community to block legislation if three-quarters of its representatives voted against it.

The background was that Congress had called a 1928 all-party meeting to draw up a constitution for India (the 'Nehru Report'), having boycotted the Simon Commission. But Congress and the League could not agree. Congress rejected the League's appeals for residuary powers to be vested in each province, rather than a central state. That fuelled fears that a Congress-controlled centre might impinge on Muslim-controlled provinces. At the same time, Fazl-i-Husain, the chief minister of Punjab, was, if anything, overshadowing the Muslim League's Muhammad Ali Jinnah by calling for more stringent safeguards.

As late as 1937, the Muslim League had not yet won a majority of Muslim votes in Bengal, or in Punjab, where a coalition of landlords and middle-class Sikhs, Muslims and Hindus had formed the Punjab Unionist Party. But, fantasist or not, Choudhary's 1946 pamphlet *India: The Continent of Dinia or the Country of Doom* (the complete pamphlet is available as the optional Primary Source 19.9) came close to prophecy in showing not just a Pakistan, but a Bangistan (Bang-i-Islamistan) in East Bengal (Bangladesh after 1971). His argument was that 'India' was a **Brahman** (high-caste Hindu) fiction meant to enslave separate non-Brahman, **Dravidian**, Sikh, Christian and other identities, all of whom should have their own states. Where Congress saw 'India' as one state and nation, he transposed the 'd' to make Dinia ('abode of religions') (Choudhary, 1945; Jalal, 1995).

We have already seen that the balance tipped in the League's favour partly because of the war, when Congress resignations allowed it to take power in more provinces, and to entrench itself as a vital ally to the British. This cemented a 1937–39 trend, when some Muslims reacted defensively to Congress's attempts to target Muslims for individual recruitment by 'mass contact', and to the likes of the Hindu Mahasabha and the RSS. In addition, Congress taking power in seven of eleven provinces shattered hopes that the 1932 Communal Award and 1935 constitution had protected Muslim interests. The former had seen the British guarantee 'minorities' fixed percentages of seats to be elected by separate electorates. The latter had promised that, if and when any central legislature became operative, Muslims and princely states would each have a third of the seats in the federal assembly, leaving Congress a minority.

Yet, after 1937, United Provinces' politically ambitious Muslims, for instance, were denied any place in a Congress-led coalition and ministry. Congress was also pressing princely states to join the federation and select seats by election not nomination: in other words, opening up another one-third of seats for Congress to compete for. Muslims were increasingly nervous, especially as their vote seemed divided, with the League securing only a minority of Muslim seats in the 1937 elections.[23]

Jinnah declared at the Muslim League's October 1937 conference that a 'Congress Raj' was trying to squeeze everyone else out. Religious leaders also reacted to what they saw as a threat by the secular Congress. Jinnah won over provincial leaders, and took Muslim League membership from a few thousand to several hundred thousand, under the banner of demanding equality of power in any parliamentary regime (Moore, 1983, pp. 531–5).

This battle over communal representation demonstrates how 'decolonisation' is more than mere 'anti-colonialism'. Garnering anti-colonial power, by alliance, all-territory organisation and an increasing repertoire of anti-colonial methods, is important. But so too are attempts to define what the 'nation' is, and how it will arrange its post-independence affairs. Benedict Anderson (1991) describes such nations as 'imagined communities'. People who might never see each other have to imagine themselves as sharing an identity and certain events, to feel part of a community. According to him, 'imagined communities' hardened as the proliferation of newspapers helped to create a sense of shared identity.

But in colonies such as the Netherland East Indies, Malaya and India there was to some degree a 'plural society' (Furnivall, 1948). Groups who mingled in the marketplace did not mix so much socially. In the case of India's Hindus and Muslims, purity and food rules meant they rarely married. They might read different newspapers, and form distinct, if overlapping, commercial and other networks. In India, separate elections had further entrenched these tendencies. By the 1920s, some Muslims were arguing there were 'two nations' in India: Hindu and Muslim.

In 1940, the Muslim League's Lahore congress demanded that:

> geographically contiguous units are demarcated into regions which should be so constituted ... that the areas in which the Muslims are numerically in a majority, as in the northwestern and eastern zones of India, should be grouped to constitute 'independent States' in which the constituent units shall be autonomous and sovereign.
>
> (Muslim League, 'The Lahore resolution', in optional Primary Source 19.10, p. 2)

This has subsequently come to be known as the 'Pakistan' motion. What was the League and its increasingly dominant leader, Bombay lawyer Muhammad Ali Jinnah, thinking? Some have argued he was in earnest. Others that this was

---

[23] Including just one in Punjab and none in Sind and North West Frontier Province. It did much better in United Provinces.

a negotiating ploy, a threat of the worst, designed to maximise Congress concessions (Moore, 1983) both for the majority provinces (perhaps as a block within a loose federation), and for where Muslims were minorities. Moore, meanwhile, has argued that we should not over-personalise events. Jinnah was following, rather than leading, regional power brokers such as those of the Sind United Party (Moore, 1983, p. 537). From 1938 to 1940, separation was coming to be the most dramatic option of a range still being debated: starting with a federation with residual powers going to states; through Muslim and non-Muslim blocks of states or cultural homelands within a loose federation; to full independence for 'Pakistan'. In supporting the Lahore Resolution, and emphasising Islam and Hinduism as two distinct nationalities and social orders, Jinnah was leading by following: speech writing by synthesising the ideas of Muslim poets, scholars and politicians of the day.

The Congress counter seems to have been that any such 'Pakistan' could not take whole provinces where populations were mixed, as in Bengal and the Punjab. If it came to a partition, these provinces would have to be partitioned. Gandhi, released from prison in 1944, offered only those parts of such provinces as might vote to go with a Pakistan. Jinnah rejected this as offering a 'moth-eaten Pakistan'. In June 1945 at Simla, Wavell tried to entice Congress and League to participate in the viceroy's executive council, but the League refused to enter unless it was the sole Muslim representative. The meeting failed. Jinnah was determined only to negotiate details *after* the principles of League representation of all Muslims, and the right to form a Pakistan, were ceded: in other words, from a position of strength.

By 1939, Britain had accepted that any postwar constitution for a new dominion would be settled by Indians, but it still hoped to cajole them to remain within some all-India framework. A united, peaceful and grateful India might be a help to the Commonwealth in international politics and defence; a divided or angry one would greatly weaken British world power. But Britain's influence was declining. The return of a Labour government in July 1945 presaged more rapid decolonisation in India. The League fought the 1945–46 elections on the basis of the demand for a Pakistan now precisely defined as the four northwest provinces plus Bengal. Whereas the League only won 25 per cent of Muslim votes in 1937 provincial elections, it won 89 per cent in 1946. A March to May 1946 cabinet mission was then sent, as yet another attempt to cajole Congress and League into meaningful negotiations.

a negotiated settlement.

EXERCISE

Read the 1946 Cabinet Mission proposals in 'Cabinet delegation and Viceroy Viscount Wavell: joint statement, 16 May 1946' (Primary Source 19.11). What was the new proposal for breaking the League–Congress deadlock?

SPECIMEN ANSWER

The central proposal was for a layering of authority within one India. There would be layer A, a central, loose federation responsible for defence and external affairs but little else. In layer B provinces would 'group' themselves.

This meant a Muslim group might counter-balance a Hindu group of provinces. Each might function as an internally self-governing unit within the federation. Beneath that, layer C would consist of individual provinces, to whom all residual powers would devolve.

Both League and Congress agreed these proposals in May 1946, presaging their entry into an interim government. Then Congress insisted provinces could refuse to 'group', including perhaps North West Frontier Province and Assam, so undermining the prospect of any coherent group of contiguous Muslim states emerging. The Muslim League withdrew cooperation. Congress alone entered an interim government in September, a reluctant League following after. So while this shows the League was to the end willing to consider some sort of compromise, from this time on partition was all but inevitable. Whether Congress accidentally or deliberately killed this last compromise proposal is unclear. Did they miscalculate? Or were they simply not willing to weaken the centre as much as Muslims now demanded?

The endgame was now on. By April, Wavell was being advised that imperial forces might not be able to control a 'Quit India' scale revolt if it came. The ICS, police and army might all be pushed if communal violence was involved. Wavell consequently suggested emergency plans for a withdrawal through Muslim provinces. These spooked cabinet, who appointed Mountbatten to replace him as viceroy from March 1947. But the latter only took the post on condition he got what Wavell had asked for anyway: a cabinet declaration that Britain would leave at a specified date. On 20 February, cabinet named June 1948 as the end date, when Britain would hand over power to one or more governments. Mountbatten made futile attempts to bring back an all-India solution. In June 1947, in frustration he brought the end date forward to August. India would become independent at midnight on 14–15 August as separate dominions, with a boundary commission to settle disputed areas (see Figure 19.8). Indian states would have the option of choosing which state to accede to, or of remaining outside.

In the resulting, tragic, end-game, Muslim leaders who believed in the idea of one India accepted instead a division.[24] Millions of Muslims moved from Hindu territories, and Hindus and Sikhs from Muslim (see Figure 19.9), with violence variously said to have claimed half a million to one million lives. It was a murderous, frustrating, nightmarish end to a 'negotiated' process: albeit one that spawned one long-lasting democracy (India), another initially stable state (Pakistan), and extricated Britain from what promised to be an even worse wreckage.

---

[24] Jinnah initially argued there was one India. As late as 1954, Fazlul Huq, chief minister of East Bengal, told a Bengal audience that 'it is idle to pretend that I am a Bengali, someone is a Bihari, someone is a Pakistani ... India exists as a whole' (cited in Park and Wheeler, 1954, p. 131).

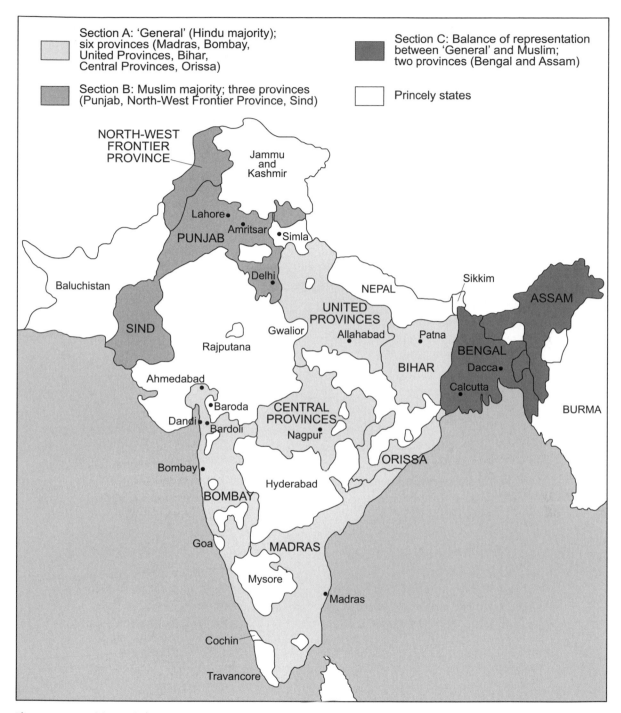

Figure 19.8   Cabinet mission proposals in the partition of India, adapted from Porter, A.N. (1991) *Atlas of British Overseas Expansion*, London, Routledge, p. 176.

Figure 19.9   Sikhs migrating to the Hindu sector of Punjab, October 1947. Photographed by Margaret Bourke-White. Photo: Time Life Pictures/Getty Images.

Untouchables

'Untouchables' (also known as *Harijans* or **Dalit**) also campaigned for separate representation, based on discrimination against them due to the caste and *jati* system. The British, in their censuses from 1871, recorded religion, but also **varna** and *jati*. Varna or 'caste' meant groups defined by occupation and *dharma* or merit. *Jati* meant smaller kin, trade and locality subgroups. Both Mogul successor courts and the British relied heavily on members of the literate Brahman (priestly) caste as administrators. These Brahmins encouraged a view of caste based on Hindu scriptures which made it seem more fixed than it had been. This is hardly surprising, since the *varna* categories favoured them. These were:

Brahman (priestly)

Ksatriya (warrior)

Vaishya (merchant)

Shudra (peasant)

The Untouchables' status related both to class exploitation, and to Hindu notions of purity, which saw alcohol, meat and certain occupations as polluting. Lower-caste groups might be employed for polluting activities, such as removing household waste and the dead, and tanning.

Gandhi, the Hindu Mahasabha and RSS attempted to reach out to Untouchables, for instance incorporating them into the caste system as Shudras. But lower-caste groups organised as well, for instance demanding 'temple entry' where higher-caste groups barred them. B. R. Ambedkar (1891–1956), the first Untouchable lawyer and provincial legislator, won British promises of separate electoral representation in 1932, prompting Gandhi in the Pune (Poona) Pact to agree instead that a proportion of general seats would be reserved. The resulting 'reservation' of seats, and later of educational places, persisted into post-independence India. Congress was thus only partly successful in capturing 'Untouchables' (Bayly, 1999).

CONCLUSION

India is, to a degree, an example of the 'negotiated' end of empire. The British, by conceding representative institutions and electoral arenas, had unintentionally conferred on Congress (and later the Muslim League) democratic legitimacy. It proved a potent example. Henceforth, transferring increasing doses of power to nationalists who had demonstrated an electoral mandate became the default mode of British decolonisation. However contested and difficult the journey to 1947, India had finally made it, and now formed the bridge by which the 'dominion example' extended from being merely for white settler colonies, to being for occupation colonies and non-whites as well.

At the same time, there always seemed to be good 'reasons' to delay full self-government: be these unresolved communal tensions, British defence and financial interests, or even the atavistic reflexes of some metropolitan politicians. Britain's preferred model was not of scuttle, but of gradual, managed decolonisation, until foes were banished and the keys to the citadel could be handed over to trustworthy friends: friends who would be willing Commonwealth allies. In Malaya, Kenya, Cyprus and elsewhere, Britain waged counterinsurgencies before leaving. In Aden, it more or less abandoned the colony in 1967 in the face of local pressure. So there is debate over how far Britain went willingly in India and elsewhere, and how far it had to be pushed by nationalism, by non-violent resistance, the threat of violence, and the strains of major wars.

Indian nationalists, frustrated by what they saw as imperial footdragging, developed a growing repertoire of nationalist and anti-colonial tools. These ranged from petitioning, through *swadeshi*'s boycotts and withdrawal from posts, and Gandhian civil disobedience, to Bengali traditions of terrorism, and finally Bose's Indian National Army. It can be extremely difficult, at any one point, to say how far the British were unfolding their own design, and how far responding to each of these strands.

As we have seen, debate continues to rage over the weight of each strand in accelerating decolonisation. Was nationalism little more than a bundle of disparate local interests and power brokers, with the thinnest veneer of all-India sentiment, as the Cambridge School might suggest? Or did Congress gradually become a counter-hegemonic body, a central reference point and meeting place for many, if not most, Hindu nationalists? Some Indian historians would have us believe the latter, so that it was not British policy, but the successively higher waves of Indian nationalism and agitation that won freedom.

But beyond British policy, and Indian nationalism, there were bigger forces at work. Was the key accelerator actually war? In 1939, there was a handful of Indian officers in the Indian army; by 1946, there were 15,000 (Misra, 2007, p. 228). In 1939, Indianisation of the ICS was already at 25 per cent, but by 1946 it was 50 per cent. Had war turned snail's pace into hare's sprint where Indianisation was concerned? What we can be certain about is that far-reaching concessions were made in the shadow of war. In 1917–19, concessions led to provincial diarchy; in 1942, there was the Cripps offer of dominion status after the war. But did war really remove stalemate (as in the 1935 constitution), or just accelerate underlying, self-accelerating processes of concession and Indianisation?

Finally, at the end, what came to the fore was not negotiation between Britain and Indians, nor external events, but rather relations between Muslim and Hindu leaders. This highlights that 'decolonisation' is not just about expelling foreigners and strengthening anti-colonial power. It also involves filling in the positive content of nationalism, defining what the 'nation' or 'imagined nation' is, and debating what kind of post-independence constitution and society will be installed.

From this we can take a number of issues and concepts that are applicable not just to the Indian case, but to 'decolonisation' and ends of empire more generally. First of all, the troika of imperial policy, nationalism and international context (especially in the form of major international conflicts) is relevant to decolonisation in general. The question is not usually whether these three were present, but what their relative weights and roles were, and how they interacted. Secondly, the interaction between imperial policy and local players is particularly important, each playing off the other. The more skilfully the colonial power balances concession and coercion, the longer it will retain enough local elite support to underpin continuing control. The more key local elites need the colonial power for their own profit or protection, the larger the scope for compromise. Thirdly, while not all colonies suffered from the level of intercommunal meltdown that India did, it remains true that 'decolonisation' is often a struggle to define what the postcolonial state and society will be, as much as it is a struggle to oust foreign rule. For that reason, the end of empire often witnesses not just anti-colonial war, but a degree of civil struggle if not civil war among the local population. As we shall see in Unit 20, on Algeria and Angola, these 'civil wars' can all too easily generate into nasty insurgencies, with unpleasant consequences and legacies for all sides.

REFERENCES

Anderson, B. (1991) *Imagined Communities*, London, Verso.

Bayly, S. (1999) *Caste, Society and Politics in India from the Eighteenth Century to the Modern Age*, Cambridge, Cambridge University Press.

Brown, J. (1985) *Modern India: The Origins of an Asian Democracy*, Oxford, Oxford University Press.

Burton, A. (ed.) (2001) *Politics and Empire in Victorian Britain: A Reader*, Basingstoke, Palgrave.

Butler, D. and Butler, G. (1986) *British Political Facts 1900–1985*, London, Macmillan.

Chandra, B., et al. (1989) *India's Struggle for Independence*, Penguin, Harmondsworth.

Chandrasekhar, S. (1946) *India's Population: Fact and Policy*, New York, John Day.

Choudhary, R.A. (1945) *India: The Continent of Dinia or the Country of Doom*, Cambridge, The Dinia Continental Movement.

Darwin, J. (1980) 'Imperialism in decline? Tendencies in British imperial policy between the wars', *Historical Journal*, vol. 23, no. 3, pp. 657–79.

Darwin, J. (1988) *Britain and Decolonisation: The Retreat from Empire in the Post-War World*, London, Macmillan.

Duffett, W.E., Hicks, A.R. and Parkin, G.R. (1942) *India Today: The Background of Indian Nationalism*, New York, John Day.

Epstein, S. (1982) 'District officers in decline: the erosion of British authority in the Bombay countryside, 1919 to 1947', *Modern Asian Studies*, vol. 16, no. 3, pp. 493–518.

Etemad, B. (2007) *Possessing the World: Taking the Measurements of Colonisation from the 18th to the 20th Century*, New York and Oxford, Berghahn.

Foster, A.L (1995) 'French, Dutch, British and US reactions to the Nghe Tinh rebellion of 1930–1931' in Antlöv, H. and Tønnesson, S. (eds) *Imperial Policy and Southeast Asian Nationalism, 1930–1958*, Richmond, Curzon Press, pp. 63–82.

Furnivall, J.S (1948) *Colonial Policy and Practice: A Comparative Study of Burma and Netherlands India*, Cambridge, Cambridge University Press.

Gallagher, J. and Seal, A. (1981) 'Britain and India between the wars', *Modern Asian Studies*, vol. 15, no. 3, pp. 387–414.

Gandhi, M.K. (1938 [1909]) *Hind Swaraj*, Ahmedabad, J.T. Desai; also available online at http://www.forget-me.net/en/Gandhi/hind-swaraj.pdf (Accessed 23 May 2008).

Jalal, A. (1995) 'Conjuring Pakistan: history as official imagining', *International Journal of Middle Eastern Studies I*, vol. 27, pp. 73–89.

Jeffrey, K. (1981) 'An English barrack in the Oriental seas? India in the aftermath of the First World War', *Modern Asian Studies*, vol. 5, pp. 370–87.

Low, D.A. (1991) *Eclipse of Empire*, Cambridge, Cambridge University Press.

Madden, F. and Darwin, J. (1993) *The Dominions and India Since 1900: Select Documents on the Constitutional History of the British Empire and Commonwealth*, New York and London, Greenwood Press.

Misra, M. (2007) *Vishnu's Crowded Temple: India Since the Great Rebellion*, London, Allen Lane.

Moon, P. (ed.) (1977) *Wavell: The Viceroy's Journal*, Delhi, Oxford University Press.

Moore, R.J. (1983) 'Jinnah and the Pakistan demand', *Modern Asian Studies*, vol. 17, no. 4, pp. 529–61.

Naoroji, D. (1901) *Poverty and Un-British Rule in India*, London, Swan Sonnenschein.

Park, R.L. and Wheeler, R.S. (1954) 'East Bengal under governor's rule', *Far Eastern Survey*, vol. 23, no. 9, pp.129–54.

Potter, D.D. (1973) 'Manpower shortage and the end of colonialism: the case of the Indian Civil Service', *Modern Asian Studies*, vol. 7, no. 1, pp. 47–73.

Sarkar, S. (1989) *Modern India 1885–1947*, Basingstoke, Macmillan.

Seal, A. (1973) 'Imperialism and nationalism in India', *Modern Asian Studies*, vol. 7, no. 3, pp. 321–47.

Short, A. (1995) 'Pictures at an exhibition' in Antlöv, H. and Tønnesson, S. (eds) *Imperial Policy and Southeast Asian Nationalism, 1930–1958*, Richmond, Curzon Press, pp. 15–33.

Silvestri, M. (2000) '"The Sinn Fein of India": Irish Nationalism and the policing of revolutionary terrorism in Bengal', *Journal of British Studies*, vol. 39, no. 4, pp. 454–86.

Spodek, H. (1979) 'Pluralist politics in British India: the Cambridge cluster of historians of modern India', *American Historical Review*, vol. 84, no. 3, pp. 688–707.

Thomas, M. (2005) *The French Empire Between the Wars*, Manchester, Manchester University Press.

Tomlinson, B.R. (1979) *The Political Economy of the Raj 1914–47: The Economics of Decolonization in India*, Palgrave Macmillan, London.

UNIT 20
THE END OF EMPIRE IN ALGERIA AND ANGOLA

Bernard Waites

AIMS

1   To compare and account for the end of French rule in Algeria and Portuguese rule in Angola.

2   To enable you to analyse the emergence of Algerian and Angolan nationalism.

3   To explain why the French and Portuguese military were able to contain the insurgencies but not able to impose a favourable political solution.

4   To help you assess the impact of colonial war on metropolitan politics and society.

5   To help you assess the impact of colonial war on African politics and society.

INTRODUCTION

(i) The European colonial empires dissolved in basically two ways after 1945. The more common way was by the imperial state negotiating an orderly and conservative transfer of power to a nationalist political party enjoying an electoral mandate. The second, less common way was by a revolutionary *(2)* movement acceding to power without an electoral mandate, after protracted insurgency had forced the imperial state to withdraw.

This unit compares the 'revolutionary' end of empire in French Algeria and Portuguese Angola. They make an illuminating comparison for several reasons. Constitutionally, both were integral parts of the imperial state's national territory; the ideological and emotional investment in them was as important as the economic. Their citizens were French and Portuguese nationals, though, as we shall see, citizenship was so constructed as to exclude the indigenous majority. In theory, the political future of Algeria's Muslims and Angola's Africans lay in being assimilated to the national state, once they had acquired 'civilised' attributes (such as literacy in French and Portuguese) and eschewed 'native' law and custom. In Algeria, the European community or *pieds noirs* were the biggest obstacle to this policy of assimilation: through their parliamentary representatives and their allies in the local administration, they sabotaged efforts to raise the political status of the Muslim majority. The Algerian nationalists resorted to violence because they despaired of the French Republic honouring its democratic principles. In Angola, the white settlers were, with rare exceptions, hostile to African political advance, but the real obstacle was the Salazarist dictatorship in metropolitan Portugal. Its obduracy left the Angolan nationalists, who would have much preferred negotiation, no alternative to insurgency.

[margin note: Similar to America ??]

[margin note: politics of mother country]

By refusing negotiation, both imperial powers were drawn into protracted colonial wars (please consult the datecharts on the website). Most analysts accept that the French and Portuguese military defeated the insurgencies: in the wars' final phases nationalist guerrillas controlled only isolated pockets of territory; they were not able to engage the colonial forces in significant numbers and could not seriously interrupt commerce and communications.[25] Yet neither the French nor the Portuguese were able to turn their military superiority into a negotiating advantage and shake their opponents' inflexibility. The Algerian National Liberation Front (FLN) never wavered from a set of demands its collective leadership drew up in the autumn of 1956, and which the French eventually conceded at the Evian peace negotiations. When the Portuguese decamped from Angola, the rival nationalist movements were locked in civil war. In both cases, the failure of the metropolitan power to secure the interests of European settlers led to their wholesale flight.

What 'nationalism' is, often.

There is a two-fold explanation for this paradoxical sequence of political capitulation to nationalist insurgency following its military containment. First, waging colonial war placed intolerable strains on the French and Portuguese political systems, which finally led to regime change. Political crises in Paris and Lisbon brought to power men who, for different reasons, were determined to extract their countries from African imbroglios and reorient them to Europe. General de Gaulle returned to office on 1 June 1958, when the parliamentary Fourth Republic collapsed before the threat of military coup, and was given authority to draw up a presidential constitution for the new Fifth Republic. The result was a more powerful executive, able to impose a political solution on the Algerian problem beyond the grasp of feeble, party governments of the Fourth Republic. In April 1974, the Portuguese dictatorship crumbled before the '**revolution of the flowers**' in Lisbon, fomented by army officers disillusioned by the seemingly endless, costly and socially debilitating colonial wars. In Mozambique and Angola, radicalised officers in the Armed Forces Movement fraternised with the left-wing FRELIMO (Front for the Liberation of Mozambique) and MPLA (Popular Movement for the Liberation of Angola), so easing their accession to power.

The second reason for the political capitulation to revolutionary anti-colonialism was the insurgents' success in internationalising the conflicts. The FLN found foreign patrons in President Bourguiba of Tunisia and Colonel Nasser of Egypt, who provided sanctuary, arms, training grounds, diplomatic protection for the Algerian provisional government in Cairo, and the means to wage a propaganda offensive against French imperialism. A similar role was performed on behalf of the anti-Portuguese insurgents by central African heads of states (Nyerere of Tanzania, Kaunda of Zambia, Mobutu of Zaire). More remotely, the Soviet Union and communist China were sources of diplomatic accreditation, money, arms and training in revolutionary warfare. At the United Nations, the Afro-Asian bloc of states became a solid, anti-colonial phalanx,

---

[25] This is not true of Portuguese Guinea, where the PAIGC (African Party for the Independence of Guinea and Cape Verde) guerrillas controlled most of the territory by the end of war and Portuguese forces were pinned into military strongholds. In Mozambique, FRELIMO had established 'liberated zones' in the north, though their strategic and political significance was much exaggerated.

thanks partly to the skill with which FLN agents publicised the Algerian cause in New York. And we must add that international public opinion – especially intellectual opinion – was overwhelmingly anti-colonialist and generally sympathetic to revolutionary insurgency. The leading spokesmen of the 'African revolution', Frantz Fanon and Amílcar Cabral, enjoyed extraordinary reputations as political theorists of, and for, the Third World.

When we look inside the nationalist insurgencies we find further similarities. Both were acclaimed as 'peoples' wars' that would bring social revolution as well as independence. The reality was more complex: the insurgencies were as much internecine as anti-colonial struggles. The FLN came to dominate the Algerian insurrection by extirpating rival nationalist organisations and killed more Muslims than Europeans. There was an underlying tension within its ranks between Arabs and Berber-speaking Kabyles. Several key figures in its highest echelons were liquidated in the course of bitter disputes between guerrilla commanders on the ground and political leaders in exile. In Angola, internecine conflict was magnified because the three nationalist movements (the MPLA, the FNLA and UNITA) never coalesced under a single umbrella. Apart from their sharp ideological differences, each drew its support from distinct ethnic and confessional groups in Angola's African population.

THE ALGERIAN WAR OF INDEPENDENCE

France and Algeria on the eve of the insurrection

EXERCISE

Soon after the Algerian uprising began on 1 November 1954, the London *Times* commissioned two background articles from its special correspondent in North Africa entitled 'Rule and riot in Algeria' (10 and 11 November 1954). These are available on the course website as Primary Source 20.1. They offer a well-informed survey of the political and economic situation in Algeria, and its distinctive administrative system. Unsurprisingly, their tone is pro-French, but not uncritically so. Read them now and answer the following questions:

1   Was nationalist terrorism in Algeria an isolated problem for French administrators in North Africa? If not, what historical and political factors made it different from terrorism elsewhere?

2   According to the correspondent, the French claimed that, since the passing of the Algerian Statute in 1947, the Muslim population 'now possess the full status of French citizens'. Was this true? What had happened to the statute?

3   What do we learn about Algerian nationalist organisations? Which was held responsible for the uprising?

4   What economic and social advantages were there for Muslims in Algeria remaining part of France?

SPECIMEN ANSWER

1   No, the French were also confronted with nationalist terrorism in Tunisia and Morocco. The difference was that these were protectorates, each with a long-established monarchy and political unity that pre-dated the French

occupation. Their governments had entered treaty relationships with France. Algeria was a conquered territory, which – according to the French – had not existed as a political entity before their arrival. It had no political future outside France.

2   It is true that the 1947 Statute had granted all Muslim adult *males* the right to vote for the Algerian and National Assemblies (the correspondent mistakenly refers to this as 'universal suffrage', so must have been a man!) But there were two electoral colleges: one predominantly European, the other wholly Muslim. Each college had equal representation in the Algerian Assembly and each sent fifteen deputies to the National Assembly in Paris. Since Muslims outnumbered Europeans by more than eight to one, the electoral system was heavily weighted to give the *pied noir* minority an effective veto on the political system within Algeria. The great majority of Muslims did not have equal political rights and were not, in any meaningful sense, full citizens. Furthermore, the local self-government envisaged in 1947 had never been introduced; the statute had been in 'permanent gestation'. Most of Muslim Algeria was administered in colonial style by French officials.

3   Algerian nationalism was divided between the more radical MTLD[26], led by Messali Hadj, and the more moderate 'Algerian Manifesto'[27] group, led by Ferhat Abbas. There had been a 'spectacular split' in the former over whether or not nationalist representatives on municipal councils should cooperate with the French authorities on such matters as housing. We are not actually told which organisation was held responsible for the uprising but we would infer that it was the MTLD or a faction within the movement.

4   The nationalists would have said that the great majority of Muslims suffered economic and social exploitation, but there were clearly some advantages: unemployed Muslims could move to metropolitan France in search of work and Muslim families were entitled to the allowances paid under the French social security system. Any discrimination against Muslims in employment was illegal; the wages of Muslim employees were protected against inflation by compulsory indexation, just as the earnings of European workers were.

Retreat from empire in Indo-China, Tunisia and Morocco

The articles in Primary Source 20.1 provide a good introduction to the broader context of the Algerian insurrection. The correspondent cannot be faulted for having only the haziest notion as to who instigated it, since the French security services were not much better informed. We will return to the uprising's immediate origins later, but here I want to emphasise that it occurred while the French were retreating from their empire in southeast Asia and North Africa, for this background conditioned their response to Algerian nationalism.

---

[26] Mouvement pour le triomphe des libertés démocratiques.

[27] Its full title was Union démocratique du Manifeste algérien – Democratic Union for the Algerian Manifesto.

prior to source 20.1

In May 1954, the 'dirty war' France had been waging since 1947 in Indo-China ended in catastrophe when the garrison at Dien Bien Phu capitulated. After the Geneva peace agreement of July, all French forces were withdrawn and the independence of Vietnam, Laos and Cambodia was recognised. The war had claimed 92,000 lives from France and the French Union, cost more than 3000 milliard francs, and embittered relations between the Republic and its army (Rioux, 1987, p. 228).

The French premier, Pierre Mendès-France, followed the settlement of the Indo-Chinese war with a public declaration that France recognised the internal autonomy of Tunisia and was ready to transfer sovereignty to the representatives of the Tunisian people. (Refer to Figures 20.1 and 20.2, and, for European economic interests in Tunisia, Table 20.1.) This was prompted by a series of tit-for-tat massacres in the 'private war' between Tunisian nationalists and settler terrorists, but Mendès-France had other reasons for his initiative. For him, France's destiny lay in Europe; he wanted to 'liquidate' imperial problems the better to concentrate on economic modernisation at home. And he felt the 'wind of change' blowing through the Arab world. The overture to Tunisian nationalism came soon after the announcement that Britain intended to evacuate the Suez Canal zone and when a resurgence of pan-Arab nationalism was transforming Middle Eastern politics. By conciliating the moderate nationalists, France could hope to preserve essential interests in Tunisia and ward off the more radical forces emanating from Cairo.

political decisions at home

The French government faced similar dilemmas in Morocco. (Refer to Figures 20.1 and 20.2, and, for European economic interests in Morocco, Table 20.1.) Political assassinations were an almost daily occurrence in

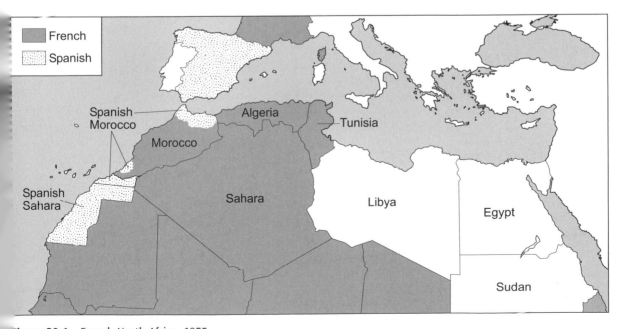

Figure 20.1   French North Africa, 1955.

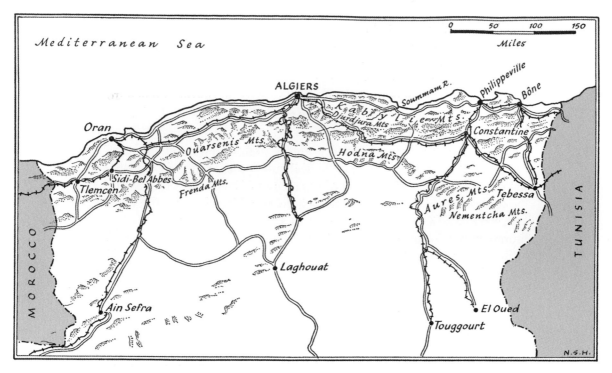

Figure 20.2   Algeria showing some relief and communications, from O'Balance, E. (1967) *The Algerian Insurrection, 1954–62*, London, Faber, p. 8.

Table 20.1   The population of French North Africa in 1955 (millions)

	Total population	Non-Muslim population	Non-Muslim share of the national income (%)	Rural population* (European and Muslim combined)	Urban population (European and Muslim combined)
Algeria	9.7	1.0	47	7.2	2.5
Tunisia	3.9	0.3	43	3.1	0.8
Morocco	10.4	0.7	33	8.0	2.4

* 'Rural' includes settlements of fewer than 20,000 inhabitants.
(Source: Amin, 1970, pp. 33, 61)

Casablanca by mid-1954; many were perpetrated by settler terrorists with the connivance of the French-dominated police and security services. In a debate on his North African policy in the chamber on 10 August, Mendès-France implored all Moroccans to end 'the horrible violence' which was 'delaying the modern evolution of their country' but by the time his premiership ended in February 1955, the powerful French North African lobby had frustrated any overture to the nationalists. Nevertheless, by the summer of 1955, chaos and violence in Morocco were making the French position unsustainable. In July, the new premier, Edgar Faure, appointed a new resident-general with a brief to reach an accommodation with the sultan, who was aligned with moderate nationalists in the Istiqlal (or 'Independence') party. European right-wing extremists tried to wreck this initiative by blatant military and administrative sabotage, openly encouraged by Gaullist ministers in Faure's government and conservative parliamentarians (Williams, 1964, p. 47). This only exacerbated the vicious circle of violence: in August, over fifty French civilians (including children) were massacred by nationalist terrorists; in riposte, French troops in Morocco 'counter-massacred' Moroccan civilians. Fear of social anarchy and criticism of France at the United Nations persuaded the Faure government that it had to end the protectorate; in November, it initiated negotiations that led to Moroccan independence on 2 March 1956. In June, Tunisia became independent. Both states signed treaties of cooperation with France, but supported the Algerian rebels. Tunisia, in particular, became a crucial ally in the independence struggle; the FLN set up offices in Tunis and the ALN (Armée de Libération nationale, or National Liberation Army) was allowed safe havens and training grounds on Tunisian territory. On several occasions during the insurrection, the French army unsuccessfully sought authorisation to invade Tunisia.

The emergence of Algerian nationalism

The *Times* correspondent's assessment of the Algerian nationalist movements was reasonably accurate, but gives no sense of nationalism's historical evolution. It emerged not in Algeria, but among immigrant workers in the industrial suburbs of Paris in the early 1920s. Unsurprisingly, Muslims in the diaspora were more receptive to nationalism than Muslims in Algeria, where indigenous society was a mosaic of clans, tribes and inward-looking communities. Exile, and the common lot of the migrant worker, encouraged Algerians to overlook their differences and identify themselves as 'North Africans': when founded in 1926, the first newspaper to call for an independent Algeria and the first nationalist party both took the name Étoile nord-africaine (North African Star). The party's dominant figure soon became Ahmed Messali Hadj (1898–1974), a factory worker and communist. Messali left the PCF in 1929, but continued to regard it as a model for political action and organisation; the ENA aimed to be a mass movement of class-conscious militants led by a disciplined party hierarchy. Its programme called for social revolution; the ENA proposed, for example, confiscating all property acquired by the French government and *colons* (colonists) in Algeria. The ENA was dissolved by the government in 1937 and reconstituted as the Parti du peuple algérien (PPA). That, in turn, was banned at the outbreak of war in 1939, when Messali was interned as a subversive. De Gaulle's provisional government[28] re-legalised the party but it was again banned after the Sétif 'incident' in May 1945 (discussed below), by when the focus of its activities had shifted from the immigrant community in France to Algeria. It soon re-emerged as the MTLD and swept the board in the Muslim

[handwritten margin notes: "Workers' ideas", "social aspect"]

---

[28] General de Gaulle established a Free French administration in North Africa in June 1943 which declared itself the provisional government of the French Republic in June 1944.

constituencies in the municipal elections of October 1947. Returning immigrants were vital to this success: they brought with them a propensity to organise and a collectivist ideology.

Algeria

Nationalist sentiment had a concurrent Islamic source associated with a religious reform movement known as the *ulama* (meaning scholars and teachers) which had been active since 1931. Their teaching highlighted the irreconcilable cultural differences between Algerian Muslims and *pied noir* society. They set up a network of youth-cum-religious organisations under the slogan: 'Arabic is my language; Algeria my country; Islam is my religion'. The intent was to make participation in the universal community of Islam an inspiration for modern patriotism.

intellectual ideas?

The final current of modern nationalism emanated from the frustrations of the western-educated professional middle class, personified by Ferhat Abbas (1898–1985). He studied pharmacy at Algiers University, where he was president of the Muslim Students Association, spoke French better than he did Arabic, and married a French woman. In 1936, he wrote that he could not die for the Algerian nation because it did not exist, and there was nothing in the Koran to forbid a Muslim integrating himself with a non-Muslim nation; assimilation was the only way forward (Horne, 1996, p. 40).

What drove Abbas, who volunteered for the French army in 1939, to renege on these sentiments and embrace nationalism was the cavalier arrogance with which the Free French authorities called on Muslims to enlist in the democracies' re-conquest of Europe, while turning a deaf ear to their democratic aspirations. In early 1943, Abbas drew up the Manifesto of the Algerian People modelled on the Atlantic Charter; its rejection pushed him into a more militant stance. In early 1944, most nationalists were briefly unified in a new grouping around the manifesto, though the differences between Messali's movement, for whom total independence meant social revolution, and the middle-class professionals who envisaged a federal Algeria aligned with France, could not be disguised. But with astonishing ineptitude, the French administration did its utmost to deny moderate nationalism constitutional expression. In the last general elections under French rule, in June 1951, officials used blatant fraud and intimidation to ensure that no Algerian nationalists were elected to the National Assembly: all the Muslim deputies returned were 'stooges' of the administration (derisively known as '*Beni-oui-ouis*' or 'yes men').

The 'dual' economy and colonial society

In the debate on the Algerian uprising on 12 November 1954, Mendès-France memorably concluded a feisty speech with '*Ici,*[Algeria] *c'est la France*'. The premier had been accused by the right-wing colonial lobby of selling out over Tunisia and, in asserting Algeria was part of France, he was denying that the two countries' situations were in any way comparable. Algeria's secession was as inconceivable as Brittany's; no form of negotiation with the rebels could be contemplated. Despite his uncompromising tone, Mendès-France subsequently countenanced secret 'feelers' to the nationalists. He also recognised that Muslim disaffection was inevitable while unemployment and poverty were rife, and advocated massive public investment to create jobs and improve the social infrastructure. Whether prompt state intervention could have cut the ground from under the FLN we cannot know: Mendès-France fell from office in February 1955 before his reformist programme could be implemented. The man he appointed governor-general to oversee a 'new deal' for Muslims, Jacques Soustelle, was so appalled by the FLN massacre at Philippeville in July (see datechart) that he decided nothing should impede crushing the insurrection by force.

To which we must add that the structural distortions in the colonial economy could not have been corrected without redistributing land that had been appropriated for European settlers, which would have been hugely controversial. State-promoted colonisation had created a 'dual' agrarian economy in Algeria: the traditional Muslim sector was subsistence-oriented, under-capitalised and subject to diminishing returns as rapid population growth pushed small farmers onto marginal land. The modern European sector was export-oriented (its principal product, wine, was not consumed by most Muslims) and organised in large, highly capitalised estates, many owned by French companies. Mechanisation was well advanced in the modern sector by 1954, and its demand for wage labour was static. True, the 'dualist' picture is an over-simplification: Muslim agrarian society was internally differentiated, with an elite of substantial landowners (numbering around 25,000) accounting for one-quarter of all the income received from agriculture by Muslims. But many economic data corroborate 'dualism' and demonstrate the great divide between the Muslim peasantry and European capitalist agriculture. The average European holding was ten times the size of the average Muslim holding and, in the most productive areas around Oran, Bône and Philippeville, four-fifths of the land was in European hands. More than two-thirds of Muslim farms were too small, given the difficult conditions for agriculture in much of Algeria, to provide a livelihood for the average family. In 1954, of the 2.7 million Muslim men of working age in the rural population, only 1.7 million were employed for more than 100 days a year; probably 80 per cent of the rural population were undernourished.

For the *fellahin* who could no longer eke a living from their plots, the alternatives were moving to the towns in search of casual labour and migrating to France for work. There was little demand for industrial labour in Algeria and Muslims were generally ill-equipped for work in the service sector. After 120 years of colonial rule, 'native' society was largely illiterate. Only 12.75 per cent of Muslim children of primary school age were being educated in 1954. Muslims were four-fifths of the population, but only 18 per cent of lycée and college students, and 11 per cent of those enrolled at Algiers University. The great majority of Algerians could not speak even rudimentary French. Likewise, only one-fifth of European men could speak Arabic, and only one-tenth of European women (Rachid Bencheneb, 1986, pp. 415–30).

Although Algeria was not an overtly segregated society, the casual racism of many Europeans underlined the mutual incomprehension of colonist and colonised. The dominant attitude among the *pieds noirs* towards Muslims was expressed in a rich vocabulary of contempt: they were '*sales ratons*', '*bicots*', '*figuiers*', '*melons*', in other words, dirty, lazy and stupid. A Muslim was almost invariably addressed as '*tu*', the familiar form the French use for children and their social inferiors (Horne, 1996, pp. 54–5). Algeria could not have been governed without Muslim 'collaborators' but they were drawn predominantly from the old, tribal leadership in the rural areas who served as *caids* (local governors) and *cadis* (Islamic judges). The former were a by-word for corruption.

The road to rebellion

Sétif

The Sétif uprising of 8 May 1945 was the key event in the years preceding the insurrection. It has been analysed by Anthony Clayton in an article on the website.

EXERCISE

Read Anthony Clayton's article 'The Sétif uprising of 8 May 1945' (Secondary Source 20.1) and answer the following questions:

1   What does the uprising tell us about Muslim attitudes to Europeans in the Constantine region?
2   What primarily determined those attitudes?
3   Why did the uprising not evolve into a general insurrection?

SPECIMEN ANSWER

1   Muslim insurgents evinced a visceral hatred for Europeans: victims were frequently sexually mutilated; women and children were raped; disembowelled bodies were left on display. Many settlers were killed by their Muslim employees, which gave the lie to the stereotype of easy familiarity on the farm. While the insurgents were only a minority, most Muslims were passively complicit in the atrocities. Muslim ex-servicemen generally remained loyal and middle-class professionals tried to restore calm, but the prevailing atmosphere was menacing even where violence did not break out.

2   French officials attributed this socio-psychological climate to disastrous economic conditions, and the glaring contrast between the settlers' comparative prosperity and the hunger and deprivation in Muslim households.

3   The French military's response ensured that the uprising was contained in the Constantine region and fairly soon repressed. But, equally importantly, the violence erupted spontaneously and took Messali Hadj's PPA by surprise. There was no coordinating organisation with an insurrectionary strategy.

The 1954 rebellion was organised by a paramilitary splinter group – *Organisation spéciale* (OS) – from within Messali's MTLD, which had an uneasy relationship with the veteran leader and eventually sought to destroy him and his movement. One objection to Messali was the cult of his outsize personality, but they also clashed over political strategies: for Messali and his following the key to the revolutionary overthrow of colonialism lay in mass organisation and raising the people's consciousness, which could not be effected clandestinely. For the OS, colonialism could only be overthrown by armed struggle, which had to be the work of dedicated conspirators. This basic strategic difference became evident when the Messalist 'tendency' within the MTLD repudiated the OS after its existence had been revealed to the police and key figures were imprisoned. They included Ahmed Ben Bella, but he escaped in 1952 and fled to Cairo, where the OS mutated into the Revolutionary Committee for Unity and Action (CRUA).

With the low-key patronage of Colonel Nasser, Ben Bella worked closely with the conspirators known as the 'historic nine' (see Figure 20.3), who formed the central committee of the CRUA and provided the insurrection's internal and external leadership (the latter was known as the **External Delegation**). They hoped to launch it with the backing of the faction-ridden MTLD (if not Messali himself) and organised several meetings in Switzerland to this end. They failed. The uprising began without the support of Algeria's largest, most militant nationalist movement; the insurgents numbered no more than 3000 and most were initially unarmed. The 'historic nine' were still young men (their average age was thirty-two) and mostly unknown outside their own conspiratorial circle. Although all were literate, they had little formal education beyond elementary school. Mohamed Khider, a former deputy in the National Assembly, was the exception; he was given responsibility for political strategy. Three had served in the French army (Ben Bella with great distinction). They were not from the poorest in Muslim society, but their socially modest backgrounds set them apart from cultured professionals such as Ferhat Abbas. They divided Algeria into six semi-autonomous military zones (***wilayas***) whose commanders had considerable latitude on tactics and choice of targets (see Figure 20.4). Their overall strategy – modelled on Mao Ze Dung's – was to establish rural fastnesses ('liberated zones') in the mountains from which to surround the towns and cities.

EXERCISE

The FLN made itself known to the world with the insurrectionary proclamation of 1 November, which I would now like you to read (Primary Source 20.2, 'The FLN initial proclamation').

1   What does the document reveal about the FLN's attitude to the rest of the National Movement?

2   What were the Front's external objectives?

3   What were its terms for opening negotiations with the French?

4   Did it offer the *pieds noirs* a future in independent Algeria?

SPECIMEN ANSWER

1   The proclamation asserted that the National Movement had become immobile, badly oriented, deprived of popular support and overtaken by events; internal 'conflicts of persons and influence' had brought it to an 'impasse'. By implication, this was pretty damning of the Messalist leadership of the MTLD.

2   Its external objectives were to internationalise the Algerian problem and pursue North African unity in a context of Arab and Islamic solidarity; and to use the UN Charter to create solidarity with other national liberation movements.

Hocine Ait Ahmed (b.1921):
a Kabyle; member of the FLN's
External Delegation; attended
Afro-Asian Bandung
Conference in April 1955;
interned 1956–62

Larbi Ben M'hidi (1923–1957):
commander of Wilaya V; arrested
by the French police in February
1957; later tortured and murdered
by a squad of paratroopers [the
squad leader, Paul Aussaresses,
caused a huge scandal when he
admitted to this, and many other
such incidents, in his memoirs,
published in 2001]

Mourad Didouche (1927–1955):
commander of Wilaya II; killed in
combat, January 1955

Ahmed Ben Bella (b.1916):
former warrant officer in French
army; member of the FLN's
External Delegation; interned
1956–62; first president of the
Algerian Republic, 1963–65

Rabah Bitat (1925–2000):
commander of Wilaya IV; captured
by French police in February 1955

Mohamed Khider (1912–1967):
former deputy in the National
Assembly; member of the FLN's
External Delegation; interned
1956–62

**Mostefa Ben Boulaid
(1917–1957):** former warrant
officer in French army;
commander of Wilaya I, based
on the Aurès Mountains;
captured by the French,
February 1955

Mohamed Boudiaf (1919–1992):
member of the FLN's External
Delegation; interned 1956–62

Belkacem Krim (1922–1970):
a Kabyle; former corporal in French
army; commander of Wilaya III; the
only one of the nine to survive the
war and remain at liberty

Figure 20.3   The 'historic nine' who led the CRUA and organised the insurrection.

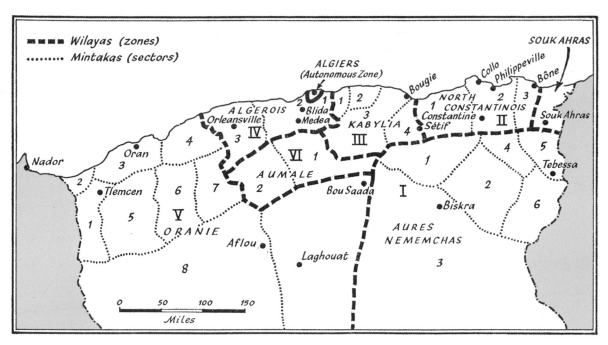

Figure 20.4   Map of the ALN's *wilayas*, from O'Balance, E. (1967) *The Algerian Insurrection, 1954–62*, London, Faber, p. 55.

3   Recognition of Algerian sovereignty and the release of political prisoners were preconditions for negotiations.

4   Yes; they could remain either as French nationals, or opt for Algerian nationality in a state that would be committed to 'preserving all fundamental freedoms, without distinction of race and religion'.

The course of the war

The Algerian war was too complex to summarise in a brief compass, so please refer to the detailed datechart. My discussion will try to answer the apparently simple question: 'Why did the FLN win?' In retrospect, it may appear that no other outcome was possible. But in early 1959 few would have wagered on an FLN victory. The organisation had, apparently, been 'decapitated' in October 1956, when the French captured Ben Bella and other members of the External Delegation after the Moroccan plane on which they were travelling was lured to Algiers (see Figure 20.5). The collective leadership did not allow this body blow to disrupt its cohesion but it exacerbated the difficult relationship between the revolution's 'external' and 'internal' forces. The decision to wage urban guerrilla warfare in Algiers in late 1956/early 1957 had been a catastrophic error: Muslims died in terrorist outrages as well as Europeans and popular support for the FLN in the city declined. General Massu's paratroopers destroyed its urban network by painstaking intelligence, torturing suspects and extra-judicial killings: 3000 of those picked up by the paras 'disappeared'. In mid-May 1958, the expectation that de Gaulle would return to power inspired

Figure 20.5   The External Delegation: Ben Bella and other leaders of the FLN after their arrest, 1956. Unknown photographer. Photo: akg-images/ullstein bild. Left to right: Ahmed Ben Bella, Mohamed Boudiaf, Hocine Ait Ahmed, Mostefa Lacheraf and Mohamed Khider.

extraordinary scenes of 'fraternisation' in Algiers, as Muslims and Europeans mingled in crowds chanting the general's name and waving the Croix de Lorraine.

EXERCISE

These scenes of 'fraternisation', and others discussed below, are shown on the course DVD. You should watch this now.

The FLN experienced equally severe reversals in the guerrilla war waged by its military wing (ALN) in the countryside. You would not gather this from the film made by the FLN of guerrilla operations (which you can see on the DVD), but I suspect this was shot in training camps in Tunisia. It is fascinating as propaganda, but gives an over-sanguine impression of the guerrillas' effectiveness. The completion of the Morice line in September 1957 sealed the frontier with Tunisia and, though it did not altogether stop the infiltration of ALN fighters, it made their detection and destruction by French mobile units much easier. In late 1958, the new French commander-in-chief, General Challe, re-invigorated counter-insurgency strategy by targeting the ALN's political and administrative organisation, deploying

Muslim units (known as *harkis*) in hunt and destroy missions, and using
helicopters to lift troops into combat zones. With the extension of military
service, Challe had ample men at his disposal. Moreover, the French army
made determined efforts to win 'hearts and minds'; special units set up rural
dispensaries and village schools. In 1956, French doctors on military service
held 20,000 consultations with Muslim Algerians under the system of
assistance médicale gratuite (AMG – free medical care); in 1959, such
consultations ran to 16.702 *million* (Jauffret, 2000, p. 182). (You have
interesting visual testimony of this on the DVD.)

There is evidence that demoralisation and desertions brought the 'internal' ALN
close to capitulation in late 1959, early 1960. Challe believed that a large group of
guerrillas were willing to surrender after the commander of Wilaya 4, Si Salah,
entered secret peace negotiations; in an extraordinary move, he and his lieutenants
were flown to Paris for a clandestine meeting with de Gaulle. But it is doubtful
whether Si Salah would have broken with the external leadership, which
sentenced him to death for treachery on learning of the negotiations. If there was
widespread defeatism, the ALN seems to have cauterised it. Whatever the real
significance of this episode, it is certain that the insurgency was contained to
isolated strongholds. At the end of the war, the ALN mostly consisted of
regular soldiers kicking their heels in training camps in Tunisia and Morocco.
They moved into Algeria when independence was declared and, after a
chaotic interlude, enabled Ben Bella's faction of the FLN to secure its hold on
the country.

So, perhaps we should rephrase our question: 'Why did the French government
feel compelled to negotiate away Algérie française to the FLN?' This was
evidently a political war in which non-military factors determined the
outcome; what were those factors?

Crucially, the FLN made sure the French had nobody else to negotiate with by
eliminating all its nationalist rivals and insisting that those who joined the
organisation did so as individuals, not as parties or groups. Ferhat Abbas, and
the moderates in the UDMA, who had initially condemned the insurrection,
rallied to the FLN in late 1955. Abbas had been placed under intense personal
pressure when the FLN murdered his nephew, a prominent spokesman for
Franco-Muslim reconciliation. Moreover, the Front's internal leadership had
told him that any negotiation with the French had to be through its
organisation. Reasoning that there was no alternative way to end the war and
secure independence, Abbas joined the External Delegation in Cairo and was
made titular head of the provisional government in September 1958.

The MTLD (and its successor) never rallied to the FLN and was destroyed in a
vicious 'war within the war'. The MTLD was dissolved in November but
reconstituted itself as the Mouvement national algérien (MNA) and was as
determined as the FLN to be the sole organisational representative of Algerian
nationalism. The two organisations waged a bitter but non-violent contest for
Muslim loyalties until late April, when Abbane Ramdane, the most forceful of
the FLN's commanders, informed the External Delegation in Cairo: 'We are

resolved to destroy all the Messalist leaders.' In May, an MNA 'tribunal' condemned key FLN figures to death. In June, a veteran of Messali's movement was assassinated in Paris. It was the first of many internecine killings: according to the French police, between 1956 and the end of 1961, 3889 Muslims were killed and 7678 wounded in France in the course of inter-Algerian political violence, while in Algeria, about 6000 were killed and 14,000 wounded (Stora, 1991, p. 144). The FLN's ruthlessness in ordering the massacre of MNA supporters in rural Algeria actually drove their male relatives into pro-French irregular units which hunted down ANL guerrillas, but savagery achieved its objective: if the French government wanted to end the war, it had to do so with the FLN and on its terms.

So what drove the government to accept these terms? Negotiation with the FLN had been inconceivable in 1954–55 when attachment to the idea of Algérie française was a near universal article of faith in the French political class. Even the communists, though vigorously condemning colonial repression, adopted an equivocal attitude towards Algerian nationalism. The evidence suggests, however, much indifference, even apathy, towards Algeria *among the French public*; in August 1955, when questioned by the polling organisation IFOP, only 5 per cent of respondents said they took any interest in the news from Algeria in their newspapers. The gravity of events there was not generally appreciated until April 1956, when the government called up (or re-called) nearly 200,000 national servicemen to serve in Algeria. Conscripts had been fighting since November 1954, but this great 'surge' in France's military commitment brought the war home to everybody with a son or relative of military age. When, in April 1956, the opinion pollsters asked: 'In your opinion, will Algeria still be French in ten years time?', 32 per cent said 'Yes', 27 per cent said 'No', and the rest did not know (or did not answer). By July 1957, a majority of the French public was in favour of negotiation with the FLN (Ageron, 1990).

Unsurprisingly, de Gaulle's return to power boosted public expectation that Algeria would remain French for the foreseeable future. European demonstrators in Algiers, with the support of senior officers, had been instrumental in bringing down the Fourth Republic and persuading the general out of retirement. (There is a vivid filmic record of these extraordinary events on the DVD, as well as excerpts from an interview with General Massu, whom demonstrators put at the head of the ad hoc Algiers Committee of Public Safety in May 1958.) De Gaulle's attachment to Algérie française in the early 1950s was a matter of public record. Privately, however, his views had changed; in October 1957, he told Foreign Minister Pineau that independence was the only solution to the Algerian problem. The war was a brake on the modernisation of the French economy and institutions; it diminished French prestige and influence abroad; and it was unpopular at home. Moreover, the general had moved with the times and now saw the colonial empire, whose retention he had vigorously championed in 1944–46, as an incubus on the renovation of France; nuclear weapons were a more effective statement of her international power and prestige than overseas dependencies. Historians and biographers are undecided as to his intentions in the summer of 1958, but over the next twelve months he concluded that there was no alternative to Algerian self-determination. The army's task was to crush the FLN militarily, so that French negotiators could extract the maximum advantage from peace talks. The French government hoped to retain sovereignty over the Sahara, where oil had been discovered in the later 1950s, and contemplated securing a *pied noir* enclave by partition.

De Gaulle's personal role in ending the Algerian war can scarcely be exaggerated: in early 1960, he established a Committee of Algerian Affairs under his own chairmanship in which all important decisions relating to Algeria were taken, thus bypassing the council of ministers. This autocratic procedure must be seen in the context of the revolution in French government that began when the National Assembly gave him authority to rule by decree for six months and devise a new constitution with an executive presidency. De Gaulle had never been a member of parliament and, while he was president, parliament atrophied. He coupled the presidency's new-found power with an uncanny instinct for communicating his authority directly to the nation on television (as you can judge from the DVD). De Gaulle first offered Algerians self-determination in a television broadcast of 16 September 1959, after the most perfunctory consultation with his ministers. At two critical moments, when *pied noir* ultras and rebellious army officers threatened to usurp power in Algeria, he used television to masterly effect to reassert the state's legitimacy and his own authority: the first was during 'barricades week' of late January 1960, when a European mob took over the government buildings in Algiers; the second, in late April 1961, when four retired generals launched an unsuccessful putsch. His imperious contempt for the plotters, and refusal to waver, confirmed his utter indispensability.

Yet, for all his mastery of French politics, the army and the mass media, de Gaulle's strategy failed; despite the overwhelming military superiority of the French forces, the FLN did not compromise on its essential demands. During thirteen months of intermittent negotiations, the French declared a unilateral ceasefire (while FLN terrorism escalated), conceded sovereignty over the Sahara, and failed to secure dual citizenship for the European settlers. It is no exaggerated to say that the war ended with France's total surrender. Why? The most important reason was the escalation of political violence in Algiers, Oran and mainland France in early 1961, following the emergence of the OAS (Secret Army Organisation). This was a terrorist network of die-hard settlers and dissident former officers dedicated to thwarting Algerian independence by murdering the leaders of Muslim civil society, European 'moderates' and public officials. (They twice came close to assassinating de Gaulle.) Between the death of Ali la Pointe in October 1957 and January 1961, Algiers had been remarkably peaceful: the indiscriminate slaughter of the OAS shattered the inter-communal peace, led to a revival of FLN urban violence, and effectively destroyed all prospect of the Europeans' feeling secure in an independent Algeria. Before the Evian agreements were signed, the mass exodus of the *pieds noirs* had begun. Many Muslims who had collaborated with the French authorities and now feared popular retribution also departed, wisely as it transpired: tens of thousands of *harkis* who stayed behind were murdered, often in the most atrocious circumstances, while the French military stood helplessly by.

French Algeria ended in anarchy because the FLN, which had maintained a united front up to July, imploded at independence, and its factions narrowly avoided full-scale civil war. The split was between revolutionaries led by Ben Bella (released from French custody in March 1962) who were determined to seize power after the fashion of Lenin in October 1917 and those in the provisional government who wished to hand over powers to the people's elected representatives. Ben Bella's faction triumphed by allying with Colonel Boumedienne (the 'external' army's chief of staff whom the provisional government had tried to dismiss) but at a terrible cost to the new nation. Throughout the late summer of 1962, warring cliques struggled for control; some took to the mountains, where they were later destroyed in brutal counter-insurgency operations. About 15,000 lives were lost in this 'war after the war' (Horne, 1996, p. 537). The chaos created ideal conditions for settling scores: some 2000 Europeans who had opted to remain in independent Algeria 'disappeared', which hastened the departure of nearly all the rest.

A stable central state was not established until late September 1962, after Boumedienne's forces had occupied Algiers and the newly elected Constituent Assembly approved the Ben Bella government by 159 votes to one. No member of the former provisional government was included and five key posts were taken by military men. The new government declared its intention of implementing with all speed a socialist revolution. It prohibited all political organisations save the FLN, which was declared 'the one and only party of progress'. A presidential and authoritarian constitution was approved by referendum in September 1963; the National Assembly was marginalised.

The Algerian war in retrospect

What did the war mean for France? It was a great moral crisis for the intelligentsia and a major disruption in the lives of the two million national servicemen who served in Algeria between 1954 and 1962. It was the immediate cause of the Gaullist revolution of 1958 to 1969, which transformed French politics and greatly accelerated economic modernisation. For French society, the war's most important consequence was the repatriation of a million or so Europeans, who were re-integrated into the booming economy with unexpected ease. This was not true of the Muslims who fled in 1962; they were poorly housed, had great difficulty obtaining skilled employment and their children usually left school with few educational qualifications. But the Muslim refugees aside, the war left few permanent scars on French national community. Economically, it was a trifling matter; French public finances comfortably absorbed the military costs and the war had no perceptible impact on the growth of gross national product (Marseille, 1990). The French economy has never expanded more rapidly that it did in the later 1950s and 1960s.

For Algerians, by contrast, the war was a huge social tragedy and a great trauma of forced modernisation. The number of Muslims who died has long been contentious: the staggering total of one and half million deaths still claimed by the Algerian government is a demographic impossibility; the official French tally of a quarter of a million is very close to estimates arrived at by counter-factual demography (Yacono, 1982).[29] But this was still an appalling mortality; as a proportion of Muslim males, war-related deaths greatly exceeded war-related deaths in Britain in 1914–18. The killing and maiming were accompanied by massive upheavals in Algerian rural society: more than two million peasants were displaced during the French drives to isolate them from the guerrillas. Fear of being up-rooted led to acute anxiety about the preservation of one's family patrimony, and was a common reason for enrolling as a *harki* or joining a pro-French civil defence group. With so many men absent, Muslim women took on new social roles and many discarded the veil. The Muslim family became more egalitarian, more accepting of modern medicine, and more receptive to the radio, which both the French and FLN used to communicate with the masses. From July 1962, these masses were deemed to have legitimised the FLN government by popular acclaim. No attempt was made to heal the deep divisions in Algerian society by dialogue or a process of 'truth and reconciliation'. The official lie that the Algerian people had been at one in throwing off French colonialism stifled debate within the FLN and public criticism without; frenetic commemoration of the war sanctioned the army's domination of society and the emergence of a militarised state.

THE ANGOLAN REVOLUTION

Portugal and Africa

The Portuguese were the first Europeans to establish colonies in sub-Saharan Africa and the last to leave. From the map in Figure 20.6 you will see that in the early 1970s Portugal still claimed sovereignty over three mainland territories (Angola, Mozambique and Guinea-Bissau) as well as the Cape Verde islands, and São Tomé and Principe. Luanda, the Angolan capital, had been a Portuguese-speaking settlement for about 400 years. Yet, for the great majority of its African subjects, Portugal's rule was of recent origin: the modern frontiers were internationally recognised during the late nineteenth-century 'scramble', but effective occupation of the interior took decades of campaigning. Around 1910, colonial officials directly and regularly controlled

---

[29] The total resident Muslim population in October 1954 was 8.47 million; had it grown at 3.4 per cent for 7.66 years it would have reached 10.676 million in July 1962. The actual population at that date was 10.420 million, giving a 'demographic deficit' of 256,000.

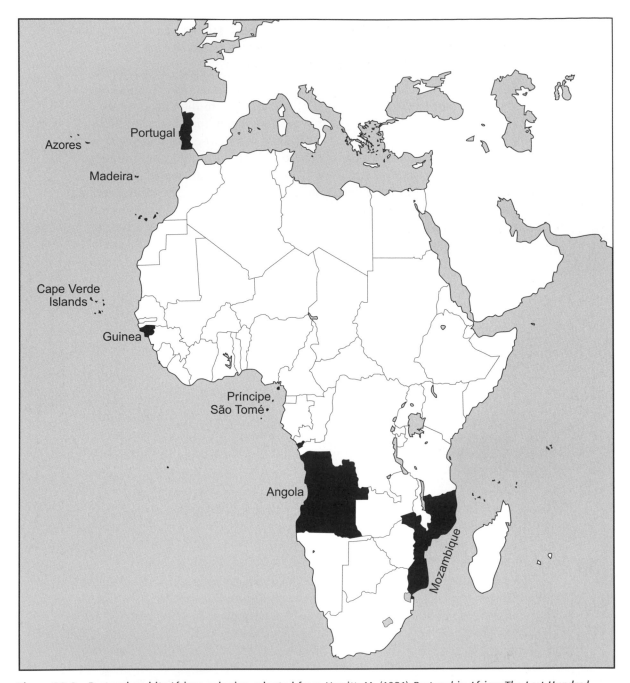

Figure 20.6   Portugal and its African colonies, adapted from Newitt, M. (1981) *Portugal in Africa: The Last Hundred Years*, London, Hurst, p. viii.

only about 10 per cent of Angola's territory and most African societies still retained considerable autonomy.

Two points about the northern colonial frontier merit special attention. First, it cut across the BaKongo ethnic community, who straddled the borders between Angola, Leopold II's Free State and the French Congo (now the Democratic

Republic of Congo and the Congo Republic). The BaKongo are one of
Africa's historic nations, with a common political tradition, and were
unsurprisingly drawn towards ethnic nationalism during the war of
independence. Secondly, during the colonial partition, the Cabinda enclave
(see Figure 20.7) was allotted to Portugal in recognition of her ancient 'title'
to the Congo estuary and the presence there of Portuguese and Luso-African
traders. It is an instance of 'deep' history having quite unanticipated
consequences for the present. In recent decades, Cabinda has acquired an

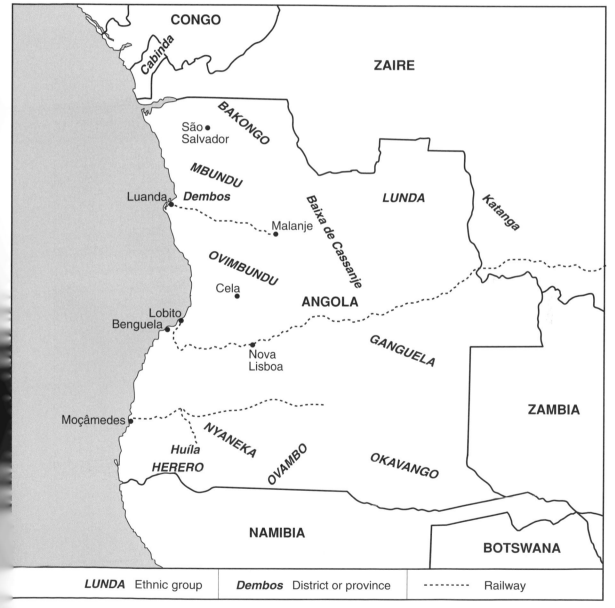

Figure 20.7   Angola, showing major towns, administrative divisions and ethnic areas, adapted from Newitt, M. (1981)
Portugal in Africa: The Last Hundred Years, London, Hurst, p. viii.

economic importance quite disproportionate to its size with the discovery of enormous off-shore oilfields. Understandably, Angola has been determined to maintain its sovereignty, despite a Cabindan separatist movement and neighbouring states' designs on the territory.

Of equally recent origin was the central purpose of Portuguese 'late' colonialism in Angola, which was to make it an attractive colony of settlement for metropolitan immigrants. In 1913, the total white population had been a mere 12,000, and the overwhelming majority of Portuguese emigrants were destined for Brazil, not Africa. Angola was primarily a dumping ground for ***degredados***, or exiled criminals. They formed the largest element in the white population until 1932, when the new Portuguese prime minister, António de Oliveira Salazar (see Figure 20.8), ended the exiling of metropolitan convicts to Angola as an economy measure. His regime soon asserted the centrality of empire to its ideology with the Colonial Act of 1933, which stated: 'It is the organic essence of the Portuguese Nation to carry out the function of possessing and colonizing overseas domains and of civilising the indigenous populations' (quoted in

Figure 20.8   António de Oliveira Salazar, 1961. Unknown photographer. Photo: © Bettmann/ Corbis.

Bender, 1978, p. 96). Given this grandiose ambition, one would have expected a drive to accelerate white immigration, but Salazar prioritised financial retrenchment at home over colonising the empire, and suspended the bounties paid to new immigrants.

Partly for this reason, the results of the regime's planned settlement schemes were fairly modest up to 1950, when whites were less than 2 per cent of Angola's population and many were transient (Table 20.2). European settlement of the interior was inhibited by the rudimentary physical infrastructure: in 1953, Angola – which is larger than France and Iberia combined – boasted only fifty-three miles of asphalted roads. But from around this time widening economic opportunities attracted growing numbers of Portuguese emigrants: the white population of Angola doubled in the 1950s and doubled again between 1960 and the early 1970s. One factor stimulating white immigration was the creation of farming communities (known as *colonatos*) where smallholders were heavily subsidised by the government. Settler families were supposed to live alongside, but not employ, African farmers, for the *colonatos* were intended to showcase both interracial harmony and peasant thrift and fecundity. However, they absorbed only a minority of immigrants and generally failed to retain them after they had fulfilled their obligations to the state. Most new arrivals settled in the coastal cities, many in the *muçeques* (slums) alongside African rural immigrants.

Table 20.2   The population of Angola

	Whites	*Mestiços*	**Total population**
1940	44,083	28,035	3,737,947
1950	78,826	29,648	4,145,161
1960	172,529	53,392	4,830,283
1970	290,000	n/a	5,673,046
1973	335,000	n/a	n/a

(Sources: Bender, 1978, p. 20; Newitt, p. 164)

The 1961 uprisings and their aftermath

When violence erupted in February–March 1961, there were two fledgling nationalist movements in Angola, one located among the BaKongo and the other centred on Luanda. African political organisation was illegal, and ruthlessly broken up by the political police, so even before the uprisings the nationalist leadership was based outside Angola. The Portuguese authorities immediately held them responsible for fomenting unrest, and they certainly played some role. But the evidence indicates the violence was largely unpremeditated and its underlying causes were social, not political. We must examine them to grasp the impact of Portuguese colonialism on African labour and put the rebellions in their wider social context.

To make their colonies 'pay', all imperial regimes had to compel Africans either to work for wages or to produce cash crops for export, which placed a huge stress on local societies. Europeans had occupied sub-Saharan Africa while epidemics were devastating the population and Africans were simply too few to meet the colonialists' demands for labour *and* sustain their own economies. Angola was no exception. We lack reliable figures, but the black population probably fell from about 5.4 million in 1850 to less than 3.7 million in 1940. Like all colonialists, the Portuguese sought to dragoon Africans into industrious habits by fiscal coercion, obligatory labour on public works and compulsory cropping. But they relied on punitive sanctions to exact labour long after other colonial regimes had turned to market incentives. Under the labour laws in force between 1899 and 1961, all Africans had a 'moral and legal obligation to work'; anyone not cultivating the land or exercising a trade had to contract themselves to an employer. The conditions imposed on contract workers were notoriously harsh. To escape ill-paid servitude, many Angolans migrated for better-paid work in South Africa, Northern Rhodesia and the Belgian Congo. By 1954, about half a million were living outside Angola, which exacerbated the labour scarcity and meant more frequent resort to obligatory contract labour on the part of white employers, who expected the authorities 'to give them blacks' (Bender, 1978, p. 143).

The northern coffee plantations were particularly dependent on Ovimbundu workers, conscripted in the central highlands and trucked up-country by white and *mestiço* gang masters. On 14 March 1961, a group on one plantation sparked a massive rural conflagration when they asked their bailiff for six months' overdue wages: he denounced this reasonable request so violently that fighting ensued. Some of the violence was black on black: BaKongo peasants whose land had been expropriated by white planters turned on the migrant wage labourers. By sheer coincidence, the nationalist movement then known as the UPA (Union of the Peoples of Angola) had chosen 15 March for a 'demonstrative' uprising to coincide with a UN Security Council meeting on Portuguese Africa. UPA militants were instructed to burn crops, bridges and houses, but not harm people. But there was no coordination of their poorly armed gangs and the two streams of violence converged in an indiscriminate deluge. In total, about 750 Portuguese civilians were killed in northern Angola in 1961, how many with 'political intent' and how many in anarchic rage is impossible to say. Many bodies were sexually mutilated, which Salazar's publicists seized on to trumpet a war of civilisation against barbarism. When suppressing these rebellions, the armed forces used their NATO-supplied aircraft to bomb villagers indiscriminately, while white vigilantes were allowed to murder at will. Probably 20,000 Africans died in six months of sporadic uprising and reprisal. In the first great displacement of peoples during the Angolan wars, around 150,000 Africans (mostly BaKongo) fled to the Congo before the end of the year (Marcum, 1969, p. 145).

Meanwhile, compulsory cotton cultivation had already provoked a quite separate uprising to the south. Cotton is very labour intensive and the returns were generally too poor to tempt farmers to grow it voluntarily. In theory, Portuguese officials 'encouraged' Africans to satisfy their labour obligations by growing cotton for sale at a fixed price to monopoly concession companies; in practice, they did so under duress. In January 1961, cotton farmers in the Kwanza and Kwango basins, driven to despair by the paltry price paid for their crop, attacked European stores, burnt the cotton seed and barricaded the roads. The uprising escalated under the inspiration of António Mariano, leader of a local Christian sect, and became known as 'Maria's war'. No nationalist movement claimed credit for what was a spontaneous rebellion with religious (but anti-Catholic) undertones. The Portuguese accused American Methodist missionaries of fomenting unrest and, while that charge was baseless, it is true that evangelical Protestantism was important in creating a 'network' of protest. Yet the rebels had some knowledge of the political ferment elsewhere in Africa, for they sang militant hymns to Patrice Lumumba, the Congolese leader who was already an iconic figure (Marcum, 1969, p. 125).[30] Portuguese forces restored order at the cost of hundreds, perhaps thousands of African lives, and about 10,000 refugees trekked into the Congo's neighbouring Kwango Province.

Yet another, again quite unconnected, violent eruption had broken out in early 1961, though this was located in Luanda and had clearly political origins. It was set in motion in late January when democratic opponents of Salazar hijacked a Portuguese luxury liner, apparently intent on sailing to Luanda and precipitating a coup (though in the event they abandoned the vessel in a Brazilian port). The authorities were confident they could nip this bizarre threat in the bud and allowed foreign journalists into Luanda to put their mastery of the situation on public record. However, the MPLA – hitherto not much more than a clandestine discussion group – seized the occasion to publicise and radicalise the nationalist struggle. The movement's core support lay in Luanda and several hundred militants – armed only with knives and clubs – attacked the city's main prison on 4 February in the hope of freeing political prisoners due to be deported to Portugal. The assault failed, but about forty Africans and seven Portuguese policemen died. Interracial violence escalated in the following days and, after another unsuccessful attack on the prison, the authorities allowed white vigilantes to terrorise the African slums. The authorities hustled the foreign journalists out of Luanda and imposed a news blackout, which lasted until the 'revolution of the flowers' in Lisbon, in April 1974.

The uprisings were disastrous for Africans, particularly African Protestants. Although only 17 per cent of the black population in 1960, they tended to be the better educated and more skilled. A disproportionate number of nationalist leaders came from Protestant families and were educated at Protestant schools.

---

[30] Ironically, Lumumba was murdered on 17 January 1961 in the breakaway province of Katanga; a Belgian police officer oversaw the execution and disposed of the body.

The Protestant churches were usually led by African pastors, unlike the Angolan Catholic Church: only 70 of its 452 priests were Africans in 1961 (though nearly half the black population was Catholic). The Catholic Church was seen as the religious arm of the state, and many churches were sacked during the uprisings; Protestant chapels were left untouched by African insurgents, though frequently burnt down by white vigilantes. The authorities in Lisbon and Luanda blamed the insurrections on both an 'international communist conspiracy', for which there was no evidence, and an 'international Protestant conspiracy'. However fantastical the idea, the colonial state acted as if it believed in it: by the end of 1962, 130 of the 165 black Methodist pastors and teachers in the region around Luanda were dead, in prison or missing (Marcum, 1969, p. 149). Protestant networks elsewhere were similarly persecuted.

Yet, in certain key respects, the uprisings achieved a great deal for Africans. In September, the government decreed the abolition of forced labour and outlawed the expropriation of African land. It also abolished what was known as the *indigenato* ('native') statute, which had marked out legal and civil distinctions between those who had assimilated Portuguese 'civilisation' and were citizens of Greater Portugal, and the 'non-civilised' who were subject to African customary law, paid the native tax and were liable for obligatory labour. Only the 'civilised' had access to jobs in the bureaucracy, freedom of movement and the right to participate fully in the Greater Portuguese community. Though raising Africans to 'civilised' status was theoretically the long-term purpose of colonial rule, less than 1 per cent had achieved it in 1950 (whereas all whites and nine out of ten **mestiços** were deemed 'civilised'.) Abolishing the *indigenato* statute meant all had equal rights before the law.

Why Portugal chose to fight

By mid-1961, it was widely expected that, whatever Portugal's success in crushing the uprisings, the decolonisation of its African territories would soon follow. In April, the UN General Assembly had passed a resolution urging the Portuguese government to prepare them for independence; to the consternation of the Portuguese, the US representative voted with the large majority. During the previous year, European rule had ended over a great swathe of tropical Africa with the negotiated departure of the colonial powers and the formation of twenty new states. Yet, rather than negotiate with the nationalists, the dictatorship of António de Oliveira Salazar chose to fight. It imposed on Portugal, the poorest country in western Europe, the economic burdens of counter-insurgency, subsidised white emigration and African rural development, which far richer countries had refused. Why was this? One theory has it that Portugal could not de-colonise because it was too weak to *neo-colonise*. Thus, whereas France, Britain and even Belgium could relinquish their colonies with the confidence that they had sufficient economic and 'soft' power to defend their essential interests in Africa after 'flag' independence, Portugal was too weak to contemplate this.

There is something in the theory; Portugal did not have the means to embark on an ambitious neo-colonial strategy. Yet the theory assumes that the decision to fight was essentially a calculation of economic interests, that the African territories were so integrated into Portugal's political economy relinquishing them was unthinkable. Salazar and his ministers may have believed this, but whether retaining the territories by force was *objectively* in Portugal's economic interests (or the economic interests of its dominant elites) is debatable.

By the early 1960s, the fundamentals of the Portuguese economy were changing rapidly. Industrial production was increasing by 9 per cent annually and exports of manufactures were overhauling agricultural exports. African markets were too poor to absorb more than a fraction of the output of Portugal's newly industrialising economy, unlike increasingly prosperous western Europe. Trade with the European Free Trade Association (which Portugal joined in 1960) and with the Common Market Six increased more quickly than trade with Africa, and invisible earnings from tourism and from emigrant workers in Germany and France came to dominate Portugal's international exchange position, relegating her favourable trade balance with the colonies to relative unimportance (Newitt, 1981, p. 221 – see Table 20.3). Meanwhile, the **Estado Novo** (New State) had relaxed its neo-mercantilist stranglehold on the African territories and allowed them to develop manufacturing and processing industries, which reduced their dependence on the metropole. Restrictions on foreign investment and trade were eased in the later 1950s. In short, when Portugal chose to fight for its African empire, its economic, neo-mercantilist rationale was beginning to look shaky.

Table 20.3   Direction of Portuguese trade

Destination of exports from metropolitan Portugal (%)

	1959	1969	1973
EFTA/EC	40.3	50.9	60.5
Colonies	29.8	24.4	14.8

Source of imports to metropolitan Portugal (%)

	1959	1967	1973
EFTA/EC	51.7	56.4	56.9
Colonies	14.2	14.3	10.1

(Source: MacQueen, 1997, p. 51)

EXERCISE   Salazar defended his African policy in a lengthy radio address of August 1963, broadcast shortly after the Organisation of African Unity (OAU) had recognised the Angolan government in exile (the Portuguese acronym is GRAE). Obviously evidence of this kind must be treated circumspectly, since politicians are not always honest with their audiences; nevertheless, I think the speech provides authoritative reasons for why Portugal chose to fight. Read the extracts from the speech that are available as Primary Source 20.3 (António Salazar, 'Declaration on overseas policy August 12, 1963') and say what they were.

SPECIMEN ANSWER

The Portuguese had a historic civilising mission to raise the cultural level of the peoples they colonised and include them in a common 'fatherland', whatever their race, indigenous language and religion. They also had a unique capacity for peacefully assimilating other cultures and embedding themselves in other environments. Angola was a Portuguese creation and those who lived there were Portuguese. If Portugal were to be excluded, then Angola would fragment into ethno-regional states. Africa faced a prolonged crisis of instability and the Portuguese were duty-bound to stand fast against the atavistic forces threatening the civilising mission. Portugal's multiracialism meant that it occupied the high moral ground in Africa: avenues to the 'highest posts' were open to the African elite and these should grow wider to counter the 'centrifugal forces' threatening to pull Greater Portugal apart. Salazar accepted the need for 'administrative decentralisation' but within a unified nation with 'one capital, one Government, one policy'.

DISCUSSION

I do not doubt the sincerity of Salazar's words, but they reveal an astonishing capacity for self-deception. It is true the Portuguese did not criminalise interracial sex and marriage (as did South Africa) nor institute a formal 'colour bar' (as did the British colonies) but 'multiracialism' in Angola was a sham. The overwhelming majority of black Angolans were excluded from white society and positions of power by a plethora of extra-legal mechanisms, such as the denial of educational opportunities: only 7 per cent of school-age children attended school in 1960; scarcely 1 per cent of adults were literate in Portuguese. Such racial integration as occurred in Angola was mostly the result of poor whites living alongside Africans in Luanda's slums, not of Africans moving into its exclusively European quarter. Even the minuscule minority of Africans who assimilated Portuguese culture and were deemed 'civilised' were disdained by Portuguese officials.

Yet, despite its patent inconsistencies, 'multiracialism' had a central place in Salazar's authoritarian nationalism and his conception of Portugal's 'civilising mission'. It legitimated resisting the claims of African nationalism and it was for this ideological mirage, rather than any clear economic interest, that Portugal chose to fight. Defending the 'civilising mission' against all comers was to have extremely unfortunate consequences for the regime's African strategy: the wars in Angola, Mozambique and Guinea were lumped into a single conflict, and defeat in one seen as the prelude to retreat from all. In point of fact, the Portuguese would have done well to walk away from Guinea, where there were no settlers to defend and no economic interests to speak of, without firing a shot, for the war in this small enclave sucked in military resources and brought the colonial army close to capitulation. It was the campaign in Guinea, not Angola or Mozambique, that corroded the officer corps' morale and built up the resentments behind the Armed Forces Movement. The decision to fight for Guinea reveals the ideological fixation behind Salazar's African policy.

The sources of Angolan nationalism

The insurgency in Angola exhibited many similarities with, but one striking difference from, the struggles that began in Guinea in 1963 and in Mozambique in 1964. In both, a single party came to dominate the independence movement and had no serious rivals when the colonial power structure collapsed in 1974. In Angola, no organisation achieved undisputed leadership: the half-hearted war the nationalist movements were waging against the Portuguese was seamlessly followed by a full-blooded civil war.

Angolan nationalism never cohered under a single umbrella organisation, principally because of the simultaneous emergence in the mid-1950s of two powerful nationalist currents, each with distinctive political, social and religious characteristics that made a confluence unlikely, and in the event impossible. The MPLA, formed in late 1956 out of the merger of several illegal groups, was the handiwork of cosmopolitan urban intellectuals and was notably interracial. Its 'founding fathers', Agostinho Neto (see box and Figure 20.9) and Mário de Andrade, belonged to the small number of 'assimilated' blacks educated at Portuguese universities in the 1940s and 1950s. The MPLA was Marxist from its inception and ideologically committed to non-tribalism, though its popular support was always concentrated among the Mbundu, whose homelands are to the east of Luanda. The movement's influence was spread inland through the regional network of Methodist chapels and schools. The leadership came from a younger, better-educated generation, which was 'progressive' in outlook, dedicated to fashioning a modern secular nation state and drawn increasingly to the Soviet bloc (and Soviet model of development) during the independence struggle. Since several prominent figures were *mestiços* and whites, the MPLA's rivals were able to depict it as the political vehicle of the old coastal elite and neglectful of 'real' African interests. (See Figures 20.10 and 20.11.)

Agostinho Neto, 1922–1979

Agostinho Neto was an Mbundu and the son of a Methodist pastor. After completing his secondary education in Luanda, Neto went on a Methodist scholarship to Portugal in 1947, where he trained in medicine. He joined an anti-Salazar youth group, was arrested and briefly jailed for subversion. After completing his medical degree, he returned to Angola with his Portuguese wife in 1959 and went into practice. He became president of the MPLA steering committee and was rearrested in June 1960, flogged before his family, and jailed. Neto escaped from a Portuguese jail in 1962 and reassumed the leadership of the MPLA in exile. Headquarters were eventually established in Tanzania, under the friendly eye of President Julius Nyerere. The movement's internal coherence and discipline came under great stress during the long years of ineffectual guerrilla war; when the Lisbon coup broke out in April 1974, the leadership was beset by crippling internal dissension. Neto was almost displaced by the guerrilla commander, Daniel Chipenda, and survived as MPLA president largely because he retained Soviet support. Neto became the first president of independent Angola when the MPLA, with Cuban assistance,

Figure 20.9   Agostinho Neto, 1976. Unknown photographer. Photo: © Bettmann/Corbis.

defeated the FNLA and UNITA (National Union for the Total Independence of Angola) in late 1975, early 1976, but he never had a popular mandate because scheduled elections were not held (see Figures 20.10 and 20.11).

The other organisation, which was relabelled the Front for the National Liberation of Angola (FNLA) in 1962, originated in BaKongo ethnic nationalism. Unusually for a black African independence movement, it had a social basis in the indigenous peasantry and mirrored the peasants' hostility to outsiders and the white world. Its forerunner, and the first Angolan political party, was the Union of the Peoples of Northern Angola (UPNA), set up illegally in 1955 as an avowedly BaKongo movement by the Baptist-educated elite. Its headquarters were in Léopoldville and its leaders originally envisaged a common future with their co-ethnics in the Belgian Congo. In 1958, the party attempted to broaden its appeal by renaming itself the Union of the Peoples of Angola (UPA), while acquiring a more radical edge. Holden Roberto (1923–2007), a Baptist mission-educated BaKongo who spent much

Figure 20.10   MPLA supporters listen to a speech by Neto, Luanda, September 1975. Photographed by Françoise de Mulder. Photo: © Françoise de Mulder/Corbis.

of his youth and early manhood in the Belgian Congo, emerged as a key activist at this time. He was given money to attend the first All African Peoples' Conference held in Accra, Ghana, in December, where he was befriended by Fanon and Lumumba. He later travelled to New York to put Angola's cause before the United Nations. His closeness to Fanon was reflected in rhetoric of revolutionary populism and the ambition to make the UPA a truly national movement. In 1961, the leadership co-opted non-BaKongo to the party hierarchy. For three years, Jonas Savimbi (see Figure 20.12), an Ovimbundu from Huambo, served as 'foreign minister' in the 'revolutionary government in exile' set up by the FNLA. But it remained a 'northern' movement, strongly identified with its original ethnic base and closely connected with the existing African socio-political order.

Figure 20.11   MPLA training at the Revolutionary Instruction Centre at Cabinda, 1974. Unknown photographer. Photo: Keystone Features/Getty Images.

The FNLA has been described as 'traditionalist', in that it envisaged a post-colonial state rooted in African 'traditions' and was suspicious of the modern urban world (Chabal et al., 2002, p. 7). Partly to please foreign patrons, but also out of conviction, Roberto sought to distance Angolan nationalism from communism and disparaged the 'self-styled intellectuals' in the MPLA; they dubbed him a reactionary 'tribalist'.

As a guerrilla organisation, the UPA/FNLA had a head start on the MPLA, which waited until January 1963 to begin military operations, when it targeted Portuguese bases in the Cabinda enclave. Throughout the insurgency, the FNLA always had more men in the field and it enjoyed the advantage of secure sanctuaries in the Congo. The Congolese government refused the MPLA access to the border regions and it was compelled to launch military incursions into thinly populated eastern Angola from Zambia, which entailed huge logistical problems. The local population was overwhelmingly rural and illiterate, and an unpromising milieu for Marxist freedom fighters, especially when led by *mestiço* officers from distant Luanda. In what each organisation

Figure 20.12 Jonas Savimbi, 1975. Unknown photographer. Photo: © JP Laffont/Sygma/Corbis.

regarded as 'its' territory, the rival was no more welcome than the Portuguese: both resorted to fratricidal violence. The FLNA eliminated MPLA guerrillas who 'trespassed' into the northern Dembos sector and set up detention camps in the Congo where MPLA militants were tortured and executed. Although the FLNA retained its strength in numbers, its political and organisational failings were increasingly evident, especially after Colonel Mobutu seized power in the Congo in 1965. Roberto became over-dependent on Mobutu's patronage and out of touch with events on the ground; he never ventured across the Congo–Angola border between the 1961 uprisings and the Lisbon coup. The party failed to develop a programme of political education and mobilisation within Angola. In 1972, the MPLA was prompted by military setbacks to seek a common front with the FLNA but was rebuffed by Roberto whose leadership had become stubbornly autocratic.

The disarray in the nationalists' ranks had been further complicated by the emergence of a third organisation, UNITA (National Union for the Total Independence of Angola), which sprang primarily from the Ovimbundu people of the central highlands. They were Angola's largest ethnic group, but had no tradition of ethnic nationalism. An important medium for spreading modern ideas among them were American Congregationalist missionaries. UNITA was set up by Jonas Savimbi in March 1966, about eighteen months after his break with the FNLA, with some assistance from communist China. After meeting

China's ambassador to Egypt, Savimbi and a few followers had been invited to Beijing in late 1965 for training in guerrilla techniques and political indoctrination, and supplied with arms and money. That Savimbi was then claiming to be a Maoist seems very incongruous in the light of later events, for he had no compunction about allying with apartheid South Africa after 1975 and was favoured by the Reagan administration with lavish military funding in the 1980s. Yet Maoism was consistent with his central political message during the anti-colonial struggle, which was the need to mobilise the exploited peasants and agricultural labourers rather than the urban workers. He was the first Angolan leader to recognise the futility of exile politics and lead his movement from within the country: from late 1966 until the 1974 Lisbon coup, most of his time was spent building political networks in eastern Angola, where he came to represent the 'unassimilated' blacks of the rural hinterlands against the creolised, Portuguese-speaking Africans of the cities. In April 1974, UNITA was not yet a significant military presence in the south, but Savimbi quickly evinced ruthless opportunism in his pursuit of power by secretly communicating to Portuguese intelligence officers his willingness to enter a neo-colonial settlement. Had the planned elections been held in 1975, UNITA would almost certainly have emerged as the largest political party.

The Portuguese way of war

EXERCISE

In early 1971, Basil Davidson, a distinguished commentator on African politics, published an account of a journey he had made on foot in MPLA-controlled territory in eastern Angola the previous summer. The report is called 'Angola in the tenth year: a report and an analysis, May–June [*sic*; this should read 'July'] 1970' and is available as Secondary Source 20.2 (though, since this is first-hand testimony, you should regard it as primary evidence). Read it now and answer the following questions:

1   Davidson did not disguise his sympathy for the MPLA; what was his assessment of its military campaign?
2   How did he view its relationship with the local population?
3   What judgement did he form of Portuguese military effectiveness?
4   Davidson acknowledged that he had visited just a small area of remote, eastern Angola for a relatively brief period. He could not know that the insurgency had more than four years to run: what enabled the Portuguese to continue a war they were (according to Davidson) losing in mid-1970? (You will have to speculate a little but there are several indications as to how the Portuguese were seeking to improve the effectiveness of their counter-insurgency campaign.)

SPECIMEN ANSWER

1   Davidson considered that, notwithstanding their great logistical difficulties, strategically the MPLA had the upper hand and were normally 'masters of the countryside'.
2   There was 'an obvious and intimate link' between the MPLA guerrillas and the local people, and a mutual trust which overcame ethnic differences. The MPLA – according to Davidson – was the only genuinely national movement in Angola; the only one to have won the support of most ethnic groups in most parts of the country.

3   Except for their commandos, he thought the Portuguese fighting morale was low and that of their African levies even lower. The policy of resettling villagers in strategic hamlets in order to isolate them from guerrilla infection had largely failed.

4   The Portuguese could improve their military effectiveness by investing more in technology (helicopters, defoliants) and a more systematic policy of resettlement. They could also seek to 'Africanise' the war by recruiting black soldiers and militiamen.

Davidson could not know that the MPLA's guerrillas would suffer severe reversals after his visit, partly because internal divisions reduced their effectiveness. But even in 1970 it should have been evident that the nationalist armed struggle posed no critical threat to the Portuguese presence. The major European centres were quite untouched and, as we have seen, white immigrants were arriving in unprecedented numbers. One indicator of the guerrillas' very limited impact is the remarkably low number of Portuguese military deaths over the course of the war: 3455 in all, of whom only 1369 were killed in action. Moreover, the trend was downwards, not upwards: in 1973, the Portuguese military in Angola suffered eighty-one deaths, of which only fifteen resulted from direct engagements with the guerrillas. The reason behind this was that the Soviet leadership had become disillusioned with the factional conflict in the MPLA leadership and ordered a sharp reduction in military aid.

The analysis by John Cann, a military professional turned academic, demonstrates that the Portuguese commanders had absorbed the lessons of counter-insurgency elsewhere. The key to their success in containing the guerrillas was not the 'high technology' assaults with aircraft, napalm and herbicide bombs (though these were tried), but routine foot-patrolling by lightly armed infantrymen. Companies of thirty to forty would be dropped by lorry or helicopter with sufficient iron rations for a five- to eight-day sweep through the bush. By the latter stages of the war, many of these troops were Africans: 42 per cent of the army's manpower in Angola was locally recruited during 1971–74. If we include self-defence militias and other paramilitary units, then the African contribution to the counter-insurgency forces was 50 per cent (Cann, 1997, p. 88). Davidson had a low opinion of black recruits but they were, in fact, a key element in the counter-insurgency campaign. The Portuguese were very resourceful in husbanding the metropole's exiguous manpower and using it effectively: most national servicemen passed their obligatory two years in Africa in what was termed 'psychosocial activity' (building roads, schools and dispensaries). The resettlement policy led to about one-quarter of the rural population living in **aldeamentos** (protected villages) by 1970; Africans resented being uprooted but their new locations at least had potable water, specially built latrines and access to all-weather roads. Although illiteracy and morbidity rates were still high at the end of the war, many more Africans were being schooled and receiving medical care than had been the case in 1960. In the north, the Portuguese administration cultivated allies among the BaKongo elite by encouraging black farmers to enter the export market for coffee, and supporting marketing and transport cooperatives managed by the Baptist church leaders. Prosperous rural capitalists would, it was thought, be immune to Marxist and Maoist blandishments.

Perhaps the most telling evidence for the insurgency's limited impact was that the Angolan economy boomed, thanks to buoyant demand for its exports (coffee, iron ore, diamonds and oil) and the 'Keynesian' stimulus of deficit-financed public expenditure on roads, social infrastructure and military equipment. Yet economic growth had the unintended consequence of loosening colonial ties. Portugal was granted associate status by the European Economic Community in July 1970, which required dismantling the barriers that had reserved colonial markets for Portuguese exports and lifting the remaining restrictions on foreign investment. Large-scale foreign capital was attracted to the Cassinga iron mines and the Cabinda oilfields. The major Portuguese corporations began to liquidate their investments, usually by selling out to Belgian, South African and US business interests. With the reorientation of the Portuguese economy towards Europe and the internationalisation of Angola's, the economic rationale for empire was nullified before the nationalists seized political independence.

None of this is to deny that the African wars put Portugal's society and economy under severe stress. Military service became deeply unpopular after it was effectively extended to four years in 1968. By 1970, one in five of those summoned was 'draft dodging', usually by migrating to Common Market countries. Military spending accounted for about half the Portuguese budget by early 1970s and was equivalent to 7 per cent of GNP. Resentment of these burdens undermined popular acquiescence in the dictatorship, but more importantly it lost the confidence of the officer corps and business circles, which saw Portugal's economic and political future lying squarely in Europe. In February 1974, General António de Spínola, the former governor and commander in Guinea, published a myth-shattering book, *Portugal and the Future*, in which he declared flatly that Portugal could not win its colonial wars. Publication triggered the disintegration of the dictatorship (Marcum, 1978, p. 242).

The 'revolution of the flowers' and the dissolution of the Portuguese empire

On 25 April 1974, Marcelo Caetano (who had succeeded Salazar as prime minister in 1968) and his closest colleagues were overthrown by career officers belonging to the Armed Forces Movement and allowed to go into exile. Spínola was asked to head the new government. The coup was prompted by narrow professional grievances relating to promotion and the loss of status relative to national service officers, but the malaise went much deeper. The dictatorship's will to govern had been eroded by disagreement with the Vatican over its African policies, industrial strife and the effects of the world recession following OPEC's quadrupling of oil prices after the Yom Kippur war. In Guinea, Portugal's military situation had become irretrievable after the PAIGC (Partido Africano da Independência de Guiné e Cabo Verde) began using surface-to-air missiles. The party declared independence on 24 September 1973 and within weeks Guinea had been recognised by over eighty states.

But in Angola, where all the nationalist movements were in severe difficulties in April 1974, there was nothing to suggest a military debacle. The Spínola government had no intention of abandoning it (or Mozambique) and envisaged reconstituting Greater Portugal as a Euro-African federation. The radicalisation of the Portuguese revolution and the demotivation of the colonial forces rendered this chimerical. Spínola, whose politics were conservative, resigned in September when further political cohabitation with the Portuguese left became impossible. Angola's white settlers were already nervous about their future and Spínola's departure rendered them desperately insecure: extremists attempted a coup with the aim of declaring unilateral independence, in imitation of the Smith regime in Rhodesia. Though never a serious threat, it provoked an African backlash, particularly in Luanda, and a sharp rise in interracial violence. Sensing they would soon lose the protection of the Portuguese military, whites began leaving in droves. Departing businessmen sabotaged their factories and offices rather than let them fall into African hands and their wanton destruction exacerbated racial hostility. Meanwhile, newly appointed left-wing officials in the colonial bureaucracy were openly siding with the MPLA, which was allowed access to the radio network. The colonial state undermined its own authority by releasing hundreds of political prisoners and allowing total freedom of political organisation and assembly.

As a prelude to transferring power, Portuguese officials negotiated the Alvor agreement with the rival nationalist movements in January 1975. This committed the parties to preserving a unitary Angola and established a coalition government, with a mandate to draft a constitution and conduct democratic elections before independence on 11 November 1975. However, the three nationalist organisations were arming and training new recruits and seeking allies in the coming struggle for power and none negotiated in good faith. President Mobutu was resolved to forestall a Marxist government in Luanda and stepped up his aid to the FNLA, which also began receiving covert financial funding from the US Central Intelligence Agency and military expertise from China. American confidence in the organisation seemed well-founded: it had about 21,000 well-armed guerrillas in early 1975, while the MPLA and UNITA had 8000 apiece. The MPLA, moreover, was in the throes of a damaging split, with the expulsion of Chipenda and his adherents in February. In March, sporadic fighting broke out when FNLA troops tried to dislodge the MPLA from its stronghold in Luanda. The Portuguese were unable to contain the escalating violence; they must have sensed their whole world was falling apart because metropolitan Portugal was teetering on civil war in the spring of 1975.

Soviet officials had been sufficiently alarmed by the rise of the FNLA to overcome their misgivings and increase the flow of military aid to the MPLA. How much each side in the incipient civil war received from its superpower patrons is a matter of debate. John Marcum argued that there was no significant difference in the scale of outside assistance, once aid to the FNLA and UNITA from China, France, Britain, West Germany and South Africa is factored in (Marcum, 1978, p. 263). But what does seem significant is the greater scale of Soviet as opposed to US military aid: the MPLA received from $100m to $200m in Soviet arms and equipment between March and December 1975; even if we take the lower total, it comfortably exceeded the $48m in money and arms that the USA committed to the FNLA in 1975. The discrepancy can be explained by the effect of the USA's defeat in Vietnam on American political opinion. 'Containing' communism in the Third World had led to national humiliation; Congress was so scarred by the experience that, in 1976, it passed the Clark Amendment outlawing military aid to any government or organisation with which the USA was not formally allied. There were no such domestic constraints on Soviet aid to Third World revolutionary movements at this time.

In the event, the decisive outside interventions came from Cuba and South Africa. Whether they were 'proxies' for Moscow and Washington or relatively autonomous agents is debatable. Cuban links to the MPLA went back to the meeting of Che Guevara with Neto in late 1965, when the celebrated revolutionary toured central Africa. In the following January, the MPLA was Angola's exclusive representative at the 'Tricontinental Conference' held in Havana, which was intended to give the 'Third World' effective political presence in international affairs. Cuban military advisers began training MPLA guerrillas, although they made little difference to the organisation's military capacity before early 1975 when Fidel Castro increased their number and the flow of weaponry. Thanks partly to the training and support of Cuban experts MPLA troops expelled the FNLA and UNITA from Luanda when full-scale fighting erupted in July. With its Zairian allies, the FNLA remained in control of the north, but the MPLA advanced rapidly southwards against UNITA, which appeared on the brink of extinction. The prospect of an MPLA victory led to an escalation in external intervention. The US secretary of state, Henry Kissinger, covertly organised a motley mercenary force to bolster the FNLA in the north. The operation was incompetently managed and the mercenaries were soon worsted.

More consequentially, in military and political terms, the South Africans restored Savimbi's fortunes by supplying UNITA with arms and advisers and, in October, invading Angola with two columns of armoured cars. South Africa was waging its own counter-insurgency in the mandate territory of Namibia and its helicopter units had been allowed to operate over southeast Angola since 1968; stopping the MPLA seizing power would deny arms and bases to the SWAPO (South West Africa People's Organisation) guerrillas in Namibia. Savimbi embraced South African allies chiefly to compensate for UNITA's military weakness; in retrospect, it was a gigantic political miscalculation.

The South Africans pushed back the MPLA but were halted before reaching Luanda by the rapid deployment of Cuban ground forces, who were airlifted from Havana in Soviet transport planes.

When the Portuguese governor departed on 10 November, he did not – and could not – formally transfer power to an independent Angolan government. The MPLA and its Cuban allies were fighting the FNLA and the Zairians for control of Luanda and the north; the resurgent UNITA, strengthened by South African troops and with some FNLA allies, was entrenched in Huambo, in the central highlands. The MPLA won the battle for Luanda and proclaimed the People's Republic of Angola; Savimbi set up the Democratic Republic of Angola in Huambo. In the 'war of intervention' that followed, three factors determined the MPLA's victory: the size and quality of the Cuban military contingent; the ineffectuality of American efforts to shore up the FNLA and the Zairians in the north; and South Africa's pariah status in international affairs. The last was decisive in terms of African international politics since the Huambo regime was utterly discredited when it was revealed to be a South African protectorate. Conservative African states, such as Nigeria, which had hitherto been wary of recognising the Marxist MPLA government now hastened to do so. Sensing that the 'Democratic Republic' was a hopeless cause, South Africa withdrew its forces to Namibia; as it did so fighting broke out between the UNITA and FNLA 'allies'. By early 1976, the MPLA had taken control of most of the country, though bands of dissidents roamed unchecked in the southeast.

CONCLUSION

EXERCISE

I began this unit by noting the structural resemblances between decolonisation in Algeria and Angola. What in your view were the most significant differences?

SPECIMEN ANSWER

These are two of the most significant differences:

1   The FLN came to dominate the Algerian revolution and excluded its rivals from negotiations with the French. Once de Gaulle had decided on Algerian self-determination, there was no realistic alternative to handing power to an FLN dictatorship, though the movement nearly disintegrated at independence. In Angola, the endgame of empire was different because none of the rival nationalist movements had achieved anything like the FLN's dominance. As Portuguese power drained away, all jockeyed for position in the post-colonial order and prepared for civil war.

2   Independent Algeria had little to fear from its neighbours, but Angola's geo-political situation in 1975 exposed it to intervention from South Africa and Zaire, which hoped to tip the military balance in favour of the FNLA and UNITA. Without Cuban and Soviet assistance, the MPLA would not have secured its hold on the country; for this reason, many Angolans never accepted its legitimacy.

Why the colonial empires in Africa ended is not hard to discern: they were agents of their own dissolution because they disseminated the principles of state sovereignty and national self-determination in a region of the world where they had never existed. Although the colonies were not states, they exhibited many of the attributes of sovereignty: they were political units within continuously bounded territory where a central authority claimed a monopoly of legitimate violence and imposed a common identity and common body of law on ethnically and culturally diverse populations. African empires also disseminated some of the features of what Europeans called 'civil society': free markets in goods and labour; voluntary association by religious and commercial groups; secular education; a relatively free press. This quasi-civil society was the matrix of anti-colonial nationalism. Western-educated nationalists 'imagined' their nations as the communities caged within the territorial boundaries imposed by the colonialists, and demanded the right to self-determination. As this unit has demonstrated *how* they ended is as important as why they ended.

REFERENCES

Ageron, C.-R. (1990) 'L'opinion française devant la guerre d'Algérie', in Rioux, J.-P. (ed.) *La Guerre d'Algérie et les Français*, Paris, Fayard, pp. 25–44.

Amin, S. (1970) *The Maghreb in the Modern World: Algeria, Tunisia and Morocco*, Harmondsworth, Penguin.

Bender, G.J. (1978) *Angola under the Portuguese: The Myth and the Reality*, London, Heinemann.

Cann, J. (1997) *Counterinsurgency in Africa: The Portuguese Way of War*, Westport, Greenwood Press.

Chabal, P., et al. (2002) *A History of Postcolonial Lusophone Africa*, London, Hurst.

Horne, A. (1996) *A Savage War of Peace: Algeria 1954–1962*, Basingstoke, Macmillan Papermac.

Jauffret, J.-C. (2000) *Solats en Algérie 1954–1962: Expériences contrastées des hommes du contingent*, Paris, Editions Antrement.

MacQueen, N. (1997) *The Decolonization of Portuguese Africa*, Harlow, Longman.

Marcum, J. (1969) *The Angolan Revolution: The Anatomy of an Explosion (1950–1962)*, Cambridge, MIT Press.

Marcum, J. (1978) *The Angolan Revolution*, vol. 2: *Exile Politics and Guerrilla Warfare (1962–1976)*, Cambridge, MIT Press.

Marseille, J. (1990) 'La guerre a-t-elle eu lieu? Mythes et réalités du fardeau algérien' in Rioux, J.-P. (ed.) *La Guerre d'Algérie et les Français*, Paris, Fayard, pp. 289–303.

Newitt, M. (1981) *Portugal in Africa: The Last Hundred Years*, London, Hurst.

Rachid Bencheneb (1986) 'L'Algérie à la veille du soulèvement de 1954' in
    Ageron, C.R. (ed.) *Les Chemins de la décolonisation de l'empire français,
    1936–1956*, Paris, Editions du CNRS.

Rioux, J.-P. (1987) *The Fourth Republic 1944–1958*, Cambridge, Cambridge
    University Press.

Stora, B. (1991) *La Gangrène et l'oubli: La mémoire de la guerre d'Algérie*,
    Paris, Editions de la Découverte.

Williams, P.M. (1964) *Crisis and Compromise: Politics in the Fourth
    Republic*, Harlow, Longman.

Yacono, X. (1982) 'Les Pertes algériennes de 1954 à 1962', *Revue de
    l'Occident Musulman et de la Méditerranée*, vol. 34, no. 2, pp. 119–33.

CONCLUSION TO BLOCK 5

Paul Lawrence

This block has considered four different 'ends of empire', ranging in time from the eighteenth to the twentieth centuries, and dispersed geographically over four continents. The differences between these case studies perhaps seem, on first glance, to outweigh any similarities. Does anything really link, for example, the revolt of the American colonies during the eighteenth century with the break up of the huge land empire of Austria-Hungary after the First World War? Your study in this block has demonstrated that there are common threads to be found but no easy answers. Violence of some kind is often a factor in imperial endings, but is not always a decisive one. The rise of new types of identity in nations under imperial rule has a role to play, but was often contested and fragmented. Changing international contexts clearly affected the viability of imperial systems, but perhaps only ever framed the extent of the possible. How, then, to begin to tackle the more general question of why empires end?

Thinking back to the introduction to this block (and perhaps rereading it if necessary) you will recall Darwin's idea that, while the precise circumstances in which different imperial systems unravelled were very different, they can be analysed by looking at the interactions between three broad types of factors – metrocentric, pericentric and international. No 'end of empire' can ever be attributed solely to events in the metropolis. Empires are never simply 'given up' by the imperial power. Equally, it is never the case that a colony simply wrestles control away from an imperial power (by force or other leverage). Likewise, while a changing international context may have made the maintenance of an empire (whether land or maritime) more or less advantageous, this too was never a decisive factor on its own. However, when all three types of factor (and particularly the interactions between them) are considered together we begin to edge closer to an explanation.

For example, in the case of America, metropolitan decisions over taxation clearly acted to rouse the colonists' ire, which in turn acted upon a nascent sense of American identity. In addition, a changing international context (primarily the defeat of France, which paved the way for expansion eastwards) in turn meant that this fledgling national identity was perhaps more politically significant in 1783 than it would have been in 1763. Equally, to take another example, in the case of India it is again possible to see all three types of factor at work together. The British, by conceding representative institutions and electoral arenas, had unintentionally conferred on Congress (and later the Muslim League) democratic legitimacy. At the same time, it seems unlikely the British would have granted full self-government without the growing repertoire of nationalist and anti-colonial tools developed by frustrated Indian nationalists. That said, in the case of India (and many other colonial regions) the process of decolonisation was as much about infighting over the shape of the future nation as it was about wresting power from Britain. It is debateable whether the fractious development of nationalism in India would have been as significant as it became without the accelerator of the Second World War and the changed international context this brought.

Thus, when considering the ends of empire, all three 'types' of factor need to be considered over both the long and short term. It is important to remember, however, that the significance of different factors varied over time and place. The need to consider the interactions between different types of factor does not mean that they were all equally important, that the end of an empire was a vague by-product of a soup of different causes. It is possible to construct cogent and meaningful explanations of the 'end of empire', but only by using a nuanced and analytical approach.

Conclusion:

In America 'nationalism' dictated the outcome by providing the impetus to go to war.

Other factors:
–
–
–

In India 'nationalism' dictated the pace of because the differing groups of nationalists decolonisation argued over the future shape of India.

Other factors:
–
–
–

BLOCK 6
CONCLUSIONS AND LEGACIES

INTRODUCTION TO BLOCK 6

Chris A. Williams and Karl Hack

> ## Learning outcomes
>
> When you have completed your study of this block, you should:
>
> - have rehearsed the skills you need to engage with previous units in a systematic manner
> - know how to use the preceding units as foundation stones, on which to build a sense of the topic of empire as a whole
> - be prepared to use these skills to get the most out of the course materials when writing your final extended assignment.

Why introduce these approaches now? Well, we have chosen to teach the history of empires through a series of in-depth case studies. This has the advantage that you are in a position to understand in some detail examples of all the major episodes and themes that we see as essential for the topic as a whole. But a corollary of this approach is that it takes some skill to make connections across these case studies, in order to answer more general questions. If this course is to achieve its aim of being about 'empires' as a category, rather than merely being a lot of unrelated empire case studies, we need to ensure you can make such connections.

Hence Unit 21 is designed to help you to extract information and analyse it in order to answer more general and thematic questions. It will help you to make connections between the discrete case studies that you have been exposed to: to 'join the dots' so to speak. Don't worry, we will start by rehearsing basic skills you are already familiar with, and gradually build up to more complex approaches.

First, Unit 21 will give you a set of exercises in how to look up different types of information – from basic names and dates to different interpretations – from within the course materials. Successful students (such as you) generally evolve ways of working through course material, making notes, and using other resources (databases, encyclopaedias and tutors), in order to make their own judgements about problems and disputes. This section will remind you of some techniques for solving these problems, and with luck it will suggest a few that you have not yet tried.

The second section of the unit will revisit the course's first block, where we introduced you to 'big questions' about empire, and to a number of approaches and concepts that help you to understand it as a phenomenon. The subsequent units have all contributed in their various ways to giving you answers to the questions, and examples to illustrate the approaches. In this section we will look again at both the questions and the approaches in the light of what you have studied over the last few months. Broad generalisations are always hard to understand in the abstract; now that you have a number of examples to relate to them, you should find that they make more sense to you than they did when you first came across them.

In the third section, the unit departs from our self-imposed rule that we will not use it to introduce new material. Here we will ask you to read extracts from two secondary sources dealing with aspects of imperial history that you have not yet covered in the course, and ask you to relate their content to topics that you *do* know about. The purpose of this exercise is two-fold: first, it's a way to give you more practice in looking through the course as a whole to find relevant concepts. Secondly, it's a reminder that although the case-study method of presenting history has left some gaps, what we have taught you so far will enable you to understand what you find in these gaps without much extra prompting.

The fourth and final part is a discussion of primary sources, and a reminder of how you can connect some of the topics raised by the course to some of the sorts of primary sources you will deal with as you complete your end-of-course assessment (ECA). We would not like you to see this unit merely as preparation for your ECA, but also as a way that you can consolidate your knowledge of historical approaches more generally.

Unit 22, by contrast, shows how you can use the information you already have to tackle big questions and problems. It focuses on three of these in particular.

- What was the impact of empire in the period you have studied, namely 1492 to the twentieth century?
- How do you use the concepts and approaches the course has equipped you with to compare and contrast different empires, colonies and situations?
- What sorts of imperial issues have persisted after the course's chosen end date of 1975?

The impact of empire is refracted through the debate between Niall Ferguson and others on how far empire provided 'public goods', such as the conditions that favoured the growth of world trade and so 'globalisation', and how far these overshadowed empire's more destructive impacts. It encourages you to use material from earlier units to answer this sort of question at different levels, by looking at the global, empire and colony-specific scales.

As you tackle this question about the impact of empires, you will be encouraged to think about the sorts of techniques you can use to compare and contrast different imperial situations. Like Unit 21, this unit will recall and use some concepts introduced at the beginning of the course, such as typologies of colonies. At the same time, it will introduce other approaches, such as looking for concrete counter-examples. Hence it briefly introduces the fate of countries such as Japan and Thailand, which maintained their independence.

Finally, Unit 22 encourages you to go beyond the strict chronological boundary of the course. Any end date is to some degree artificial, and the same is true of ours: 1975. The legacies of empire, and techniques of empire, did not suddenly cease at that magical date. Instead, the unit encourages you to think about how imperial legacies continue, for instance in plural populations of postcolonial countries, in issues of land rights, and by looking at the place of once-marginalised aboriginal or 'first' peoples in countries such as New Zealand. It also asks how far present-day conflicts, such as that over the identity and future of Tibet, can or indeed cannot be analysed as 'imperial' situations.

So, while Unit 21 concentrates on the practical skills you need to answer precise questions, and achieve specific results, Unit 22 encourages you to tackle open-ended and challenging problems. Can you hope to achieve definitive answers to the latter? Not at all. But you can hope to achieve a greater ability to understand and analyse issues that shaped, and continue to shape, the modern world.

UNIT 21
EMPIRES IN HISTORICAL PERSPECTIVE

Chris A. Williams

AIMS

- To help you effectively manage the information contained in the course materials.

- To show how you can integrate your knowledge about the course and apply this knowledge to general questions.

- To develop your ability to understand and contextualise primary and secondary sources related to the history of empires.

INTRODUCTION

This unit is different from the rest of the course, in that it is not intended to tell you about anything new: instead, its aim is to summarise the key themes that have emerged from the course as a whole. It will stick with the examples and issues that you have already covered, but will draw links and parallels between them in ways that might not have been apparent when you were working through them in detail.

The unit's aims are printed above. This is how I will help you achieve them:

- *Effective management of the information contained in the course materials* – this unit will give you hands-on practice in looking things up, and remind you of what you have learned over the last few months, in order to give you an opportunity to re-examine and revise your own understanding of the course as a whole.

- *Integration of knowledge about the course and its application to general questions* – we will re-examine a number of the 'big questions' set by the course to give you practice using your knowledge of the course material to address a range of general questions about the history of empires, linking the themes of the course and exploring how much they can explain.

- *Ability to understand and contextualise primary and secondary sources related to the history of empires* – in the third part of the unit I will set you some exercises in closely reading secondary sources, in order to demonstrate the way that you can use what you already know to more fully understand what they contain.

EXERCISE

This unit is supported by an audio CD, around 25 minutes long, that provides an introduction to the sorts of exercises that you will be carrying out in the unit. It consists of discussion between some of the A326 course authors on the ways that we can link up our knowledge of the course's different elements. It is divided into two tracks – the first approximately 12 minutes long, the second 13 minutes. Listen to the whole audio now. It will make clear the way that this unit differs from the others in the course, and the way that you ought to approach it. The two texts we discuss on the audio (optional Primary Sources 21.1 and 21.2) are available on the primary source database, accessible via the course website.

When we were writing this course, it quickly became apparent that we would never be able to produce a 'total history' of even one colonial empire, let alone more than one. The scope of such an undertaking would be immense: it would have to cover five centuries, and nearly the whole of the planet at one time or another. Most of the substantial European colonial empires are all dealt with on some level, but we have been unable to cover crucial episodes in each of them. To take some examples, by now you know how the Spanish empire began, and you might have an inkling of how it operated in its initial stages and some idea about the major factors that led to its initial downfall in the 1820s. But this course has not told you about how and why it continued in Cuba and the Philippines until their conquest by the United States following the Spanish–American War of 1898. Nor has it told you about the survival of a Spanish occupation colony in Western Sahara until 1975, or the two enclaves in North Africa, Ceuta and Melilla, which are part of Spain to this day. Italian empire-building in North and East Africa is absent, as are the efforts of Germany in Africa, China and the Pacific. Nor have we even mentioned Danish colonial efforts in Greenland and (until 1917) the West Indies. We have told you enough about similar events that, if you were to learn about these for the first time, you would be able to see that they formed a part of the same long-term trends in European imperialism that you do know about.

Even given these limitations, our decision to study 'empire' largely in terms of the European colonial empires has left out large areas of what is arguably imperial history. The Habsburg empire is described, but we have not considered the Ottoman empire. Japan's empire in China, Korea and the Pacific is absent. India's Mughal empire is mentioned in Units 9 and 10, in order that we may understand how and why the British were able to take over; but we have not told you about the Safavid empire, which held great power between 1500 and 1747. The only major 'land empires' outside Europe that we have covered are Russia and China, but Russia's drive to the east is not compared either to the American move west or to the 'empire' that many people thought that the USSR held in eastern Europe between 1945 and 1989.

Don't feel short-changed by this approach. If we had described all of these, we would have had to do so in a very shallow way, and there would have been no room to explain anything. Instead of trying to tell every possible story, our aim has been to give you enough knowledge to be able to join the dots and look in a comparative and general manner at the ways that empires grew, existed and fell.

Although we left a lot out, we also squeezed a lot in. Over the last few months we have introduced you to a bewildering variety of things. You have come across: abstract concepts, such as 'suzerainty' and 'periphery'; archaic technical terms such as 'boyar' and 'hacienda'; descriptions of geographical areas like the Siberian taiga and the West Indian Islands; accounts of complex events such as the Amboyna massacre and the Boston Tea Party; as well as methods of explaining all of this, such as the analysis of letters home and the use of oral history from pre-literate societies. And we expect you to understand, remember and analyse it all! You could be forgiven for being confused.

But we have tried to write the course with the learner in mind. Our main aim in each unit has not been for you to memorise the factual content, but to learn and understand some of the key underlying processes and concepts. This unit is designed to help you to bring it all together better. It has three sections as well as this one:

- Using the course materials
- Re-evaluating the course materials
- Linking what you know to other historical work.

These skills will be important as you prepare for your last piece of assessed work.

USING THE COURSE MATERIALS

Being stuck for the answer to a factual question – sometimes of crucial importance, sometimes a small but significant part of the puzzle – is a very common experience among students, and indeed among historians in general. Answering complex questions requires a good grasp of where to find detail. As mentioned above, there is a bewildering variety of information contained in the course. There are, though, many different ways that you can get your hands on it, and this section is intended to help you work on the practical skills that will enable you to find it most effectively. These include the following places. I have summarised the advantages of each in Table 21.1. I am sure that by now you have made use of most of them, but the chances are that you have missed at least one.

Table 21.1

Source of information	Advantages
Contents pages: The contents pages at the beginning of each block have a useful amount of detail in the titles of the sections in each unit	You can find which unit a topic is covered in
Indexes: We have taken care to index each of the books very thoroughly. You ought to be able to find a mention of what you are looking for in an index entry in one of the course books. If you don't find what you want straight away, try to think of other terms that might describe what you are after and look them up in the indexes	Very good for names and places

Source of information	Advantages
Glossaries: The glossaries at the end of each book list any unusual or unfamiliar terms that have been used for the first time in that book	They explain technical terms and non-English words
Datecharts: There is a general list of significant events on the course website that covers the period of the course. A few of the units also have more specific datecharts associated with them; these are also on the website	You can find out what else was happening at the time you are interested in
Other course resources: Don't forget the DVD and the Visual Sources Book	Visual resources are interesting and more memorable than mere text (see Figure 21.1 for an example); they often give more information
The course's online conference: Your fellow students are an important source of information	Many hands make light work; and everyone else will be able to see the answer as well
Online course resources: These are available through the course website and will be dealt with in more detail below	Wide range of information available, which we have flagged up as relevant to your study

Now let us look at a few sample concrete questions and how you might go about finding the answers to them.

Who was Lord Linlithgow?

This is the kind of question that is best looked up in a course book index. It helps if you have some idea about *when* Linlithgow was active, so that you know which book's index to look at first. As it happens, he was the viceroy of India between 1936 and 1943, thus you can find him in the index to the third volume; so, if you were going through them in order, it would take an extra minute or so.

Did the Portuguese empire spread earlier than the Dutch one?

This is clearly a chronological question, and you can answer it quickly with reference to the online datechart. The answer is also clear from a look at Unit 6 (but that will take longer): the Portuguese empire in the Indian Ocean was established about 100 years before the arrival of the Dutch.

Are there any problems in interpreting autobiographies written by slaves?

This question is rather more complex than some of the simple factual ones in this list. It is best answered with close reference to the contents pages, in this case of Block 4 in Book 2, where we find that Unit 12, on the slave experience, has a section entitled 'Slave autobiographies and the black experience in the later eighteenth century', the first subsection of which is called 'Interpreting the sources'. If there are problems, here is the first place to look for them.

Figure 21.1 Charles de Gaulle in Algeria, 1958. Photographed by Erich Lessing. Photo: © Erich Lessing/Magnum Photos. This photograph shows Charles De Gaulle at the time of the events depicted on the course DVD related to the crisis of the Algerian War of Independence.

What is 'comparative advantage'?

A technical term like this one ought to be covered in one of the course book glossaries. You will have to guess which volume to look in first, but perhaps you would recognise it as an economic term, and therefore look in the second volume, which contains Unit 10 on the economics of the British empire. In the glossary you would find that 'comparative advantage' is a term that means the extent to which one country or area can produce goods or services cheaper than another.

When was the British Empire Exhibition?

This was the topic of one of the sections on the DVD (related to Unit 10 on 'Imperial cultures'). Rather than actually play the DVD to remind yourself of what is on it, you could consult the 'Media notes' at the end of the Course Guide. The answer is 1924.

Now I would like you to answer a short quiz I have prepared. This has two aims: the first is to get you used to answering this sort of question using the search methods I have outlined above. The second is to force you to get all the other course materials down from the shelf and onto your desk, where they will stay until you have worked your way through this unit. If you study in a place that makes this difficult, but have access to a computer, you can download the course books from the course website as PDF files. This gives you another search option: as well as using the index, you can use the software's 'find' function to look for key words and names. If you are using the printed volumes, you might want to clear a space on your desk, and collect together some book-stands, bookmarks and paperweights. Now I would like you to try the quiz, making a note of the various places where you looked for the answers.

EXERCISE

Where would be the best place(s) in the course material to look for the information you need to answer the following questions? Test this by seeing how many of the questions you can answer in an hour or so. The specimen answer lists the first places that I would go within the course material to look for the actual answers. The actual answers will be made available on the course website during your work on Block 6.

1   What is Fieldhouse's definition of a 'plantation' colony?
2   When did Singapore introduce its own version of the Contagious Diseases (CD) Acts?
3   How did British and Indian hunters dress in India in the late nineteenth century?
4   Give three examples of how, in the eighteenth century, making war in the North American continent was different from doing so in Europe.
5   Did the defeat of the Spanish Armada in 1588 swiftly open up the Atlantic for English settlement?
6   What were *malaya*, *watembezi* and *wazi-wazi*?
7   Two groups of scholars have debated the nature of twentieth-century Indian nationalism: how are they described in the course?
8   What was a *nau*?

SPECIMEN ANSWER

1   Index to Book 1.
2   Index to Book 3.
3   Visual Sources Book: related to Unit 10 'Cultures of empire'.
4   Contents page for Block 3.
5   Online datechart.
6   Index to Book 2.
7   Contents page for Block 5.
8   Glossary for Book 1.

DISCUSSION

You probably noticed that there is a limit to the immediate effectiveness of some of these ways of finding information: sometimes the nature of the problem gives you an idea of where to look, but at other times you just have to choose at random. Looking things up in the index is all very well, but you have to guess which volume to look in first. My tip is that if you have not got a very good idea where you need to look, it is better to try all the indexes and the contents pages *first*, rather than spend time flicking through the most likely book looking for something that catches your eye. This can drag on, and as a search method flicking through has the disadvantage that there is always a chance that the information is there, but you have missed it. But if you look for it in the index and can't find it, then you have got a reasonable idea that it is not there, and you can move on to look somewhere else.

Think of these as 'limbering-up exercises'. In the next section, I will begin to ask more complex questions about the material in the course units.

RE-EVALUATING THE COURSE MATERIALS

This section is intended to give you some practice in considering the main themes of the course, and working out how you can best use the course material to 'join up' your thinking across units and blocks.

I would like you to reconsider the first block of the course in the light of what you have subsequently learned. This exercise might look short on the page, but there is a lot of reading to do, so allow yourself two hours for it at the least.

Before doing the exercise, I would like you to reread some material from the first block, with a view to noting your reactions to the questions posed there. Please read:

1 the 'Introduction to Block 1'
2 the 'Conclusion' from Unit 1

You will note that there are a number of questions at the end of Unit 1, written down under headings that set out the main titles for the course's blocks. When you do the exercise, I would like you to consider two of these questions and work out how you would now go about answering them. What other parts of the course you would need to consult? At this stage, you need *not* actually set out an answer to the question. I have done a 'worked example' for you. Under 'How do empires work?' there is the following question:

> *'Questions must therefore be asked about maintenance, survival and renewal; what forces held empires together?'*

An answer to this question could be:

The most obvious place to start is Block 3 itself, which sets out the course's view of 'how empires work'. But as well as this, there are a number of other points where there is information that might be useful. Units 4–7 on the beginning of empires attempt to point out when they became mature and enduring. Block 5 on 'Why do empires end?' could also help to answer that question: for example, Unit 18 gives some idea of how the Austro-Hungarian empire survived the nineteenth century, as well as how it finally succumbed in 1919.

EXERCISE   Now try this yourself for these two questions. The detailed block contents pages are a good place to start, but don't forget the indexes. Try to identify at least three different parts of the course material, and avoid, if possible, getting bogged down in detail.

1   'How were armies paid for and colonies administered?'

2   'Was there a fundamental divide ... between land empires and maritime ones?'

1   The answers to this question are largely contained in Block 3, particularly Unit 8 on military power and Unit 9 on economic power, but also Unit 11, especially the section 'The pattern of the Chinese past', which includes details of the relative level of the Chinese tax burden. We could also argue that one way that empire was paid for – through the exploitation of people at the bottom of the pile – is also explored at length in Unit 12 on the experience of empire from below. There is also some detail on the administration of British North America in Unit 17, and on the administration of British India in Unit 19. The notion of 'indirect rule' as a way of administering colonies is introduced in Unit 2 and discussed in Unit 10 in the context of the British and French empires.

2   This question is introduced in Unit 7, covering the expansion of Russia: this is itself an implicit reply to the accounts in the three preceding units. Unit 8 on military power continues this comparison, between Britain's maritime empire and Napoleon's land empire. Unit 9's focus on economics naturally contains a lot of information about the importance of maritime trade to nineteenth-century Britain. Unit 11, with its comparison between China and western Europe, also approaches this theme. Unit 18, on the end of the Austro-Hungarian empire, offers a point of comparison for the other empires studied in this block.

All these are broad issues – questions that we have tried to address throughout the course books – and thus the above answers cover a lot of material. The next step in addressing them would be to work more closely on the contents pages and the index to identify sections within the units that are most relevant to the question.

When looking at the big questions, it is also worth returning to Unit 2, which considered theories of empire. There, we told you about a number of ways that we can categorise and theorise empires in general. These general concepts provide another way to think about the course as a whole.

In the next exercise I am going to ask you to select a unit from Blocks 2–5 and to consider which of the theoretical generalisations from Unit 2 can help you to make sense of the topics it covers. To recap Unit 2 (in a highly truncated way!), I think that the key points that it makes are as follows:

• definition of empire as having a hierarchy of societies

• significance of core and periphery

• typology of colonies: *settler*, *plantation*, *mixed*, *conquest*, *enclave*, *protectorate*

• state actors and sub-imperialist actors

• direct and indirect rule

• maritime and land empires

• global power

• formal and informal empire.

Here is a worked example, which uses Unit 5, on the genesis of the British empire in the Atlantic:

The point about an empire having a **hierarchy of societies** does not feature to a great extent, but the concepts of **core and periphery** are definitely present, in the way that Massachusetts and Barbados were financed from the core and expected to return their surplus there. Of the **typology**, New England's were settler colonies, Barbados rapidly evolved into a plantation, and there is a very brief mention of slave-trading enclaves in West Africa. Mixed, conquest and protectorate colonies do not feature. The distinction between **state actors** and others is made, but this is to explain the permeability of the early modern state, not to stress the distinctiveness of its role. **Direct and indirect rule** are not mentioned, nor are **global power** or the **formal/ informal** distinction, but the **maritime** nature of enterprise is stressed throughout.

As you can see from this answer, I have not been able to find examples of all these factors in Unit 5, and some of them (such as state action and enclaves) are mentioned there primarily to stress their limited relevance. I doubt that there is a single unit in the course where all the concepts from Unit 2 are discussed.

EXERCISE

Now select a unit from Blocks 2–5 and note down in a paragraph or so which of the theoretical generalisations from Unit 2 can help you to make sense of the topics it covers. You ought to be able to do this exercise by skim reading the unit rather than reading every word. Remember to look up all the key terms in the index first, and use the contents page to find the sections that you ought to look closely at.

DISCUSSION

There is little point including a specimen answer for this exercise: each of the units is different enough that it wouldn't be much help. I hope that you were able to find some points where you could apply the general statements, even if only at a relatively abstract level.

INTEGRATING THE COURSE WITH FURTHER SECONDARY READING

By now, you should know enough about the topics covered by the course to be able to contextualise and understand a wide range of secondary academic literature. In this section there are two exercises that will give you practice in doing that.

The first one uses an article by Opolot Okia from the *Journal of Imperial and Commonwealth History* called 'In the interests of community: Archdeacon Walter Owen and the issue of communal labour in colonial Kenya, 1921–30'. Research articles like this one have advantages and disadvantages. The advantage is that they are completely up to date: indeed, the point of journal articles is to present brand-new conclusions derived from research. The main disadvantage is their often very narrow subject coverage, but often this is offset somewhat by references the author makes to the bigger picture of academic research and historical context, usually found at the beginning and end of an article. This can be a mixed blessing; another problem (from your point of view) with articles is that they are often written with overt reference to highly obscure academic arguments, and/or to technical terms that have a narrow and sometimes opaque meaning.

I would like you to read Opolot Okia's article, which is supplied as Secondary Source 21.1. As you do so:

1   note where your existing knowledge of the course gives you an insight into the points that it is making, then

2   use this knowledge to write a short (less than 200 words) answer to the following question: How typical of empire as a whole are the structures, events and processes described in this article?

For our purposes, I have abridged the article a little (removing Part IV). When reading articles, the most important bits are usually at each end. If you want to read the whole article, you can locate a copy through the Open University library website (accessible via the course website). You will find many of the following course resources of benefit when doing part 1 of this exercise:

- Unit 16
- Unit 10
- DVD
- Unit 3
- Unit 4
- Unit 14.

1   This article overlaps in terms of its setting with Unit 16 on Kenya. The specifically 'communal' justification for the labour (p. 3) seems to be an example of indirect rule, of the kind described in Unit 10. The role of missionaries is shown in the DVD section on circumcision – Hooper and Arthur, who are featured on the DVD, are also mentioned in the article (p. 6). Owen's line of criticism – that the colonial system was not wrong in itself, but contained abuses (p. 7) – was taken by a number of the commentators in Unit 3. On p. 3 of the article, the idea that the 'communal' was used as an 'atavistic justification' has echoes of the arguments over the liberation of Indian women that were described in Unit 14. The use of forced labour was not unique to the British in Africa: as we know from Unit 4, the Spanish used it in sixteenth-century Central America.

2   As we see from the answer to part 1, there are several themes here than recur elsewhere. The indirect nature of colonial authority, which is tied up with that of 'traditional' local leaders; the role of the church in criticising exploitation; the need for empire to be cheap; the casual use of violence to enforce compliance in what looks a bit like a modern-day version of slavery: all these suggest that this kind of situation was not unique to twentieth-century Kenya. On the other hand, the extreme violence and oppression of the period of early conquest (such as in Central America) and plantation economies (such as the West Indies) are absent.

Above I warned you about the way that research articles often contain elements that are very hard for the general reader to follow. One example of this in Okia's article is the term 'articulation', which appears to form a significant part of his argument. If we follow the footnote, we can see that Okia is using it in the sense that was first used by some theorists of development studies in the 1970s. His specialist readership might well know exactly what it meant in practice; the rest of us have to take his word for it, and pay more attention to the empirical aspects of the article and what they tell us about the history. This is not because we are only interested in facts to the exclusion of analysis, but by now we know enough about the context of articles like this to fit them into our own broad generalisations.

So, you have just practised a way to examine an article dealing with a discrete and focused historical event against the content of the course. We will now take a look at a bigger picture, using a secondary source extract that deals with an area that the course has not devoted much time to: the Pacific.

EXERCISE

The extract you will read next, from *The Pacific Islands: Paths to the Present*, by Evelyn Colbert (Secondary Source 21.2) is a broad overview of the history and nature of European colonialism in the Pacific. Unlike the research article you have just studied, this is from a book intended to give a general introduction to a particular area; so you ought to find the style of the text easier going. I would like you to read it and answer the following two questions:

1   How much of this has been touched on already in the course units, and where? To answer this, you will need to range more widely through the course materials than you did in the previous exercise.

2   What parallels can you draw between the operation of empire in the Pacific and elsewhere in the world?

Table 21.2 is an answer matrix for you to use when answering question 1 – I have filled in some of these for you to give you the idea.

Table 21.2   Answer matrix

Section in Secondary Source 21.2	Relevant mention in A326 course materials
p. 1 'the Spanish Period'	Unit 4 – describes the significance of the Manila galleon
p. 1 'Explorers'	Beginning of Unit 1 – the discussion of Cook's first map of New Zealand
pp. 3–4 regarding 'traders'	
pp. 3–4, 12–14 references to 'plantation' and 'settler' societies	
p. 4 impact of disease	Units 4 and 5 – both deal with this issue in the context of the Americas
pp. 4–6 'Missionaries'	
p. 6 cultural impact of religion	
p. 7 'Expansion of Colonial Control'	
p. 5 discussion of 'erotic behaviour' among the local customs attacked by missionaries	
pp. 8, 12, 13 expansion of the French empire	
p. 11–15 'Patterns of colonial administration'	

Section in Secondary Source 21.2	Relevant mention in A326 course materials
p. 12 Guam petition for US citizenship	Unit 19 – there are echoes here of the language of 'trusteeship', which the UK referred to when claiming that Indians were not ready for home rule
p. 13 Fiji – movement of indentured Indian labour	

Figure 21.2   Nathaniel Dance, *Captain James Cook*, 1775–76, oil on canvas, 127 × 101.6 cm. National Maritime Museum, Greenwich, London, BHC2628. Photo: National Maritime Museum, Greenwich, London. Cook's voyages of exploration in the Pacific in the latter part of the eighteenth century did more than anything else to transmit knowledge of that area to Europe.

1   See Table 21.3, the completed answer matrix.

2   Outside New Zealand, the Pacific pattern is lot like the African one: Europeans had technological advantage; they were motivated by the desire for raw materials; there was not (as in mainland Asia) significant trade with locals, nor were Pacific political units strong enough to have a chance of fighting them off. In the later nineteenth century there was a scramble for colonies, which was usually settled by agreement rather than war (pp. 10–11).

Table 21.3   Completed answer matrix

Section in Colbert	Relevant mention in A326 course materials
p. 1 'the Spanish Period'	Unit 4 – describes the significance of the Manila galleon
p. 1 'Explorers'	Beginning of Unit 1 – the discussion of Cook's first map of New Zealand
pp. 3–4 regarding 'traders'	Unit 3 – one of these traders, Vernon Lee Walker, is the subject of Case Study 3
pp. 3–4, 12–14 references to 'plantation' and 'settler' societies	Unit 1 – Fieldhouse's models, which are discussed in more detail in Units 5 and 12 (plantations) and Unit 13 (settler society)
p. 4 impact of disease	Units 4 and 5 – both deal with this issue in the context of the Americas
pp. 4–6 'Missionaries'	Unit 13 – the box on 'Cook to Wakefield' talks about role of missionaries in colonisation of New Zealand
p. 6 cultural impact of religion	Unit 3 – 'Empires of the mind', in its discussion of Franz Fanon, gives another example of how 'European' ways of seeing the world interacted with indigenous cultures
p. 7 'Expansion of Colonial Control in the South Pacific'	Unit 1 and Visual Sources Book – World maps 5–9 give an idea of when the South Pacific was colonised, and by whom
p. 5 discussion of 'erotic behaviour' among the local customs attacked by missionaries	Unit 16 – there are echoes here of the debate about female circumcision in Kenya
pp. 8, 12, 13 expansion of French empire	Unit 13 – discusses this in the context of settler societies in Algeria
pp. 11–15 'Patterns of colonial administration'	Unit 10 – discusses the relevance of 'indirect rule' as an imperial strategy.
p. 12 Guam petition for US citizenship	Unit 19 there are echoes here of the language of 'trusteeship', which the UK referred to when claiming that Indians were not ready for home rule
p. 13 Fiji – movement of indentured Indian labour	Units 4 (Spain in America), 5 (English Atlantic) and 12 (British empire 1700–1830) – all show how important labour migration was to empire

Colbert's account has one slightly misleading phrase in it, since it refers to Cook's (Figure 21.2) 'mistaken belief' that observing the transit of Venus from the South Pacific would enable astronomers to calculate the distance between the Earth and the Sun. This was not mistaken: observing the transits led to a confirmation of the existing estimates for this figure. They did not lead to appreciably better estimates, chiefly because they did not have the technology to do so, but the theory was fine. You might also have had a look on the *Empire Online* database. This contains a digitised version of a particularly relevant source: the journal of Captain James Cook, whose expeditions to the region in the later eighteenth century were one of the most significant ways that Europeans gained systematic knowledge about it.

In the Introduction to this unit, I wrote about all the events we did not have room to discuss in the course materials. I hope that this section has demonstrated that the way we have written the course helps you to understand and explain many of these events, through reference to what we have taught you about the structures and trends of European imperialism.

INTEGRATING YOUR UNDERSTANDING WITH PRIMARY SOURCES

In this section, we are going to look at four primary sources, first a pair of images, then two short text extracts, to see how we can use the course material to help contextualise them.

Images are important tools for understanding the way that imperial rule was interpreted; they can also give us clues as to how it actually was. Not least important, though, is the impact that they have on our understanding, and the way that they can provide valuable cues for our memories: it is a lot easier to remember the written content of a unit that was accompanied by some striking pictures than one that was mainly text. And our understanding of events is often changed and made far more vivid if we can attach it to an image.

All the factors listed above are reasons to be wary of images, even as we welcome what they can do for us. We need to ask the same questions of an image as we would of a written primary source. The questions 'Who made it?', 'When?' and 'Why?' are essential if we want to use the image as a guide to what actually happened. To draw conclusions about the contemporary impact of an image we need to have some idea about who saw it, and how representative it was. Again, this is a skill that has been flagged up along the way in the course material. Unit 1 began by showing different ways we can look at maps, which tell us a good deal more than just where things are (this point was also made in Unit 10's discussion of James Rennell and the mapping of India). Unit 6 discussed John White's pictures of the New World; photographs of India were analysed as an example of imperial culture in Unit 10; and Unit 11 showed how William Alexander represented Macartney's mission to the Chinese empire. Bear in mind that we can also think about maps as images, rather than mere representations.

Figures 21.3 and 21.4 share a common theme: violence in the British empire, but they depict events that took place at either end of it. The first (Figure 21.3) is a watercolour, probably by John White, which appears to depict a scene from Frobisher's expedition of 1577. This is the only surviving image from this expedition, although White also painted three Inuit who were captured by it and brought to England. The second (Figure 21.4) is a photograph of British soldiers in Aden (southwest Arabia) in 1965, during the protests that were to culminate in the ejection of the British from this colony.

Figure 21.3   Unknown artist after John White, *The Skirmish at Bloody Point*, *c.*1580s–90s, watercolour with bodycolour and pen and grey ink, 39 × 26 cm. British Museum, London, Prints & Drawings, SL,5270.12. Photo: © The Trustees of the British Museum.

Figure 21.4   British troops in Aden, 1967. Photographed by Terry Fincher. Hulton Archive. Photo: © 2007 Getty Images.

Both of these images can be related to their context by looking at other sources. First, the watercolour seems to be of this event, described in George Best's account of Frobisher's voyage thus:

> And thervpon indeede our men whiche were in the boates ... forced them to put themselues ashoare vpon a point of lande within the said sound (which vpon the occasion of the slaughter there, was since named the Bloudie point) wherevnto our men so speedily followed, that they hadde little leysure lefte them to make any escape. ... And desperately retorning vpon our men, resisted them manfullye in their landing, so long as theyr arrows and dartes lasted, & after gathering vp those arrows which our men shot at them, yea, and plucking our arrowes out of their bodies, encountred afresh againe, and maintained their cause, vntil both weapons and life vtterly failed them.
>
> (Best, 1578, pp. 22–3)

The photograph, which was one of many taken at the time, shows events that were heavily reported in the British press. *The Times* describes a similar British response to riots in Aden in March 1967 thus: 'A few attempts at demonstrations were made in several parts and in the Maalla district the civil police used tear gas to disperse demonstrators who began half a dozen small bonfires and blocked streets with rocks and rubbish' ('Aden gripped again by impromptu strike. Party protest over lynchings', 1967)

EXERCISE

What is the next most significant question that we ought to ask about each image if we want to use it as a historical source?

SPECIMEN ANSWER

There are of course a number of potential answers to this question. Regarding the first image, the most important point is that we don't know if White (assuming him to be the artist) was there or not. The painting is consistent with the written report, but the most likely explanation for that is that it was composed after the fact with the report in mind.

As for the second image, we have little idea of the context in which it was taken. Had the British soldiers just come under attack, or were they about to attack the protesters? The gas masks hide their faces, making it impossible to know whether they were looking aggressive, frightened, or some combination of these emotions.

Regarding them both, we are only getting one side of the story here. A photograph of Arab protesters would produce a very different impression of the situation: we don't know if the Inuit ever made their own visual records of their encounter with Frobisher's men.

DISCUSSION

The need to contextualise visual sources should not stop us from using them; their impact and their incidental detail alike provide good reason for seeking them out in order to improve our knowledge of the past.

You also need to put written primary sources into context in order to understand them. Before you begin to draw conclusions from a primary source, it is important to ask some basic questions. What kind of a source is it – is it an official document, such as an order, a constitution or a charter, a report for public consumption, or a personal account? Who created it, when and where – how much do you know about why it was created and how? What is its immediate context – perhaps a letter is one of a personal exchange, or perhaps (remember Cortés's letters to Charles V from Unit 4?) it was deliberately composed in order to fulfil a very specific purpose. Once you have thought about these issues (it might help to make a note of your conclusions), you can move on to analysing it.

This process of analysis needs to take place on two main levels. The first level is a practical historical one. How does it fit into its *immediate* historical context? Think for a moment about the two accounts of Macartney's audience with the Chinese emperor, which you examined in Unit 11. Each of them can only be really understood if we also consider the other. To take another example, the discussion of the various letters home and published memoirs from settler empires that you studied in Units 13 and 14 showed how we need to be aware of the circumstances in which they were created. For an illustration of this, go back to the start of Unit 13 and reread what Robin Mackie had to say about the letters of Jessie Campbell.

The second level is to ask what it tells us about the questions that we are interested in. If the first level can be summarised as 'where does this fit in?' the second one deals with the question 'so what'? The answer to this question is not as clear cut, for it depends on the circumstances. If, for example, we are looking at Captain Cook's journal to investigate the role played by scientific investigation in his voyages, we might be looking for very different material from what we would need if were investigating how he treated indigenous inhabitants.

Let us look at two primary sources that allow us to explore a related theme: the nature of anti-imperialist nationalism. For each of them, I would like you to use the course materials to do two things:

1   Contextualise it.
2   Ask what evidence it provides that helps us to answer the following question: How far was anti-imperialist nationalism something that defined itself in terms of individual rights, and how far in terms of other competing claims to nationalism?

Address of W. C. Bonnerji to the First Indian Congress, Bombay 1885

[O]n more than one occasion, remarks had been made by gentlemen, who should have been wiser, condemning the proposed Congress, as if it were a nest of conspirators and disloyalists. Let him say once for all, and in this he knew well after the long informal discussions that they had all had amongst themselves on the previous day, that he was only expressing the sentiments of every gentleman present, that there were no more thoroughly loyal and consistent well-wishers of the British Government than were himself and the friends around him. In meeting to discuss in an orderly and peaceable manner questions of vital importance affecting their well being, they were following the only course by which the constitution of England enabled them to represent their views to the ruling authority. Much had been done by Great Britain for the benefit of India, and the whole country was truly grateful to her for it. She had given them order, she had given them railways, and above all she had given them the inestimable blessing of Western education. But a great deal still remained to be done. The more progress the people made in education and material prosperity, the greater would be the insight into political matters and the keener their desire for political advancement. He thought that their desire to be governed according to the ideas of government prevalent in Europe was in no way incompatible with their thorough loyalty to the British Government. All that they desired was that the basis of the government should be widened and that the people should have their proper and legitimate share in it.

(Bonnerji, 1885, pp. 17–18)

Thomas G. Masaryk 'The problem of small nations in the European crisis: inaugural lecture at the University of London, Kings College'

This is an extract from the inaugural lecture that Thomas Masaryk, the Czech nationalist, gave at the University of London in 1915 (it was published in 1916)

History is in favour of all individuals, of individualism in general; nations are natural organisations of homogenous individuals, and states being more artificial organisations, are more and more adapted to the nations. So general is this tendency that the numerical strength of the nations does not play a decisive part.

History shows that since the eighteenth century the principle of Nationality has grown stronger, and received more and more political recognition. National individualities, their language and culture have steadily gained ground all over Europe, and linguistic rights have been gradually codified. These rights have been and still are advocated by Italy, by the Austro-Hungarian and Balkan nations; they are advocated by Germany herself. How then can Germany or any other nation claim for herself this right and at the same time refuse it to others?

How strong and far-reaching national feeling and ideas have become in modern times, is proved by the revival of oppressed nationalities of all states. The Renaissance of the Bohemian nation is a specially striking instance, and a confirmation of the general national principle. The social unit of conscious nations, breaking the old political boundaries, is the real, because the all-comprising social unit, the old state being the organ of political and military conquest. The function of the state changed, therefore, and changed in accordance with the development of culture. Austria and Prussia are classical instances of the antagonism of state and nationality. The state is autocratic, ruling and domineering, the nation is democratic, administering, social, developing from within.

SPECIMEN ANSWER

1   The context for the first extract is the beginning of Indian nationalism in the later nineteenth century, as featured in Unit 19. The second one illustrates the growth of Czech nationalism, and the fact that the most passionate nationalists, such as Masaryk, sided with the Allies against the Austro-Hungarian empire of which the Czech lands were then a part. The emergence of a Czech national lobby was a key episode in the collapse of the empire, as detailed in Unit 18.

2   Unit 19 refers to two different bases of nationalism in the nineteenth century: 'reform' and 'revival', which between them can be used to explain the difference between the two examples. 'Reform' is evident in the first extract: the claim to independence is justified in terms of legal rights recognised within the empire. The second extract is less obvious, but talks about national (as opposed to individual) rights which are in opposition to imperial control; thus it falls into the 'revival' pattern.

CONCLUSION

Now look at the pile of books on your desk. I hope that you feel more able to use them than you were when you started this unit. With luck, you will also have further developed a set of routines and short-cuts that will help you to use the course material to improve your understanding. The study of history is an intellectual enterprise, but it is also a craft skill: knowing where to look next is something that improves with practice. Finally, I would like you to have another look at the maps in the Visual Sources Book, just to remind yourself of some of the many things that you now know about the worlds they represent.

REFERENCES

'Aden gripped again by impromptu strike. Party protest over lynchings' (1967) *The Times*, 3 March, p. 5.

Best, G. (1578) A true discourse of the late voyages of discoverie, for the finding of a passage to Cathaya, by the Northwest, under the conduct of Martin Frobisher ..., London, Henry Bynnyman.

Bonnerji, W.C. (1885) 'Opening speech of Mr W.C. Bonnerji, president' in *Proceedings of the First Indian National Congress*, Bombay.

Masaryk, T.G. (1916) 'The problem of small nations in the European crisis: inaugural lecture at the University of London, Kings College', London, Council for the Study of International Relations.

| UNIT 22 |
| EMPIRE IMPACTS |

Karl Hack

AIMS

- To encourage you to think analytically about the past impact of empires.
- To help you begin to think analytically about their continuing impact.

INTRODUCTION

In Unit 21, we got you to use the course materials to tackle specific problems: from mundane questions (such as 'Who was Lord Linlithgow?'), to more challenging tasks (such as integrating the course with further secondary reading). In this unit, you will ask one last question: one that goes to the very core of this course.

That question is: 'So what'? Or, to put it a little less tersely: 'What difference did empire make?' If you find this question mind-boggling you are not alone: so do I. But fear not. First of all, recall Unit 2. There we developed models and typologies for empires and colonies. We knew none would be perfect, but that nevertheless they might provide heuristic or learning devices, and useable tools for analysis. Our aim here is much the same – to test a number of interpretations and ideas that will help you to improve, though never perfect, your understanding of the impact of empires. Besides which, you have in fact been gathering material relevant to this question as you completed earlier units, even if this was not always obvious at the time. So, my first job is to help you realise how much you already know about this topic.

At one extreme, you have gathered evidence for the impact of empire on the big events and patterns in global history. In the 'Introduction to the course' in the Course Guide, for instance, we quoted empire historian John Darwin's claim that, 'empire (where different communities fall under a common ruler) has been *the default mode of political organization throughout most of history* ... The history of the world, it is tempting to say, is an imperial history, a history of empires' (Darwin, 2007, pp. 23, 491 – the words we originally quoted are italicised).

You might entertain some scepticism about an imperial historian telling you that empire is the predominant force in history. But what Darwin is really getting at is the role of empires in forming the modern world. For him, any explanation of how the globalised world of today was formed must have at its heart an understanding of the role of imperialism, especially in the period after 1750. It was in the latter period, he claims, that maritime empires finally overtook the power of Eurasian land empires such as Russia (Unit 7) and China (Unit 11). Block 3 showed how this led to the most powerful maritime empire (Britain) forcing the most populous land empire (China) to open up to world trade in stages from 1842 (Introduction and Unit 11). Unit 9 analysed how Britain tried to expand world trade more generally, in its nineteenth century 'imperialism of free trade'. As you will see below, some have argued that Britain's 'free trade' imperialism played a preeminent role in accelerating globalisation, and so in laying the foundations for the contemporary world.

At the other extreme, you have also seen evidence of empire's impact on the everyday lives of millions of ordinary people. Block 4 demonstrated this for categories as contrasting as slaves and European emigrants, and in areas of life as divergent as land use and sexual practice. But Unit 16 on Kenya also hinted at how these influences continue beyond independence, into 'postcolonial' periods (Unit 16, pp. 328–41, for instance, on changes of land ownership and use). In some cases it is difficult to imagine particular peoples, and territories, existing in anything like their present form without their imperial past. One surprising legacy of the French empire, for instance, is that the European Union's most distant citizens live thousands of miles from Strasbourg and Brussels: in South America, the Caribbean, and the Indian Ocean. They are the inhabitants of France's four overseas departments: French Guinea (South America), Guadeloupe (Caribbean), Martinique (Caribbean) and Réunion (Indian Ocean). Despite their location, they are integral parts of France, and so of the European Union. Thus the descendants of slaves living on the Caribbean island of Martinique carry euros in their pockets, speak French, and vote in French elections. In common with many other postcolonial territories, the population mix of these departments is also specifically imperial in origin. The French citizens of Réunion, for instance, include the descendants of Europeans, Indians, Chinese and others, with mixing among these groups having also produced a local Creole tongue (see Figure 22.1).[31] Indeed, prior to French colonisation, Réunion seems to have been uninhabited. In this case, then, empire did not so much impact on a population and culture, as constitute them.

Empire created many other mixed populations: in some places these were different communities living alongside one another, but with little mixing (plural societies); elsewhere they were people of different origins who mingled and intermixed. Sometimes the results have been relatively peaceful, but in many other cases the long-term impact has been more pernicious. Whether Catholics and descendants of Protestant settlers in Northern Ireland, aboriginal people and white settlers in Australia, or Maasai and Gikuyu eyeing long-lost lands in Kenya (Unit 16), millions of individuals' lives were shaped by imperialism, or are lived now in contexts shaped by its legacies.

Thus empire constituted, and continues to constitute, the contexts in which people played out their lives across the globe. It did this not just in economic and demographic terms, but often in matters of faith, language and law as well. Unit 1, you may recall, mapped the changing face of empire across centuries. It could equally well have included maps showing which religions or languages predominated across the world in different eras, or which countries' law codes imprinted on which colonies and ex-colonies. Such maps would

EMA

---

[31] Creole is usually a blend of two or more languages, in this case French with elements of Hindi, Chinese and others.

Figure 22.1   Woman reading a local newspaper, *Le Quotidien*, Reunion Island, twentieth century. Unknown photographer. Photo: © Hemis/Alamy.

show the far-reaching conquests of French, English, Spanish, Portuguese and Russian languages, and of Islam, Catholicism, Protestantism and other faiths. Though both religion and language have spread by peaceful methods as well, and though local languages have often fought back after independence, the legacy here is manifest. In this sense we can think of 1492 not just as the year that Spanish language and Catholicism launched itself across the Atlantic, but also as the year in which these twin cultural forces finally finished off the Muslim-speaking, Islamic kingdom of Granada on the Iberian peninsula. Finally, we might note the way in which the transplanted cultural forms could outlast, and upscale, their metropolitan roots. Hence there are far more Portuguese speakers today outside Portugal (notably in Brazil) than inside, and attempts to give substance to a Lusophone world (for instance with increased educational links) draw strength as much from outside Portugal as from inside.

Empire and its legacies thus represent an important constituting force in history at various levels: at the macro-scale; at the micro-scale of individual experience; and at the level of cultural forms and communities. This vast range of imperialism makes our task in this unit more than a little challenging. How can you assess impact when a phenomenon is so vast in scope? But that is not the worst of it. Imperialism is also a highly emotive topic. For many there is something of the night about empire, as expressed in mariner Joseph Conrad's novel *Heart of Darkness*. As his main character Marlow puts it, 'The conquest of the earth, which mostly means the taking away of it from those who have a different complexion or slightly flatter noses than ourselves, is not a pretty thing when you look into it too much' (Conrad, 1983, pp. 31–2).

Indeed not. For some, empires should be seen mainly as spreading death, destroying or sapping local cultures, appropriating indigenous people's lands, shackling minds and bodies, humiliating subjects, exploiting other people's labour and resources, hardening racism, and employing 'divide and rule' tactics in ways that left deeply fissured societies dotted all around the globe. You will no doubt remember, in this connection, Unit 4's description of a 'holocaust' of American indigenous peoples in the face of the sixteenth-century Spanish onslaught and disease.[32] You should also recall Unit 12's description of the horrors of plantation slavery in the eighteenth-century Caribbean. The willingness to treat humans as chattel goods, who could be worked like machines under constant threat of whipping, and to separate slave families, leaves an indelible stain on European imperialism of the eighteenth to mid-nineteenth centuries. Nor did the receding tide of slavery – with Britain banning the slave trade in 1807 and slavery itself effective from 1834 – end the combination of coercion and exploitation. Trocki has shown how easily Britain went from being a slave-dealing to a drug-dealing empire (Trocki, 1999).[33] Quite apart from the 1839–42 Opium War with China, vast amounts of opium were grown in Bengal, and opium revenues of one sort or another helped to underpin both British trade in the east, and revenues in India and satellite settlements such as Singapore (see Unit 2, p. 47; Block 3 Introduction, pp. 9, 11–13; Unit 11, pp. 145–7; and Unit 15, p. 287).

As if this was not enough, European land grabbing was growing apace even as slavery ended. Australian historian David Day has shown how 'supplanting societies' of British settlers were by the early nineteenth century already hard at work dispossessing Australian aboriginals. The concept employed to justify this taking of land, *terra nullius* (Unit 2, p. 44), had already been applied against other peoples and places. Where *terra nullius* was too big a fiction to

---

[32] As ever, however, we do need to be cautious in what we ascribe to 'imperialism' in itself. Unless the Americas had never been discovered, pandemics of European diseases were almost inevitable there after any first contact, whether warlike or peaceable.

[33] Sales of Bengal-grown opium to China played a major part in financing Britain's eastern purchases. The sale or licensing of opium for long played a crucial role in the finances of India, and of other colonies such as the Straits Settlement of Singapore, Penang and Malacca.

maintain, those to be dispossessed could be classed as 'savages', as uncivilised when measured against any one of many of the conquering state's standards of civility: in housing, dress, religion or manners (Day, 2008b, pp. 69–91). Alternatively, treaties and agreements could be undermined or evaded, and lands guaranteed nibbled away over time. This last process you saw in Unit 13 on New Zealand, where the Treaty of Waitangi (1840) proved only a partial shield for Maori land.

[handwritten margin note: EMA "land grabbing"]

A black book of imperialism's sins would thus cover many volumes. But emotion and moral judgement are not the preserves of empire critics alone. Empire's defenders can be equally determined to prove empire was 'a good thing', and many of its administrators earnest in their desire to protect and improve the lives of those they served. Empires have been defended as having expanded trade and exported the rule of law, and for laying the foundation stones of globalisation. That is even if we put aside older claims of bringing civilisation and Christianity. Hence empire forged the modern United States of America and Australia as dynamic economies with democratic freedoms, even as the land was, in large part, stolen or cheated away from their indigenous inhabitants, and even as American blacks and Australian aborigines were denied full civil rights until the 1960s.

What sorts of questions, and models, can help us analyse the impact of empire, when it encompasses so much of world and individual history, and of pride and disgust? Obviously, in terms of content we can only hope to dip into the pot here and there to illustrate trends. So it is best, I think, not even to pretend we will get any sort of representative coverage. Instead, I am going to concentrate on developing a few major themes and some useful questions for you to ask when you come across such issues in your own reading. These themes will include the impact of empire at the global, empire-wide and territory levels. Though much of the discussion will focus on the impact of empires at the time, there will also be references throughout to the legacy empires left for the post-1975 period, and for the world of today. I will also discuss this as a theme in its own right in the very last section of the unit.

I now want to begin with one of the biggest questions, and certainly the biggest scale, of all: how far did empire lay the foundations for the modern, globalised world?

GLOBAL IMPACT

At the beginning of the eighteenth century, the standard of living in Asia and Europe was not dissimilar, and the two were not technologically far apart either. Two hundred years later, the wealth, technological and health gaps between the two were immense. Why? Our first exercise will explore the idea that the reason was imperialism itself.

Read the extract from Bernard Waites's 'Europe and the Third World' (Secondary Source 22.1) and answer the following questions. All you want from this is a sense of how empire supposedly had macro impacts on European and non-European, regions. So don't fret over details. In each case, restrict your answer to one to two paragraphs.

1   In what ways does this extract suggest Europe gained by imperialism? Exclude from this particular answer any reference to Wallerstein's theory of a world economic system.

2   Explain what Wallerstein means by a 'world economic system' (pp. 2–3). How does Wallerstein argue that core areas under-developed 'peripheries'?

3   What are Waites's main arguments against imperialism being crucial to western industrialisation?

1   Obvious material gains included control of an 'unparalleled share of the earth's biological resources', including fisheries, subtropical lands, forests, prairies and granaries. It also included a more varied diet, additional bullion and cheap cotton. For Marx, mercantilism – the system of each European power trying to monopolise key flows of goods – also led both to bigger export markets and to 'primitive capital accumulation' of finance. That is, both expropriation and the monopoly profits of chartered companies provided unique sources of concentrated capital. This accumulation of extra capital (crudely put, profits) supposedly fuelled Britain's and the west's early industrialisation. In sum, colonies paid for Europe to develop its industrial and technological lead.

[handwritten: @MA]

2   Wallerstein sees primitive capitalist accumulation as a necessary condition for western industrialisation. But he adds to this by arguing that Europe itself then formed a 'world economic system', with a core, periphery and semi-periphery. Each zone was characterised by its form of labour, namely: free in the core, bonded or share-cropping in the semi-periphery, and slave in the periphery. Earlier industrialisation and specialisation allowed western Europe to focus on higher-value-added goods provided by free labour, supplied with grains, bullion, cotton and sugar from areas using sharecropping and slavery. Crucially, he argues 'core' areas were then able to impose terms of trade favourable to themselves, so appropriating most surplus value. In short, territories in the periphery were locked into their poorer, inferior status within this particular world economic system. They became permanently 'underdeveloped'.

[handwritten margin note: Counter-argument! if not profitable at all why carry on? = see book on money. Gold & silver went in time.]

3   Waites first of all mentions the Spanish problem. The country that benefited earliest and most from New World gold and silver – Spain – suffered from relative stagnation of its industry and economy. Portugal fared little better. It seems that exploiting other people did not guarantee a good ending for your own economy. Secondly, he questions how significant to the west colonial trade and capital really were. Hence total external trade was only about 10 per cent of economic activity for Britain and the Netherlands in the eighteenth century, probably less before. Of this, most trade went to other states in the core. Hence, 'The conclusion seems inescapable that as long as oceanic trade remained as a tiny proportion of total economic activity it could not propel Europe towards an industrial society' (p. 4). Individuals, companies and even whole towns may have benefited, but no structural impact is suggested.

Waites thus adopts a fairly sceptical prognosis on the impact of empire on Europe. On the one hand, 'contact with western Europe promoted underdevelopment in southern America, Asia and Africa' (p. 4). On the other hand, he thinks this enriched only discrete entities, such as particular companies, or towns such as Bordeaux and Bristol, rather than altering Europe's economy in a structural sense.[34]

We will return to the idea of 'underdevelopment', or at least impoverishment of certain groups, later on when we look at impacts on empire-wide and territorial scales. Meanwhile, I hope this first reading has given you at least a flavour of the sorts of debates that raged from the late 1960s to 1980s, both about whether imperialism was a necessary condition for western industrialisation, and about whether this also relied on the 'underdevelopment' of the non-western world.[35]

These debates generated a huge amount of interest at the time. This was partly because non-western countries appeared to have slow or negative growth after the first decade or so of independence. This was the opposite of what nationalists and many others had expected, and led people to ask whether imperialism had somehow continued sucking wealth out of these countries 'from beyond the grave'. Had it, perhaps, all along exploited by indirect rather than direct means? The device of a 'world economic system' allowed proponents to continue blaming the 'core' for 'underdeveloping' the periphery even after colonies had achieved independence. They could, of course, have come up with rather simpler explanations, such as the overdependence of many ex-colonies on a narrow range of commodity export crops, making their economies extremely sensitive to commodity price fluctuations.

By 1993, however, when the extract you used above was published, the conditions that framed these debates had already undergone dramatic change. While some post-independence states had indeed remained underdeveloped, other supposedly 'peripheral' areas had already enjoyed years of sustained, rapid economic development. A combination of improved local governance and foreign direct investment (that is, companies building factories abroad) was boosting many 'developing world' economies. Hence Japan's ex-colony Korea was quickly developing, as were select ex-British colonies such as Malaysia. Soon India as well as China would be enjoying surging growth, and gradually moving up the value-added chain in terms of its range of manufactures. To some academics it now began to seem that, far from the 'world economic system' being the problem, it was the solution. The more you combined effective governance with embracing the free market and foreign investment, the more you seemed to prosper.

EMA —

One such academic proposed a much more positive assessment of the global impact of empire. This was Niall Ferguson. Ferguson was, and remains at heart, an economic rather than an empire historian. For him, empire can be defined as an organisation for extracting goods or services people would not

---

[34] Unit 2 also discusses Lenin's and Hobson's arguments for a structural relationship between Europe and their colonies; see pp. 64–5.

[35] If you also studied A200 *Exploring history*, you may remember a similar debate over the impact of slavery on industrialisation, especially over whether it was a significant catalyst and accelerator of British industrialisation.

[handwritten: EMA]

offer voluntarily in a free market, or would not offer at the discount enforced. This might mean, for instance, that empire forced them to hand over their land, or to agree to live peaceably when they preferred war, or to agree to reduce trade barriers or tariffs, as China did in 1842.

Ferguson has taught history at Oxford and Harvard, and the book we take his argument from below, *Empire: How Britain Made the Modern World* (2003) is both accessible and thought provoking. It is also refreshingly open in outlining how his own Scottish family had 'a good empire', including a few years of his own childhood in 1960s Kenya (Ferguson, 2003, p. xiii-xvi). He confesses that he read the imperial adventure novels of H. Rider Haggard uncritically, and took it as a matter of fact that Glasgow was the 'second city' of the British empire (Ferguson, 2003, p. xvi). Now, what is his claim for Britain?

EXERCISE

Read the extract from Ferguson's *Empire: How Britain Made the Modern World* (Secondary Source 22.2) and answer the following questions. Read as far as the paragraph beginning 'The difficulty with the achievements of empire' on p. 2 to answer question 1, and then finish reading the article to answer question 2.

1   How, according to Ferguson, did the British empire above all others promote globalisation?

2   What, according to Ferguson, was the specifically British legacy of empire?

SPECIMEN ANSWER

1   The British empire above all other forces helped to impose the conditions necessary for globalisation, even where others were reluctant to accept these. It 'acted as an agency for imposing free markets, the rule of law, investor protection and relatively incorrupt government on roughly a quarter of the world' and encouraged those things in still more countries by 'the imperialism of free trade' (p. 1). Ferguson sees globalisation primarily as being about the free movement of commodities, finance and people, and argues that 'no organization in history has done more to promote the free movement of goods, capital and labour than the British Empire in the nineteenth and early twentieth centuries', as well as 'to impose Western norms of law, order and governance around the world' (p. 2). In short, the British empire helped impose both the free flows that compose globalisation, and the institutions and practices that sustain them. His suggestion is that no other power of the time was likely to have done these things to the same extent.

2   Ferguson offers us both a list of attributes and an underlying dynamic that he finds distinctively British. The nine-fold list comprises the English language, forms of land tenure, Scottish and English banking, common law, Protestantism, team sports, a limited state, representative assemblies, and the idea of the liberty. The ninth and last of these, 'the idea of liberty', is according to him the most fundamental, present as critique even when the empire was at its most authoritarian, and giving it 'something of a self-liquidating character' (p. 3). He suggests this essentially British legacy by invoking counterfactuals, for instance a Delhi where the Mughals had triumphed in the Indian Mutiny-Rebellion of 1857–58, or a dilapidated latter-day Dutch settlement.

[handwritten: 'idea of liberty'? didn't America take that? We didn't give it to them]

DISCUSSION

Ferguson does not deny that empire was guilty of massacres, racism and more, but his attitude seems to be that these things happen in all systems but that the greater good of globalisation (or 'Anglobalization' as he calls it) makes the excesses pale beside them. It is an argument that says 'it hurt, but ultimately did good'. Above all, he is arguing that major empires, such as Rome, nineteenth-century Britain and, he hopes, twenty-first-century America, provide public goods for colonies and internationally.

This idea of 'public goods' is worth taking further. You may remember that Unit 9 ended by quoting Patrick K. O'Brien on the type of 'public goods' people have claimed a 'hegemon' might provide. To refresh your memory, here is O'Brien's summary of how other historians have seen the nature, and role, of hegemons:

> Under a hegemonic system, one paramount state supposedly maintains a semblance of order and uses power and persuasion to impose flexibly enforced rules upon an otherwise potentially anarchic system of international relations, and all other nations benefit. The 'public goods' conferred, maintained and defended by hegemons include peace, access to all international waterways and air spaces, laws and institutions for the protection of property rights, the enforcement of contractual agreements that transcend national legal systems, an open and predictable regime for foreign trade, an international monetary system to minimise the risks and transaction costs of trade and investment across frontiers, institutions to mitigate fluctuations in the levels of global production and commerce, environmental protection and finally, rules to minimise governmental restraints on the movements of migrants, capital and information across frontiers.
>
> (O'Brien, 2002, p. 4, cited in Unit 9, pp. 78–9)

A 'hegemonic' power must have, to some degree at least, the will and ability to influence international behaviour and codes of conduct, in order to produce such international 'public goods'. It might be an empire in the sense of possessing colonies, or not, but it will certainly require a system of power for successfully projecting its influence on a global stage. In addition, an empire may be a hegemonic power if it possesses the resources and will, but could equally fall far short of that level of influence.

So we have overlapping categories, namely: hegemon and empire. For hegemony, O'Brien remains sceptical about how far Britain, as opposed to the modern USA, really was hegemonic, in the sense of being willing and able to set its rules on the international system. But I am not really interested here in whether Britain or the USA were, or can be, hegemonic. What interests me is the use of the concept of 'public goods' in relation to empires and hegemons (Maier, 2006, pp. 36, 65).

Hence Ferguson is anxious to argue both that Britain did achieve some sort of hegemonic role in the nineteenth century (providing public goods at an international level), and that it also provided public goods in its individual colonies, such as the rule of law. He is anxious that the USA should accept both a hegemonic role to protect international trade and order, and also a more specifically imperial role of sustained occupation of certain overseas territories. When he wrote *Colossus: The Rise and Fall of the American Empire* (Ferguson, 2004), he was worried that the USA's determination to be seen as anti-imperial would prevent it accepting such prolonged occupation, for fear of being accused of having 'colonies'. Yet for Ferguson, actual imperial occupation is sometimes required for sustained periods if new institutions and 'public goods', such as the rule of law, are to be entrenched.[36] In short, he suggests that imperialism can deliver very important public goods at international and colony levels.

So, is Ferguson's argument credible in the above terms? His conclusions can be boiled down to two main points: that Anglobalization provided global-level 'public goods' (answer 1 above); and that it also provided 'public goods' to its individual colonies, such as common law, land tenure forms and 'the idea of liberty' (answer 2 above).

The international part of the argument works best if we restrict our vision to the last 100 years or so of the British empire, omitting the years when Britain was the world's greatest supplier first of slaves, and later of Bengal-farmed opium. But it would not work very well for earlier periods. Hence the British empire of the fifteenth to eighteenth centuries, for instance, was anything but free trade. It was mercantilist, based first and foremost on the sort of unfree labour (bonded, indentured, slave) that Wallerstein identified with peripheries, and tended towards large-scale dispossession of indigenous peoples.

Nor did most of the other empires this course has covered perform such a benign hegemonic role internationally. There was a major free-trade period from the 1820s to the 1870s, at the end of which most European countries had tariffs of 10–20 per cent. But by the 1880s tariffs were rising both in European countries and in Britain's dominions. Unit 9 shows that 'By 1913, the trend towards free trade had been reversed' (Unit 9, p. 53, and also Table 9.2).

Ferguson's argument for global-scale 'public goods', therefore, are most plausible for the nineteenth-century British empire. Even then, they only began to become relevant after 1819, by when slave trading had been banned, and Singapore had just been established as a trailblazing free-trade port; and they were already of diminishing significance by the 1880s.

It is also debatable whether any empire, even the British, was ever strong enough to be truly 'hegemonic' in our period of 1492–1975 (see also Unit 2, pp. 70 and 74–6). Britain's influence over, say, the trade policies of European powers and the USA remained limited even at its mid nineteenth-century peak. Nevertheless, Ferguson clearly does make a case for Britain championing more and freer world trade and markets for a time, and with some successes.

Ferguson's argument that the British empire provided a nine-fold list of 'public goods' for its colonies is also worthy of debate. It is certainly true that the British empire spread the English language, and some legal and other

---

[36] See Unit 2, p. 75, on hegemony. Ferguson's argument (Ferguson, 2003) is that 'empire' also encompasses the use of a world system of power to control others, and the 'imperialism of free trade', even if formal colonies are lacking.

institutional forms. However, there is plenty of room for debate about how far this should be seen as conferring benefits. As we shall see below, European-style land tenure and taxation systems were often applied in ways that had ambivalent, and sometimes disastrous, results for local peasants. Peasants faced with rigid tax demands from European colonial states, combined with the withdrawal of social obligations on superiors (such as emergency rations in times of scarcity) might face severe crises when crops were poor. To demonstrate that the introduction of western-style land tenure and laws was a 'public good' we would need more than mere evidence that they were introduced. We would also need evidence that empire introduced these reforms more efficiently than other forms of government.

Other benefits, such, as 'team sports' and particular languages, could be spread without empire, and anyway could have negative as well as positive impacts. What limited educational spending there was in colonies, for instance, was often heavily skewed towards subsidising the metropolitan language. This left colonies such as India and the Netherlands East Indies (Indonesia) with a small minority educated to high standards in the metropolitan language, but a majority not literate in any language at all at independence.

Other supposed empire legacies also turn out to be more ambivalent than we might at first expect. For instance, take the idea of a limited state and of 'liberty'. Even where nascent postcolonial democracies did not break down, elections might come to be dominated by elites who offered benefits to particular ethnic groupings in return for votes. Just replicating a formal structure did not mean you replicated the way it operated. Foreign, empire-imposed institutions might be reshaped by local cultures and needs. In short, there certainly is a case to be made that empires can provide public goods within their borders – such as better communications, and free movement of people and goods, and unifying institutions and language. But a cost–benefit analysis of 'public goods' versus 'public bads' would be difficult, if not impossible, to compute in any meaningful way.

Counter examples

One of Ferguson's methods of showing that empire provided public goods is to employ counterfactuals. For instance, he suggests that without British imperialism there would have been no Calcutta (though no doubt there would have been other entrepots under Indian control in its stead). Let's employ the same method in reverse by looking at some comparisons. What happens when a country does not become part of an empire? Do these counter examples suggest that imperialism was a necessary cause of modernisation, and a more efficient route to that end?

Thailand (Siam)

Thailand opened up to increasing trade with the west from the 1850s. Its Chakri dynasty encouraged western-style education for the elite, reformed the law and army, made territorial concessions, and so preserved independence and built up strong exports in rice, and to a lesser extent tin. It modernised itself – accepting foreign advisers – while retaining control of its politics and economy. A 1932 coup led to it becoming a constitutional monarchy, after which it oscillated between civilian and military rule.

Japan

Japan was persuaded to open to western trade by US warships in the 1850s. From the 1870s it began a determined self-modernisation. Like Thailand, foreign advisers were employed for the army, navy, railways and in other areas. As a result, in 1894–95 Japan was able to defeat China and take Formosa (Taiwan) as a colony; it followed this by defeating Russia in 1904–05, and supplanting Russia's influence in Manchuria. Japan was then able to build its own empire, and to inflict ignominious defeat on British and Dutch forces in southeast Asia in 1941–42. By that stage, Japan's torpedo aircraft, large naval guns and naval aircraft were all superior to British models, and its cotton goods and cheap manufactures (cotton undergarments, bicycles, toys, etc.) were successfully competing with British goods in Asian markets.

Abyssinia (Ethiopia)

The Abyssinian story is much less successful. Though it defeated Italian forces at Adowa in 1896, the country failed to modernise in any significant way before Italian occupation in 1936–41, and showed signs of severe state failure in the face of droughts.

Egypt

Other countries, such as Egypt, ran into trouble through misjudging their modernisation, including in this case the Suez Canal and expanded irrigation. Egypt's semi-autonomous rulers ran up debts that resulted in Europeans demanding financial supervision. That supervision in turn helped to provoke an internal backlash, and the British intervention of 1882. Egypt, though notionally still part of the Ottoman empire, then came under effective British supervision. It was made a British protectorate in 1914.

Political legacies

As Ferguson raises 'the idea of liberty', it is worth briefly examining this area. Abernethy (2000, pp. 367–9) analyses the post-independence politics of ex-colonies of European powers. He ranks them on a scale of freedom from 1 to 7. A ranking of 1 implies regular, free elections, while 5 to 7 implies a lack of effective mechanisms for elections, with less freedom the higher the number. A 6 or 7 suggests a one-party state or despotism. He argues that the chances of successful post-independence democracy are influenced by how far colony-wide representative institutions had been in place, and functioning effectively, before independence. Their presence did not guarantee postcolonial democracy, but their absence all but ruled it out. Table 22.1 is my adaptation of a chart Abernethy uses to show how these countries fared.

Table 22.1

Former metropole	No. of ex-colonies ranked	Rankings					
		1–2		3–4		5–7	
		No.	%	No.	%	No.	%
Britain	53	22	42	7	13	24	45
France	25	0	0	5	20	20	80
Portugal	5	0	0	0	0	5	100
Belgium	3	0	0	0	0	3	100
Holland	2	0	0	0	0	2	100
Italy	2	0	0	0	0	2	100
Spain	1	0	0	0	0	1	100

(Source: adapted from Abernethy, 2000, p. 368, in turn compiled from Gastil,1980, Tables 1, 3, pp. 14–18)

You should bear in mind that that Table 20.1 represents a snapshot. Some ex-colonies have been more democratic at previous periods, or have become more democratic since 2000. For instance, as of 2007 the Portuguese ex-colony of Timor Leste should probably be a 3–4. Nevertheless, the broad trends seem robust.

Hence the British empire, however belatedly, did extend representative assemblies to most colonies, and a majority of its ex-colonies are shown in ranks 1–4. The French empire had a midway position. The majority of its colonial subjects could not vote, but those who were assimilated were able to vote in elections and send representatives to France. French ex-colonies include one-fifth in the range of moderate democracy, that is 3–4. Abernethy argues, in contrast, that the empires characterised by more authoritarian rule produced ex-colonies overwhelmingly in the 5–7 range.

I have some reservations about such broad generalisations of what are very nuanced differences in democratic conditions. However, even where I would contest the classification of some ex-colonies, it does not necessarily weaken Abernethy's case. For instance, I would argue that the ex-Dutch colony that is now Indonesia was democratic before 1959 and after 1999. But then, as Unit 19, p. 82 noted, the Dutch introduced representative institutions into what is now Indonesia from 1917, albeit at first with a very limited franchise and powers, and severe restrictions on nationalist parties.

The broad trend Abernethy identifies is thus not inconsistent with Ferguson's claim for the British empire. It does seem – loosely speaking – that the more the 'idea of liberty' was rendered concrete in pre-independence territories, the greater their chance of having more democracy after independence.

Ferguson, however, had much more in mind than merely praising empire past. He also wanted to call forth empire present. He was calling the USA to 'take up the white man's burden' (as Kipling called it) after the '9/11' attacks on the World Trade Center's twin towers in New York. He wanted the USA to drop its squeamishness about being imperial. In and beyond his main book on American imperialism, *Colossus and Empire* (2004), he argued that the USA should not merely strike back against specific enemies, but accept prolonged imperial responsibility in so-called 'failed states', and in rogue states such as Afghanistan that might threaten international stability.

Hence Ferguson's *Colossus: The Price of America's Empire* (2004) audaciously recast the whole of American history as quintessentially that of empire, from settlement, through its own expansion westwards, to the use of its 'global system of power' after the end of the Cold War. You may recall that you have already read an extract of *Colossus* in Unit 9 (Secondary Source 9.5). In 1898, the USA had gone to war with Spain over the latter's rule in Puerto Rico and Cuba, and subsequently took its ex-colony in the Philippines for good measure. True, it took the latter from local Filipinos who had rebelled against the Spanish as well, but let's not lose sight of the main point. Like Ferguson, Rudyard Kipling dreamed of Anglo-Saxon leadership that might impose its brand of civility on the world, urging the Americans to:

> Take up the White Man's Burden –
> Send forth the best ye breed –
> Go bind your sons to exile
> To serve your captives' need;
> To wait in heavy harness
> On fluttered folks and wild –
> Your new caught sullen peoples,
> Half devil and half child

(cited in Wilson, 1977, p. 204)

So Ferguson's arguments make two cases: first, for Anglobalization laying the foundations of our modern, free-trade world (also discussed in Unit 9); secondly, for the need for a free-trade, democracy-supporting hegemon to possess, and use, a 'global system of power' to create and sustain public goods (see Figure 22.2 for western-style education as one such public good). Together, these assertions suggest that empire – especially western empires and within that the British and then American world systems of power – were the irreplaceable midwives at the birth of our modern, globalised world.

You may have noticed that Ferguson's arguments are directed almost as much at the present as the past. His mind is on Iraq and Afghanistan, 'failed' and 'rogue' states, and the need to extend good governance and free trade in the present and future. But to my mind we need to think about empire's role in putting down even deeper roots for globalisation. That is what the next exercise is designed to explore.

EXERCISE

Read John Darwin's definition of a globalised world given below. In what ways do you think the empires described in this course contributed to the historical growth of the factors mentioned in points 1, 2 and 4? Do not spend more than 20 minutes

Figure 22.2 Demonstration lesson in a German colonial school, Dar es Salaam, 1903. Unknown photographer. Photo: © ullstein bild/TopPhoto.

on this exercise and write just one or two paragraphs for your answer. The point is just to get you thinking about these links, rather than to be comprehensive.

> But we can, nonetheless, sketch the general features of the 'globalized world' – the stage which globalization has now reached – in a recognizable form. ...
>
> These features can be briefly summarized as follows:
>
> 1 the appearance of a single global market – not for all but for most widely used products, and also for the supply of capital, credit and financial services;
>
> 2 the intense interaction between states that may be geographically very distant but whose interests (even in the case of very small states) have become global, not regional;
>
> 3 the deep penetration of most cultures by globally organized media, whose commercial and cultural messages (especially through the language of 'brands') have become almost inseparable);
>
> 4 the huge scale of migrations and diasporas (forced and free), creating networks and connections ...;

5   the emergence from the wreck of the 'bipolar age' (1945–89) of a single 'hyperpower', whose economic and military strength, in relation to all other states, has had no parallel in modern world history;

6   the dramatic resurgence of China and India as manufacturing powers. In hugely increasing world output and shifting the balance of the world economy, the economic mobilization of their vast populations (1.3 billion and 1 billion respectively) has been likened to the opening of vast new lands in the nineteenth century.

(Darwin, 2007, pp. 7–8)

SPECIMEN ANSWER

The advent of a single global market might be thought of as something specifically nineteenth century, when British 'imperialism of free trade', and naval supremacy, helped open up new areas of the world. Likewise, intense interaction between distant states developed from that period with, for instance, regular steamship routes and telegraphs making information flow freely. The mere fact that empires covered so much of the world makes it more difficult, by this point, to unpick 'imperial' causes from more general developments.

The migrations and diasporas of today, however, are prefigured, and made possible by, much earlier developments. These stretch back to the fifteenth century – from the first trickle of Europeans and their livestock onwards. The subsequent flows included both free and bonded labour from Europe to the 'New Worlds' of the Americas and Australasia from the fifteenth to twentieth centuries, and of course the massive transplantation of millions of slaves in the seventeenth and eighteenth centuries, as well as flows of indentured and migrant labour. The latter included the massive movement of Chinese and Indians to British territories as far apart as British Guinea and Fiji. Of course, capital, goods and labour could flow without empire, but it is very noticeable that European maritime empire created flows over unprecedented distances, on unprecedented scales.

Despite the problem of disentangling imperial from more general world history, the question above does raise an important problem.[37] This is: how far did empire, specifically European maritime empire, build the deeper foundations of the modern, globalised world? After all, international trade was nothing new in 1492. Columbus set off in search of a direct ocean route to the Indies and its spices (and wrongly insisted he had found it) precisely because Europe already knew of eastern commodities. A second poem captures something of the changing nature of global connections. This being John Masefield's *Cargoes*, which was written around 1910. Masefield had been sent to sea in the 1890s, at a time when sailing ships were in retreat before increasingly efficient steam.

In three short stanzas he captures three technologies – oar, sail and steam – and three sets of empires – Assyrian, Iberian and British. But he also hints at three

---

[37] A good example of this problem is the nineteenth-century cable and telegraph system. Britain controlled much of it, but it passed through independent countries as well as colonies. How much did this have to do with Britain's empire, and its 'world system of power', as opposed to general developments in technology and finance?

types of world interconnections. The poem begins with a quinquireme (a vessel powered by oar with auxiliary sail, though whether or not five-banked boats ever existed or were even possible is questionable):

> Quinquireme of Nineveh from distant Ophir
> Rowing home to haven in sunny Palestine,
> With a cargo of ivory,
> And apes and peacocks,
> Sandalwood, cedarwood, and sweet white wine.
>
> Stately Spanish galleon coming from the Isthmus,
> Dipping through the Tropics by the palm-green shores,
> With a cargo of diamonds
> Emeralds, amethysts,
> Topazes, and cinnamon, and gold moidores.
>
> Dirty British coaster with a salt-caked smoke stack
> Butting through the Channel in the mad March days,
> With a cargo of Tyne coal,
> Road-rail, pig-lead,
> Firewood, iron-ware, and cheap tin trays.

(Masefield, 1966, p. 906)

The Assyrian imagery is taken from the Bible (1 Kings 10). Assyria's core, including the city of Nineveh, was inland, but by the seventh century BC its empire extended as far as Egypt, the Levant and Cyprus. The poem therefore suggests a metropolitan-owned ship ('Quinquireme of Nineveh') returning from the Indian Ocean port of 'Ophir'. Such a ship would have had to unload its Palestine-bound cargo at the northern extremity of the Red Sea, where it meets present day Egypt or Israel close to the mouth of the Suez Canal.

The poem thus conjures a world in which goods from Africa, India and China could sail to the Red Sea, and then be transported overland to the Mediterranean. These connections were very old indeed. But they created, in a sense, not so much a global economy, as separate economic zones loosely joined for the sake of transferring small quantities of luxuries. By comparison, the world of Spanish galleons, larger trading vessels, and Portuguese moidores (gold coins) is one where different continents are directly joined in a single ocean voyage. But though this world makes possible a new level of global connections it is, as we saw in Units 1, 2 and 9, one where each empire attempts through mercantilism to keep the most profitable flows going through a single European centre. It is also still a world where most products transported are high value and small volume.

Finally, however, there is something less romantic, grubbier at first sight, but inestimably more potent. The salt-caked steamer with its mass-produced, practical manufactures of rail and iron, manufactures that can further bind the world's hinterlands to the ports, and through them into one global set of exchanges. And, of course, 'cheap tin trays' – goods that could be sold to a mass market. Masefield depicts a grubby coaster in Channel waters to maximise the contrast to the exotic goods of the past, but similarly prosaic cargoes were by now being shipped worldwide. The important point is that the third stanza is supposed to evoke the dreary globalisation of tin cans, wheat, meat, and ordinary cotton cloth moving thousands of miles.

Now, a poem is, at best, something that combines insight into real events or processes into poetic form. I want to suggest that, in many ways, Masefield's poem does capture the essence of what post-1492 maritime empire had done, and done in contrast to earlier periods. The European maritime empires had played a critical role in preparing for a globalised world, albeit in distinct phases. From their first tentative steps in the Atlantic in the fifteenth century, the Europeans eventually constructed global empires, sometimes uniting countries in Asia, the Americas, Africa and Europe into a single economic and military system. Whether mercantilist or free trading, these imperial systems did help to bind the world. As a heuristic model (a model that aids learning, as described in Unit 2) I want to propose at least four distinct, major, waves of globalisation in which the western (Europe and the neo-Europes) states played a crucial role.

The first wave, seen in Block 2 'How do empires begin?' was around 1450–1600, when oceanic threads joined together the different continents, and high-value, small-volume goods such as gold, silver and spices – including Masefield's cinnamon – were traded. In this period, maritime empires were declared mercantilist, supposedly channelling goods from colony to metropole (for instance gold to Spain, pepper from Amboyna to Amsterdam) though in reality these systems were always vulnerable to piracy and privateering (see also Unit 5), and to smuggling. This phase saw the great companies, such as the English East India Company (EIC) and the Dutch East India Company (VOC) (evolutionary precursors of today's multinationals, but with cannon too, see Unit 6), and the seeding of the great extractive and plantation economies of the Americas and Caribbean. If you imagine a globalised world as a spider's web, this era provided the anchor threads going from each centre to its particular peripheries.

The second great phase of globalisation matured between 1750 and 1870, with the neo-Europes becoming populated enough to take off as significant economies in their own right, and some asserting autonomy or independence. Even if the greatest waves of European migration to the Americas still lay ahead, they were by this point significant demographically and economically. This phase also saw the expansion of a new type of global trade, with low-value, higher-volume goods traded globally, including grains, lower-value metals, timber and Masefield's iron and 'cheap tin trays'. The modern, global world is unimaginable without the imperialism of this process, and its nastier side. That is, the subordination or removal of indigenous populations from vast areas of American, South African and Australasian temperate zones completely changed their use, from extensive (for instance hunting and roving grazing) to intensive (for instance American and Canadian grain, and South African mining). Yes, these areas could have been incorporated into a global economy over time, just as enclosure had advanced production for the market over subsistence in Britain, but that might have been a painfully slow process. In reality, the epidemics, war and exploitation caused by explosive European penetration paved the way for these neo-Europes – as integrated parts of a wider European-led economy. We might add that Russia incorporated Siberia and much of its east in its own massive expansion (see Unit 7), albeit a land-based expansion, while the Qing empire reached its maximum extent in the middle of this period.

It is not so much that the excesses of empire were regrettable sideshows, so much as they were integral parts of its awesome power to reshape the world over a mere century or so. I am suggesting, in other words, something rather unpalatable for exponents of empires: that their creative and globalising force was inextricably linked to their nastier side. We will revisit this point later, when we talk of capitalism and famines. But we are getting ahead of ourselves. The main point here is that in this period, with the USA and neo-Europes joining Britain in seeking freer trade, the concentric circles of the web were filled in, developing multiple channels for the flow of people, goods and services.

If the first major wave of globalisation replaced separate but linked trading zones with integrated, global empires; and the second laid the foundations for neo-Europes as integral parts of a European-led world economy; the third (1870–1914) saw not only the accelerating march of the neo-Europes, but also the conquest of the tropics. This is the period in which quinine became effective in preventing malaria, and steam power allowed boats and rail to penetrate hitherto relatively untroubled interiors. We saw in Units 15 and 16, for instance, how the Mombasa to Uganda railway opened up the interior of east Africa in the 1890s, with settlers following hot on its heels. In 1850, much of Europeans' map of Africa and southeast Asia, and other tropical hinterlands, was still marked unknown or left blank. By 1914, these worlds were mostly divided up. Admittedly, they were also mostly found to be economically disappointing, but that is by the by. We can debate about the degree to which these regions gained, or lost, by being integrated into the world economy on European terms as well, but it is indisputable that for most that is what happened.

The fourth globalisation was after 1945, mainly after 1965, and only weakly linked to empires. It featured a new international division of labour – with companies moving production to cheaper locations, freedom of capital movement, and finally an explosion in the volume and availability of information.

Clearly, European maritime empires, and the neo-Europes they created, were deeply implicated in at least three of these phases of globalisation. But unpicking just how far empire – actual rule over other peoples – was necessary in each stage can still be tricky. For instance, take the nineteenth century, which lies at the epicentre of Ferguson's world of Anglobalization.

from
Colony
to
neo-Europe.

Still an
economic
model.

Even for the nineteenth century, the picture was far more complex than one empire – British or otherwise – pulling the levers. By the middle of the nineteenth century, the neo-Europes, for instance, were increasing in economic scope and size of population. Those neo-Europes in the Americas that had attained independence were committed to trading with whoever they wanted. In a sense, Britain's genius was to swim with the tide. Furthermore, the progress of globalisation was not linear. When depression stalked the world in the 1930s, the British empire response was to increase trade barriers against the rest of the world – this was done in the 1932 Ottawa agreements, which raised empire tariffs. British empire countries gave each other lower, preferential tariffs, so that in the 1930s the empire actually increased its share of Britain's overall trade. In the same decade, the main impact of other, newly rising European empires, German, Italian and Soviet, was to increase autarky (economic self-reliance) in their respective zones. Japan's response to these growing barriers, meanwhile, was to intensify its attempts to carve out a safe economic space for its exploitation and development in northern China. The peak and final flourish of the British empire came in this period of rising barriers and reduced world trade, with several empires being complicit in this process.

Rather than European or American imperialism, it was American military might, reluctantly called forth in 1941, which ultimately restored movement towards globalisation. It was the same American military might that prevented that movement succumbing to the communist model offered by the Soviet Union. You could present that as American 'imperialism' taking up the mantle of free-trade champion where a faded Britain had left off, but only if you really believed that the USA really was acting as an 'empire' at this point. Since Britain and other western European powers worked hard to encourage a renewed American commitment to western defence in the 1940s – a commitment that was at first in doubt – the 'imperial' label is questionable for this period at least.

We could have similar debates about how far empire benefited Europe. That Europeans, notably individuals and companies, took vast profits, is undeniable. That some metropolitan powers derived benefits in cash and kind is equally undeniable. For instance, the Dutch state extracted significant flows of income from the Netherlands Indies in the cultivation period of 1830–70, as discussed in Unit 9 (p. 76). But it is equally undeniable that empires carried costs as well as benefits: armies had to be paid for; capable and energetic individuals were sidetracked into being district officers in distant lands; markets skewed. Even in situations where the gain may appear dramatic, the economic impact of empire can turn out to be complex. Sixteenth- to seventeenth-century Spain, for instance, gorged itself on New World silver. This helped to boost the circulation of money in Europe, but we have already noted that Spain's own economy did not do well in the longer run. It suffered inflation, and by the eighteenth century lagged behind more dynamic, less 'fortunate' northern neighbours. Debates over how far empires gain from, or are vulnerable to being overstretched and undermined by, their colonies will undoubtedly continue (Kennedy, 1989).

Empire-level impacts

What I want to do now is to change the level at which we are assessing impact. I want you to come down from the rarefied heights of the global economy, and international 'public goods', and ask what difference it made which empire ruled. Yet again, you have already gathered relevant materials from earlier units. Specifically, Unit 9 included a section on 'The costs and benefits of empire: famine and India'. That section dealt with the first and last of the three large-scale famines that struck India (and many other areas of the world) in 1876–78, 1888–91 and 1896–1902. I will now summarise what you have already read and then suggest how these events might help you to think about empire-wide impacts.

Briefly, Unit 9 and Mike Davis's *Late Victorian Holocausts: El Niño Famines and the Making of the Third World* (2001) show that:

- free market or 'laissez-faire' ideology led to a desire to minimise intervention to alleviate starvation in imperial India, lest this damage markets. Hence rations for workers on emergency works were sometimes set at or even below minimum levels needed to sustain life adequately, despite there being enough food in India as a whole (Davis, 2001, pp. 9, 28–32).

- By contrast, in eighteenth-century Qing China there were 'ever normal granaries', anti-speculative regulations, tax reductions during shortages, and a commitment to provide for peasants in times of crises. It alleviated if not avoided mass starvation. Davis also claims that the Mughal empire avoided the excesses of mass starvation seen in British Ireland and India (Davis, 2001, pp. 280–5).

- Integration with the world market tended to lead to increases in export crops at the expense of subsistence crops. Combined with the effect of rigid revenue demands (in India sometimes based on estimates of an area's average yield) this made peasants more vulnerable to subsistence crises. Because of the decline in reserves, and of locally grown subsistence crops, drops in export crop prices could leave them unable to afford rising food prices, or plunge them into ever greater debt to buy food and pay taxes.

Unit 9 also noted linked debates and problems, for instance with Indian population growth scarcely more than 1 per cent a year for much of the late Raj period, and slow per capita economic growth.

Why did the British do badly at combating famine in Ireland from 1845 to 1848 (over a million dying after potato blight broke out, and more emigrating, as the country's population plunged from around 8 to 5 million) and late nineteenth-century India (see Figure 22.3)? Why, in contrast, was the eighteenth-century Qing empire able to mitigate shortages?

The British did gradually improve their famine performance, but nevertheless the dramatic early levels of failure demand explanation. These related, in part, to the core nature of the British empire: to its economic principles. The British

Figure 22.3   Indian famine victims, unattributed photograph in *L'Illustration*, 30 November 1901. Photo: Mary Evans Picture Library.

commitment to the free-market doctrines of Adam Smith, to balanced budgets and sound finance, and in some cases to the ideas of Malthus about potentially catastrophic population explosion, made them reluctant to give aid that interfered with the market, or which might support the increase of impoverished populations. Indeed, the 1877 Anti-Charitable Contributions Act in India specifically forbade donations that might impede the grain market there.

Hence the nature of the empire in charge, and even of its domestic politics and principles of economics and governance, mattered. In this case, British policy makers were projecting abroad key attitudes they held towards their own economy and their own poor. The aim was to ensure minimum interference with the market. Therefore, though help might be given to people who participated in government-provided work schemes, this should be rewarded at below the lowest market rates. So, despite improving railways, the introduction and refinement of famine codes, and an Indian empire of increasing power and wealth, the Indian government three times saw people die in their hundreds of thousands. While factors such as potato blight in 1840s Ireland and monsoon failure in India could not have been eradicated – at the peak some 3 million were claiming famine relief of some kind in Ireland alone – there can be little doubt that their effects could have been more significantly alleviated (Young, 1996). In some famine periods, Indian grain exports actually increased.[38]

The debate on how much of an impact British famine policies had at various periods continues. Increasingly, the emphasis is not on famine-relief policies alone, but on the way Britain's tax, market, land and other policies increased rural indebtedness and vulnerability. There is an emphasis on how rural communities were integrated into capitalist markets in a way that exacerbated vulnerability for specific groups by reducing their entitlements to assistance and access to subsistence resources, and by increasing their indebtedness. A combination of these factors could make specific groups very vulnerable to sudden increases in food prices. These changes created 'spaces for famine' (Young, 1996). But the point I am trying to make here is not really about famine itself. It is that we need to consider what difference it made which empire was in charge, in terms of its particular principles, its approaches to subject peoples, and even its particular financial strength at a particular moment in time.

Hence British laissez-faire policy was of much wider significance. It impacted on approaches to immigration (favouring large-scale immigration, even where this created plural societies), it balanced budgets (even where this restricted investment) and it deferred social expenditure in order to prioritise the development of infrastructure directly related to external trade and to control (such as railways, roads, telegraphs, ports).

The wider issue at stake here is this: for many areas, and much of history, the question was not so much whether a majority would be free – the reality was one or other empire or elite group was generally in control – but what sort of ideology, principles, system and attitudes the ruling elite would have. Hence the British empire system of the nineteenth century undoubtedly accelerated globalisation, by integrating many areas into the world economy to a new extent. But the same principles that drove it to negotiate agreements for more trade, and low tariffs, also contributed to people dying unnecessarily, and to the integration of peasantries into the world market in a way that might exacerbate the subsistence crises this process had a tendency to cause in other areas. Whether or not those subsistence crises were a temporary phase or, as Wallerstein suggests, a locking of 'Third World' peasantries into 'peripheral' and semi-peripheral roles in a world economy, is another question.

In short, the *type* of empire, including any underlying ideology and approaches to economics, liberty, politics, administration and minorities, and its assumed obligations (or lack of them) to defined social groups, could be critical in determining the fate of millions.

---

[38] By the nineteenth century, a much-deteriorated Qing empire was also becoming increasingly ineffective against natural calamity. But the reason for late Qing failure was not economic principle, but rather a combination of enlarged population combined with fiscal decline and the poor state of repair of the Grand Canal.

It is worth asking, at this point, whether the differences in types of empire highlighted in Unit 2 produces tendencies (not, note, hard and fast rules) in the impact of empires. In Unit 2 we suggested two different broad types of empire, and we have tried to give examples of both types in every block. The first type was the maritime, or in Motyl's terms (Unit 2, pp. 66–7) discontinuous, empire. The second type was the land, or continuous, empire. Hence, in Block 2 'How do empires begin?', we contrasted Russia with the maritime empires of England, Spain and Portugal; in Block 3 'How do empires work?', we compared China with Britain; and in Block 5 'Why do empires end?', Austria-Hungary was the counterpoint to British, French and Portuguese decolonisation.

The introduction to Block 3 explained that another way of putting this is that some states simply were empires, while others possessed empires. Hence the great land empires of Qing China, Romanov Russia, the Ottoman realm, and Habsburg Austria-Hungary were all empires in themselves, with monarchs ruling over multiple nationalities in or near their core territories. Britain, France and many of the other maritime powers, by contrast, tended to see monarch, assemblies and 'nation' at home as sharing a 'national' identity or culture, while ruling autocratically over large numbers of other, contrasting, peoples abroad. States could *be* empires. States could *possess* empires. All of which is well and good, but what was the significance (if any) of this distinction for the ruled?

One such crude generalisation, or tendency, might declare that many of the empires-in-themselves showed considerable periods of tolerance to local customs, religions and elites, or even demonstrated external rulers adopting local methods. Hence the Manchus of Unit 11 preserved the Confucian nature of China. Orthodox Christianity was able to flourish under Ottoman rule, as did Judaism.[39] Habsburg rule also sat lightly on its various national minorities for much of its existence, who were free to remain Muslim or Orthodox Christian, despite their rulers' Catholicism. Unit 18 showed how the 1867 *Ausgleich* (compromise) allowed for a dual monarchy over Austria and Hungary, with Hungary allowed increased autonomy within the imperial structure.

Such empires tended not to bring overwhelming changes to the demographic or economic structures of the areas they ruled. An initial conquest might be nasty, brutish even, but relatively short. Some land and wealth might be transferred to support the new imperial centre and its military and ruling elites. But things then tended to settle down. In some cases even the trauma of conquest was avoided or lessened when territories were acquired by marriage or treaty.

The key ideological underpinning for many of these empires was that of a dynasty ruling over a multinational empire of different peoples, some of whom might have a degree of local autonomy or control through their own elites and

---

[39] Tolerance did not mean equality of course. Non-Turks and Arabs could rise to the top in the Ottoman bureaucracy, but only if they converted to Islam.

assemblies. They might provide common legal codes and an elite lingua franca, and allow different nationalities and religions to coexist, and larger economic structures to be fostered. Above and beyond this, in theory at least, an empire would provide 'public goods' such as extra security against external attack and internal civil war alike.

These tendencies could, of course, be contradicted by countervailing forces. For instance, growing power and wealth could foster in the metropolitan population a growing sense of its own nationality and superiority, and even of its ability to force aspects of its own culture on others. Hence late nineteenth-century Russia indulged in campaigns of russification on its margins. Also, toleration and extension of protection to multiple communities did not necessarily imply equality. Take the disabilities imposed by the Ottomans on Christians. Nevertheless, the concept of an empire of nationalities and communities united by a sovereign did imply that multiple communities and their ways of life had a durable stake in empire, and claims upon it.

Some maritime empires have, by contrast, tended towards more of a crusading spirit, determined to export their home models of religion and manners, even if this meant attacking local beliefs and customs. The early Spanish expansion depicted in Unit 4, for instance, was informed by this sense of extending Christianity, albeit in an unholy cocktail of imperial motives that mixed God, Gold, Glory, and guns too.

It was the combined rise of nationalism (the idea that nations should rule their own destiny) and liberalism (the idea that political authority should derive from individuals giving their consent) that eroded the ideological underpinnings of the great land empires. From the French and American revolutions of the late eighteenth century onwards, these forces, albeit slowly at first, started the fracturing of Europe into ever smaller nation states. Thus the Ottoman empire lost Greece to independence between 1821 and 1832, and soon found its other Balkan provinces demanding more autonomy. Austria-Hungary, as we saw in Unit 18, struggled to contain the rising forces of nationalism in the first two decades of the nineteenth century.

Austria-Hungary in the end did not dissolve slowly, but ended almost instantly with defeat in 1918, and its following division into nation states. For land empires such as Austria-Hungary, decolonisation often came in a big bang, with the implosion or defeat in battle of the imperial state or dynasty. Hence for the Romanovs, Ottomans, Habsburgs, and Napoleonic France, the end came directly or indirectly from the strain of war and defeat. For the Romanovs and Manchus, it was also fuelled by political revolution at the centre. By contrast, maritime empires have usually been able to readjust relations with peripheral colonies without the destruction of their core polity. Britain in 1947–48 (when it lost the main source of its eastern manpower, India, as well as Ceylon, Burma and Palestine) is a good example of this. These losses caused scarcely more than a ripple in domestic politics, and decolonisation continued to unfold over two to three decades.

EMA
reason why empires ended.
= same reason for its success.
Economic.
Money.

and Algeria

Colony-level impacts and differences

We should not, however, be too quick to attribute differing impacts to the type of imperial system. While such differences may be important, the above generalisations suggest tendencies rather than rules. Another variable, at work within land and maritime empires, is difference at the colony level.

We have already noted, in Unit 2 and in the section above, that the type of colony may have a big influence on the type of impact. Fieldhouse, you should remember, gave the proportion of outside settlers pride of place in his classificatory scheme. Hence settler colonies, with an overwhelming number of settlers, tend to transform the economy and culture, and sometimes also the ecology, of the occupied space. They also tend towards either the removal or the marginalisation of indigenous peoples. Where land empires aimed at settlement, their impact was potentially just as devastating as was that of maritime empires. Take Nazi Germany's imperial ambitions of 1933–45, and its empire of 1939–45. Hitler aimed to settle much of conquered Poland, and probably parts of western Russia as well, with ethnic Germans. This was especially the case after war broke out with the Soviet Union in June 1941. That aim of settlement, and the conceptualisation of the war as partly a racial war, fuelled mass killings not only of Jews but also of Poles (Mazower, 2008). Wherever it manifests – in the USA, Australia, Israel, Ireland or Poland – such settler aims have terrible implications for prior occupiers. Even though the attitudes of the metropolitan states may have varied hugely, in each case the 'supplanting' drive of the settlers was a disaster for many if not most local people. The type of colony intended was a major, if not the major, determinant of outcomes as far as indigenous peoples were concerned.

Plantation colonies, meanwhile, have been scarcely less profound in their impact, but feature a much higher proportion of imported unfree or semi-free labour, whose suffering (especially that of slaves) may be added to the sum of imperial unhappiness. By contrast, occupation colonies, with a relatively thin layer of imperial administrators and of immigrants, are more likely in land empires, or for maritime empires attempting to rule large land masses (as in India). Here the impact is likely to be less structural, and the empire may even choose to rule indirectly through local elites for a time at least. This implies less ability to restructure, or even perhaps to manage efficiently, a colony.

But Fieldhouse's model does have one flaw when it comes to judging impact. It has little to say about the nature of the host society, and the host environment. This too could have a major shaping role on the nature of imperialism, and the impact of empire. Take, for instance, Unit 4 on the Spanish conquest of the Americas, and Unit 5 on English expansion in the Americas. These units showed how some societies had been relatively isolated before 'first contact', and consequently were ravaged by disease, paving the way for large-scale European settlement. Others societies, such as those in India and China, had long been connected to Eurasian disease pools through trading routes. These were not so severely affected by pathogens, and so continued to be as or more populous than Europe. They therefore remained demographically as well as environmentally unsuitable for significant settlement, and for becoming what Units 1 and 2 called 'neo-Europes'.

Indeed, tropical areas of Africa and Asia harboured illnesses such as malaria which – until quinine's successful development as a preventive medicine in the 1850s – made them white men's graveyards. Hence, as Units 15 and 16 have shown, white settlement in Africa was mainly restricted to limited highland, coastal and other areas where Europeans could enjoy quasi-temperate conditions, and develop safe grazing for cattle, sheep and other fauna they were familiar with. So, for instance, the ecological factors in east Africa helped to ensure that Kenya, as the area eventually became, remained an occupation colony with a settler enclave. Where there were exceptions, as in Europeans' penetration inland into southern Africa's climatically varied regions, they could generally be explained by exceptional wealth-creating opportunities, here presented by the region's gold, diamond and copper mines.

In addition to disease and environmental factors, the culture and religion of the target population also mattered greatly. Areas such as the Americas were quickly conquered by Christianity, but some religions offered much greater resistance. Islam, in particular, provided populations with cultural ballast that western imperialists could make little headway against, right across northern Africa, through the Middle East and India to modern-day Indonesia.

If religion was one critical cultural factor, another was military and bureaucratic organisation. Aztec and Inca military technology, which lacked familiarity with firearms, was quickly overwhelmed by small numbers of conquistadores and their local allies. Australian aboriginals, with rudimentary military skills, and divided into many different communities, stood little chance against settlers from 1788. By contrast, Maoris, who possessed a developed military culture and had already adopted firearms from early settlers, made formidable opponents when conflict blew up in New Zealand. This difference is strongly related to the different fate of their lands, with Australia declared *terra nullius* and the fertile land gradually transferred to settlers, while the 1840 Treaty of Waitangi preserved clearer Maori claims to land. Alternatively, geography or difficulty of access might facilitate resistance, even where groups were more loosely organised or less impressively militarised. So, as well as the type of imperialism and type of colony, the nature of the host environment and population, and the tools at its disposal (cultural, military, social, environmental), were vital ingredients in determining outcomes.

Legacy and continuity

The Maori story did not, of course, end abruptly in 1975, the date chosen for the ending of our course. For them, 'imperialism' and its legacies did not die at 'independence', and continued to be matters of debate at the time of writing. On the one hand, the non-Maori groups gradually integrated Maori names and identity into their mainstream history. On the other, Maori representatives campaigned for the return of some rights over land taken contrary to Waitangi and other treaties. The ongoing working out of these tensions is seen in the Museum of New Zealand Te Papa Tongarewa opened in 1998 in the capital, Wellington. You may remember from Unit 13 that early settlers had ambivalent views about Maori culture, which often turned negative when conflict over resources arose. Te Papa, as it is sometimes called, is anything but negative about Maori history (the course website contains a link to the museum web page). It defines its key tasks as to preserve and present the *taonga* (Maori for treasures) of New Zealand's peoples and to interpret the country's heritage for national and international audiences. It contains both Maori and *Pakeha* (western) artefacts, reconstructions and history.

The New Zealand museum's relaunch (it also contains more traditional collections from its predecessors) reflects the problem of how the interests, memories and aims of 'first peoples' can be addressed. This reminds us that our final content block – on why empires end – was not really dealing with an 'ending' of empires, or at least not with the end of their legacies. We tend to talk of settler colonies as being decolonised at the point they win independence from their parent country. Hence Unit 17 takes the 'end of empire' to be the creation of an independent United States of America. In Unit 19, I talked of Britain's white settler dominions being formally recognised as autonomous and equal states by the 1926 Balfour Declaration and 1931 Statute of Westminster.

But for 'first peoples' this was certainly not the case. Take another settler colony. Australia's aboriginal population by 2000 was about 280,000 out of a total Australian population of 19 million (Denoon et al., 2000, p. 369). As we noted above, they were less able than the Maori to impose costs on European land-grabbing, and as a result had been more radically dispossessed. Their land had been declared *terra nullius*, in effect legally vacant, in 1788. They remained marginalised until the 1960s. Indeed, from the 1940s to the 1960s the so-called 'white Australia' policy actually hardened. This policy allowed officials to test immigrants in any language they chose. So if an immigration official was presented with an English-speaking Asian, for instance, they could legally test them in French and reject them. Internally, it included an assumption that the aborigines were heading for extinction, segregation or absorption. For 'half-caste' aboriginal children of sufficiently promising hue – later dubbed 'the stolen generation' of over 100,000 children – this meant a policy of taking them from aboriginal parents and placing them with white foster parents.

Australia's individual colonies, which federated in 1901, had moved early on to grant wide franchises in elections, in some cases including women. By contrast, aboriginals' right to vote in Commonwealth elections regardless of state legislation was only confirmed in 1962, and by 1965 they could vote in elections in all states as well. A 1967 referendum then voted to give the central state more powers over aboriginal affairs, and equality legislation followed in 1975. But aboriginals only really gained some control over their own affairs when the Department of Aborigines was replaced by the Aboriginal and Torres Islander Commission in 1989. More significantly, land rights have been raised. A land rights act of 1975, and the so-called Mabo judgement of 1992, effectively overturned *terra nullius* first in reserves, and latterly where aboriginal groups could show that traditional use established common-law rights before land was taken from them (Day, 2008a). Since these judgements, there has been much debate about what precisely aboriginal land claims mean. For instance, do they imply the right to repossess certain lands, or demand compensation from businesses using them, or merely to use them for certain traditional purposes?

In terms of land, citizenship, compensation, apologies for past oppression, and the rewriting of history, 'decolonisation' – seen as the removal of colonial and, in this case, specifically settler oppression – thus came late to Australia. Indeed, it is an ongoing process, with divisive arguments, for instance, over whether frontier settlement constituted a brutal and even holocaust-style campaign against aborigines, or something still vaguely describable as honourable development. These 'postcolonial' issues remain important not only to the aboriginals, but to broader Australian identity.

Similar first peoples or indigenous peoples issues occur in countries such as Canada, and there are analogous land issues in places such as Kenya (Unit 16), where they are the subject of ongoing disputes (Beinart and Hughes, 2007).

Wider 'postcolonial' issues of identity afflict ex-imperial powers as well as ex-colonies, and individuals as well as societies. On the one hand, the loss of imperial power, and migration of people from colony to metropole, could challenge nationalist myths of supremacy and of monolithic 'national identity'. On the other hand, the western-propagated imperial propaganda of the 'civilising mission' had a life beyond decolonisation. The arguments for metropolitan societies possessing superior 'modernity', rationality and governance had been entrenched in 'discourses', textbooks and literature. We saw this in Units 3 and 10, which recorded, for instance, Frantz Fanon's journey from desiring assimilation to French culture, to arguing for violent decolonisation so as to free mind and body alike.

Such ideas have led to the growth, after independence, of schools of literary analysis aimed at uncovering western discourses about others, and at exploring how the colonised and post-independence writers have tackled related issues (Loomba, 1998; Said, 1978, 1993; see also Units 3 and 10). Such 'postcolonial' issues include themes of multiple identities (sometimes expressed as 'hybridity'), diaspora experiences, and even metropolitan societies coming to terms with the more multicultural legacy empire has brought home to roost.

I do not want to end, however, with the idea that everything is now 'postcolonial', and empire is ended. Far better, I think, to end with the more sobering message that empire – the art of conquering and ruling other, distinct peoples – is far from dead.

China's post-1911 history neatly demonstrates this continuing relevance of the 'imperial' mode of analysis. It retained, or in some cases regained (after the communist victory in 1949), 'imperial' control over an arc of territories stretching from Xizang (Tibet, reoccupied in 1950) in the west, through Muslim Xinjiang in the northwest, to Mongolia in its north: a vast area whose non-Han minorities nevertheless constitute just 8 per cent of China's overall population (Hack and Rettig, 2006, pp. 20–1). Indeed, you can almost imagine the Han majority areas as a tight core clustered in the east, and running along the coast and great inner waterways, but cupped by this vast, often mountainous, outer realm of minorities. China still bases its claim to rule these territories not mainly on the consent of the ruled, or natural affinity, but rather on the basis that historically China exercised some claim of sovereignty over these peoples, and that they are strategically important.

Such claims, now as in the past, have major implications for the incorporated areas. Just as the American west in the nineteenth century was overwhelmed by pressure of European penetration, so the Chinese west in the twentieth to twenty-first centuries has seen its original inhabitants and cultures facing pressure from Han economic, cultural, linguistic and bureaucratic 'penetration' and 'investment'. As with the old chestnut about one person's terrorist being another's freedom fighter, one person's investment and peaceable movement is another's cultural repression and loss of autonomy. Clearly, the imperial issue refuses to go away. On the one hand, Chinese investment has helped to integrate its peripheral areas into the world economy, providing links and infrastructure even when these probably make little initial economic sense. Just as it is difficult to imagine a Mombasa to Uganda railway being built in the 1890s without imperial motives (see Units 15 and 16), so it is difficult to imagine a commercial case for building a railway to Tibet over permafrost, as China did at the beginning of the twenty-first century (see Figure 22.4). Arguably, China was, from 1950, accelerating any economic 'modernisation' Tibet might have been expected to achieve unaided. On the other hand, such externally led development has usually come at the cost of lost autonomy, if not worse.

China could also claim that it had helped to end old 'feudal' practices there and elsewhere by bringing more 'modern' law, much as Ferguson has claimed Britain brought its style of law and the 'idea of liberty' to its colonies. In fact, the parallels between today and previous periods go further still. When accepting Hong Kong from Britain in 1997, and Macao from Portugal in 1999, China designated them as 'Special Administrative Regions' (SARs). This means that they are technically part of China and host Chinese troops, but they retain considerable autonomy in almost all aspects of internal policy. In creating such SARs, China has devised a system with echoes of the old European one of protectorates. This SAR model is not exactly the same, in that these SARs are claimed as an integral part of China, in contrast, say, to Oman, over which Britain claimed rights mostly to advise on foreign policy. Perhaps a closer parallel is that of the princely states of India in their relationship to

Figure 22.4   China to Tibet railway, near Lhasa, Tibet, 2006. Unknown photographer. Photo: © AP/PA Photos.

'British India'. Or perhaps these SARs are *sui generis*. Whatever analogy you favour, the SARs are certainly intended to make Chinese oversight acceptable to people not ready for direct Chinese control. They are also intended to help pull Taiwan back into China's fold one day as a future SAR, and might eventually prove useful in solving problems in other peripheral areas.

Issues such as China's control of its peripheries, the USA's 'world system of power', and settler problems in Israel, certainly can be discussed without reference to empire. But I would argue that an imperial mode of analysis is in many cases appropriate, and enlightening, and that we therefore greatly impoverish our analysis if we fail to harness its potential.

CONCLUSION

The point of this unit has been to discuss some possible impacts of empire analytically, so you can accustom yourself to thinking in this way, and start to think of the course as a whole. By making free use of topics you have already studied, and categories used in earlier units, I also hope I have shown you how much you already know about this topic.

Hence you can try to differentiate the impact of empire by the type of imperial system, the type of colony, and the nature of the territory affected, both in its people and its ecology.

You can also start to apply modes of analysis you have used in this course to new situations. I slipped in Hitler's Germany and its imperial ambitions in central and eastern Europe earlier. This may seem an unfamiliar or even slightly unsettling example of empire at first, and an unusual way of thinking about Nazi Germany. But that should not hold too much fear for you by this stage. For any empire of any kind, you can now ask what system of power it possessed (fiscal, military, diplomatic and the like, as discussed in Block 3), and what particular portfolio of different types of colony it possessed. You can look to see if it had an ideology or guiding principles, and how far the end result of its imperialism was affected, in each particular territory, by local conditions.

You can also look for different areas and types of impact. What was the economic impact? What was the cultural impact? What were the effects of empire at the macro, empire, colony and individual levels? What are the ongoing legacies, after empire formally ended?

This unit and the course as a whole has, however, done more than offer ways of analysing the impact of empire. It has also hinted at possible answers to some big questions. For instance, it has suggested that maritime empires did play a major role in shaping a new, globalised world. It has also suggested that maritime empires may have accelerated the birth and intensity of that globalised world, while increasing the cost of that transformation.

Finally, I hope it has given you the reassurance that you already know a lot about the impacts of empires, and how to debate them; but also the confidence to accept that it is all right to embrace heuristic models. With a topic this vast, and this entangled with world history, final answers will often evade us. But even incremental improvements in our ability to understand, analyse and comprehend a topic as vast as empires will have a disproportionate effect on our ability to understand world history.

REFERENCES

Abernethy, D.B. (2000) *The Dynamics of Global Dominance: European Overseas Empires 1415–1980*, New Haven and London, Yale University Press.

Beinart, W. and Hughes, L. (2007) *Environment and Empire*, Oxford, Oxford University Press.

Conrad, J. (1983) *Heart of Darkness*, London, Penguin English Library.

Darwin, J. (2007) *After Tamerlane: The Global History of Empire Since 1405*, London, Allen Lane.

Davis, M. (2001) *Later Victorian Holocausts: El Niño Famines and the Making of the Third World*, London, Verso.

Day, D. (2008a) *Claiming a Continent: A New History of Australia*, London, HarperCollins.

Day, D. (2008b) *Conquest: How Societies Overwhelm Others*, Oxford, Oxford University Press.

Denoon, D., Mein-Smith, P. and Wyndham, M. (2000) *A History of Australia, New Zealand and the Pacific*, Oxford, Blackwell.

Ferguson, N. (2003) *Empire: How Britain Made the Modern World*, London, Penguin.

Ferguson, N. (2004) *Colossus: The Rise and Fall of the American Empire*, London, Penguin.

Gastil, R. (1980) *Freedom in the World: Political Rights and Civil Liberties*, Westport, Greenwood.

Hack, K. and Rettig, T. (2006) *Colonial Armies in Southeast Asia*, London, Routledge.

Kennedy, P. (1989) *The Rise and Fall of Great Powers: Economic Change and Military Conflict from 1500 to 2000*, London, Fontana.

Loomba, A. (1998) *Colonialism/Postcolonialism*, London, Routledge.

Maier, C.S. (2006) *Among Empires: American Ascendancy and its Predecessors*, Cambridge, Harvard University Press.

Masefield, J. (1966) *Poems*, London, Heinemann.

Mazower, M. (2008) *Hitler's Empire: Nazi Rule in Occupied Europe*, London, Allen Lane.

O'Brien, P.K. (2002) 'The Pax Britannica and American hegemony: precedent, antecedent or just another history?' in O'Brien, P.K. and Cleese, A. (eds) *Two Hegemonies: Britain 1846–1914 and the United States 1941–2001*, Aldershot, Ashgate.

Said, E. (1978) *Orientalism*, London, Routledge and Kegan Paul.

Said, E. (1993) *Culture and Imperialism*, New York, Knopf.

Trocki, C. (1999) *Opium, Empire and the Global Political Economy: A Study of the Asian Opium Trade, 1750–1950*, London, Routledge.

Wilson, A. (1977) *The Strange Ride of Rudyard Kipling: His Life and Works*, London, Warburg.

Young, E.M. (1996) 'Spaces for famine: a comparative analysis of famine in Ireland and the Highlands in the 1840s', *Transactions of the Institute of British Geographers*, vol. 21, no. 4, pp. 666–80.

GLOSSARY

aborigines: literally, those inhabiting a territory from its historical origin. Although most commonly used of the inhabitants of Australia whom Europeans encountered in the eighteenth century, it can refer to any peoples who predated settlers from Europe, such as the Native Americans.

ahimsa: Hindi term for non-violence or avoidance of violence.

aldeamento: fortified compound in which rural Africans were compulsorily resettled as a Portuguese counter-insurgency measure.

Anglicans: members of the Church of England as established by law. The church had been established in the reign of Elizabeth I when the queen and her successors became supreme governors of it 'insofar as the law of Christ allows'. Although replaced by a Presbyterian establishment in 1646 during the civil wars, the church was restored along with the monarchy in 1660. Anglicans were to be found in all the mainland American colonies during the eighteenth century, but the church was only established in those from Virginia to Georgia.

ashram: Hindi term for a spiritual or religious community.

Atlantic historians: until relatively recently, colonial American and early modern Britain were studied separately. This led to research being devoted to one or the other but rarely both, a practice that reinforced views of America as exceptional, differing from European norms from the start. During the last thirty years or so, research has been directed into examining both sides of the Atlantic simultaneously. This development has led historians to see continuities rather than change in the British communities that settled North America. It has also encouraged them to investigate comparisons between other European countries that colonised the New World and their colonies. The result has been the emergence of Atlantic history to describe the conceptual framework of these comparative historians.

Austro-Hungarian empire: the terms 'Austro-Hungarian empire' and 'Habsburg empire' tend to be used interchangeably, although the Habsburg empire only became the Austro-Hungarian empire after the *Ausgleich* (compromise) of 1867. The empire is sometimes also referred to as the Donaumonarchie (Danubian monarchy) or Dual Monarchy.

Brahman: 'priestly' caste, considered the highest of the Hindu *varna* or caste system.

Brahmin: a member of the Hindu Brahman caste.

cadi: Turco-Arabic term for a judge, magistrate administering Islamic law.

caid: Turco-Arabic term originally meaning 'local governor'; more generally, native Algerian administrator exercising customary authority.

Calvinism: doctrines associated with John Calvin, the sixteenth-century Protestant reformer.

cash crop: a crop that is grown specifically for sale rather than for subsistence. Some American colonies concentrated on the cultivation of particular crops that could be sold in bulk, e.g. tobacco in Maryland and Virginia, rice and indigo in South Carolina and Georgia, and sugar in the West Indies.

Cisleithania: the Austrian part of the Dual Monarchy (the Hungarian part was Transleithania).

colonato: state-subsidised agricultural colony in Angola designed to attract Portuguese immigrants.

Dalit: Hindi term for 'one who is oppressed'; another term for 'Untouchables'. Western literature sometimes uses the term *Dalit*, Gandhi coined *Harijans* (children of God), and the modern Indian state prefers 'Scheduled Castes'. Many other names, some pejorative, have been used.

degredado: exiled Portuguese convict.

Dravidian: One of the languages of southern India, sometimes also ascribed to the majority peoples of this area.

Estado Novo: New State; the nationalist regime that seized power in Portugal in the early 1930s.

External Delegation: the leadership in exile of the FLN (as opposed to the clandestine leadership in Algeria).

fellahin: Arabic term for a peasant farmer.

harkis: Arabic name given to Muslim recruits to French counter-insurgency forces in Algeria.

hartal: Hindi term for an economic stoppage, which may take various forms, such as a strike, a boycott or a sit-in.

Hindu Mahasabha: 'Great Hindu Assembly'. A Hindu nationalist organisation founded in 1915 to counter the Muslim League.

irredentism: 'a policy of seeking the recovery and reunion to one country of a region or regions for the time being subject to another country' (*Oxford English Dictionary*). (Interestingly, most of the examples of early use of this word in the *OED* refer to Austria.)

jati: sometimes considered as sub-castes within the main four orders of the Hindu *varna* or caste system. These might reflect regional, occupational or linguistic associations.

k.u.k: you will come across this German abbreviation of *kaiserlich und königlich*, referring to the Austrian part (e.g. of the army) as *kaiserlich* (of the emperor), and the Hungarian part as *königlich* (of the king), because Kaiser Franz Joseph was, from 1867, simultaneously Austrian Kaiser (emperor) and Hungarian König (king) – this is sometimes referred to as the dualist system.

khadi: Hindi term meaning home-spun cloth.

Ksatriya: 'warrior', the second highest in the Hindu *varna* or caste system.

lathi: Hindi term for a long stick used for hitting and beating.

Magyar: the name of the people of Hungary, and of their language.

mestiço: Portuguese term for a person of mixed European and African descent.

muçeque: Portuguese term for a slum.

panchayat: Hindi term for elected village-level councils, but also used for arbitration councils formed to bypass British-controlled institutions.

panslavism: 'the idea of, or movement for, the political union of all Slavs or Slavonic-speaking peoples; pan-Slavic solidarity, feeling, belief, etc.' (*Oxford English Dictionary*). Similarly, you may come across the term pan-Germans or pan-Serbs.

Protestant dissenters: Protestants who dissented from the Church of England and were otherwise known as non-conformists. These included Baptists, Congregationalists, Presbyterians and Quakers. Until the Toleration Act of 1689 they were not allowed to worship separately from Anglicans, and were pressurised to conform to the established church. Although they were permitted to meet in chapels and places other than the established churches after 1689 they still could not hold office under the crown or in local government. Many went to the colonies to escape these restrictions, e.g. Congregationalists to New England, Presbyterians to the middle colonies and Quakers to Pennsylvania.

purna swaraj: Hindi term for complete independence, sometimes as opposed to merely 'self-government' within the empire.

Rashtriya Swayamsevak Sangh (RSS): National Volunteer Union – a Hindu nationalist organisation founded in 1925, with anti-Muslim overtones.

revolution of the flowers: popular name for the Portuguese revolution that broke out in April 1974.

satyagraha: Hindi term meaning soul force or truth force. Gandhi also conceptualised this as demonstrating the superiority of one's cause by accepting suffering, often brought on by breaking unjust laws.

Shudra: labouring or peasant caste within the Hindu *varna* or caste system.

swadeshi: Hindi term for self-reliance and restricting to one's own country, region or surroundings. The word was used by Indian nationalists to encourage the boycott of British goods and cultural forms, in favour of local cultural forms and goods, such as home-spun cloth.

swaraj: Hindi term for self-rule, home rule, self-government or independence.

Untouchables: see *Dalit*.

Vaishya: trading caste within the four-fold Hindu *varna* or caste system.

varna: Hindu order or caste. Refers to the four-fold division of society into Brahman, Ksatriya, Vaishya and Shudra.

Weltpolitik: literally world policy, implying the desire to establish or extend an empire abroad.

wilayas: the military zones set up by FLN–ALN in Algeria.

ACKNOWLEDGEMENTS

Grateful acknowledgement is made to the following sources for permission to reproduce material in this book.

Text

pp. 58–9: Beller, S. (2006) 'AEIOU, 1439–1740', *A Concise History of Austria*, Cambridge, Cambridge University Press. © 2006 Cambridge University Press, reproduced with permission.

p. 205: Masefield, J. (1966) 'Cargoes', *Poems*, London, Heinemann. Reproduced by permission of The Society of Authors as the literary representative of the Estate of John Masefield.

Figures

Figure 20.4:
Hocine Ait Ahmed, 1961. Photo: © STF/AF/Getty Images.
Larbi Ben M'Hidi, 1957. Photo: Photos12.com/Oasis.
Mourad Didouche, 1954. Photo: Photos12.com/Oasis.
Ahmed Ben Bella, 1961. Photo: © STF/AFP/Getty Images.
Rabah Bitat, 1961. Photo: © STF/AFP/Getty Images.
Mohamed Khider, 1961. Photo: © STF/AFP/Getty Images.
Mostefa Ben Boulaid, 1954. Photo: Photos12.com/Oasis.
Mohamed Boudiaf, 1961. Photo: © STF/AFP/Getty Images.
Belkacem Krim, 1961. Photo: © STF/AFP/Getty Images.

Tables

Table 19.1: Adapted from Chandrasekhar, S. (1946) *India's Population: Fact and Policy*, New York, John Day.

Table 20.4: MacQueen, N. (1997) *The Decolonization of Portuguese Africa: Metropolitan Revolution and the Dissolution of Empire*, Harlow, Addison Wesley/Longman Limited.

Table 22.1: Abernethy, D.B. (2000) *The Dynamics of Global Dominance: European Overseas Empires 1415–1980*, New Haven and London, Yale University Press.

Every effort has been made to contact copyright holders. If any have been inadvertently overlooked the publishers will be pleased to make the necessary arrangements at the first opportunity.

INDEX

Spanish–American War (1898) 170, 202

Untouchables (*Dalit*) 98, 107, 116–17, 223

UPA (Union of the Peoples of Angola) 144

Vaishya 224

varna (caste) 94, 98, 116–17, 224

Versailles Peace Conference (1919) 81

Victoria, Queen 53

Vienna, diamond jubilee parade (1908) 53, 54–5, 56

Vietnam War 158

virtual representation, and the American colonies 27

visual sources, contextualising 183–5

VOC (Dutch East India Company) 206

Waitangi 215

Waites, Bernard, 'Europe and the Third World' 194–5

Wallerstein's world economic system 194, 198

Wank, Solomon 62, 67–8, 75–6, 77

Washington, George 17, 23, 40

Wavell, Lord, viceroy of India 94–5, 113–14

Weltpolitik 65, 224

White, John, pictures of the New World 182, 183

wilayas 131, 224

Wilhelm II, German Kaiser 57

Wilkes, John 28

women, Muslim women in Algeria 139

world economic system, and globalisation 194–5, 198, 211

Yugoslavia 72

Zaire 159